Freedom for the Poor

Freedom for the Poor

Welfare and the Foundations of Democratic Citizenship

Timothy J. Gaffaney

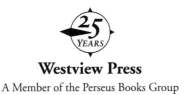

Westview Press

A Member of the Perseus Books Group

For Josette

Copyright © 2000 by Westview Press, A Member of the Perseus Books Group

Published in 2000 in the United States of America by Westview Press, 5500 Central Avenue, Boulder, Colorado 80301-2877, and in the United Kingdom by Westview Press, 12 Hid's Copse Road, Cumnor Hill, Oxford OX2 9JJ

Find us on the World Wide Web at www.westviewpress.com

Library of Congress Cataloging-in-Publication Data
Gaffaney, Timothy J.
    Freedom for the poor : welfare and the foundations of democratic citizenship / Timothy J. Gaffaney.
       p.   cm.
    Includes biliographical references and index.
    ISBN 0-8133-6781-6
    1. Public welfare—United States.   2. Conservatism—United States.   3. Liberalism—United States.   4. Citizenship.   5. Equality.   6. Liberty.   I. Title.

HV95 .G32   2000
362.5'0973—dc21
                                                                            99-059999

The paper used in this publication meets the requirements of the American National Standard for Permanence of Paper for Printed Library Materials Z39.48-1984.

10   9   8   7   6   5   4   3   2   1

Contents

Acknowledgments   vii

Introduction   1

PART ONE
Liberal Citizenship and the Critique of Welfare

1 Bentham on Utility and Poverty Relief   11

   Liberty and the Principle of Utility, 12
   Pauper Management, 15
   The Rationality of the Indigent, 21
   Citizenship and the Extension of the Suffrage, 22
   Conclusion, 25
   Notes, 26

2 The New Right and Market Citizenship   29

   The Economic Liberals, 30
   The Libertarian Critique, 46
   The Moral Conservatives, 50
   The Prepolitical Conditions of Citizenship, 55
   Market Citizenship, 63
   Credits, 70
   Notes, 70

PART TWO
Liberal Citizenship and the Basis of Welfare

3 T. H. Green on Freedom and the Common Good   79

   Individual Self-Development and the Common Good, 80
   A New Model of Citizenship, 88
   The Objects of State Intervention, 92
   The Limits of Citizenship, 94

Conclusion, 97
Notes, 99

4 Citizenship and the Right to Welfare   103

The Nature of Rights, 104
Property Rights in Welfare Benefits, 105
The Social Rights of Citizenship, 109
Contracting to Welfare Provision, 115
The Duty to Provide, 122
Conclusion, 128
Notes, 129

PART THREE
Freedom, Poverty, and Democratic Citizenship

5 Autonomy and Participation   135

Freedom and Democratic Citizenship, 136
Autonomy, 139
Participatory Democracy, 145
Autonomy and Citizenship, 154
Participatory Democracy and the Legitimate State, 156
Notes, 159

6 Citizenship and Welfare Provision   161

Autonomy and Welfare Provision, 161
Welfare Benefits and Citizenship, 164
The Terms of Distribution, 166
Notes, 171

Conclusion   172

References   181
Suggested Readings   191
Index   193

Acknowledgments

The ideas expressed in this book originally took form as a dissertation under the direction of Professor Carole Pateman at UCLA. Her prodding and patience with me as I struggled to clarify my thoughts were truly heroic. For that, as well as her encouragement since leaving Los Angeles, I am truly grateful and indebted. At UCLA, I also benefited from the invaluable constructive criticism of Professor Victor Wolfenstein of the Political Science Department and Professor Barbara Herman of the Philosophy Department. I am also grateful to my fellow graduate students and friends, John Medearis, Bill Niemi, and Dan O'Connor, for their insights on political theory, their wit, and their sarcasm. Another friend, Mike Murashige, was also a source of both inspiration and endless suggestions for reading. Finally, from UCLA, I wish to acknowledge the powerful intellectual influence of the late Professor Richard Ashcraft, who showed me that the project is never really finished.

Since coming to Washington, D.C., I have had the opportunity to discuss my ideas, in part or in whole, with a number of talented and friendly political scientists, among them, Stephen Elkin at the University of Maryland, Mark Warren at Georgetown University, Ingrid Creppell at George Washington University, and Joe Soss at American University. Whether they will recognize it or not, this book clearly bears the marks of their helpful suggestions.

Aside from this intellectual support, the writing of this book has depended on the material support of a number of generous people. John Bader of the UCLA–Washington Center for Politics and Public Policy provided comfortable office space during the early stages of writing. Karen O'Connor of American University provided space for writing and financial support to present my ideas at professional meetings. And my friend Martha Weiss of Georgetown University generously allowed me to take advantage of the solitude and printing facilities of her ecology laboratory. I would also like to thank David McBride and Kay Mariea of Westview Press for their assistance in shepherding this project through the editorial process.

I am most grateful, however, to my wife, Dr. Josette Lewis. Her love, encouragement, and patience have truly enabled me to write this book. I dedicate it to her.

Timothy J. Gaffaney

Introduction

The boundaries and nature of government action have never been settled issues in American politics. Public political discourse over the past two decades, in particular, has been informed by the effort to reorient the focus of government, curtailing its reach in some matters and strengthening its hand in others. The Reagan administration, for instance, led an assault on a range of government bureaucracies and policies that the administration believed was increasingly at odds with the market and the family, at the same time pouring unprecedented sums into the defense buildup, the war on crime, and the war on drugs. Even the centrist Democratic party of the 1990s has fallen in line with this effort to redefine the role of government action. Perhaps nowhere has the effort to curtail the breadth and depth of the government been waged more vocally than in relation to the question of public assistance for the nonworking poor.

The rhetoric of big government and the need for welfare reform is not entirely a matter of public or political debate, however. Behind these debates lies a long tradition of liberal democratic theory engaged with normative and empirical questions on the meaning of fundamental political values such as liberty, equality, and rights. So, for instance, the attack on public assistance is not inspired simply by a concern for the distribution of scarce fiscal resources. Even in the most bullish of times, liberal theorists have reasons against welfare, or public assistance, for the nonworking poor.

In this context, my first aim in this book is to identify and critically examine the way in which New Right liberal theorists in the United States have employed a conception of liberty in their attack on welfare provision for the poor, and to contrast that concept with liberal justifications for public welfare that are typically grounded in equality.[1] Placing these theorists side by side demonstrates how egalitarian liberals have failed to address the heart of the New Right's position, and why they may have failed to garner political support for their version of liberalism. By grounding their arguments for public assistance almost exclusively in the language of rights and entitlement, egalitarian liberal theorists have neglected the language of freedom. Although I find the New Right's conclusions disturbing, it seems to me that their appeal to liberty, in conjunction with their distinctive claims for equality and the rights to property, has given them a stronger standing in the public debates. Egalitarian liberal justifications for public assistance seem to focus too much on equal standing and entitlement for the tastes of the American public. In theoretical terms, the New Right brings into relief the long-standing tension between equality and liberty inherent to liberal democratic theory, and in the policy debate they have paved the way for the triumph of the latter in American politics. By the 1980s it could plausibly be put forth in both scholarly and public debates that one woman's poverty threatened not only another man's pocketbook, but his liberty as well.

Given the prominence of the New Right in the last decades of the twentieth century, a defense of public welfare provision is urgently needed that is able to address the inegalitarian liberal theory of the New Right on its own terms. People committed to a policy of public assistance to the nonworking poor have a great deal to gain by retrieving the language of liberty from the constraints of New Right liberal theory. Still, for reasons that I will make clear, simply patching the familiar language of liberty onto the egalitarian liberal language of rights may not be sufficient. The future of public assistance—the income that will feed, clothe, and house the nonworking poor—seems to depend on a radical reconceptualization of the terms underlying this policy.

Yet much more is at stake than conceptions of freedom and equality, and the internecine liberal debates over public assistance reflect more than a tension between liberty and equality. Given the central place of these two values in liberal conceptions of citizenship, normative or prescriptive claims about the provision of public assistance have distinct implications for models of citizenship as well. It would be incomplete, therefore, to discuss the meaning of liberty and equality in relation to the policy of public welfare provision without placing them in the wider, more complex, context of citizenship. It is difficult to ignore the way in which liberal critics, reformers, and defenders of welfare provision either imply, or explicitly draw upon, specific conceptions of citizenship.[2] Indeed, even for theorists who are not explicit about the connection with citizenship, it is possible to read a conception of citizenship through the particular way that they use the language of liberty, rights, or both. Accordingly, this examination of the interrelationship of political terms clustering around the policy of public welfare provision to the nonworking poor provides an ideal opportunity to critically assess typical liberal conceptions of citizenship. The case of public assistance provides an ideal opportunity to understand the problems in the liberal political theory of both the New Right and its more egalitarian alternatives.

So, whereas my first aim is to understand the scholarly and political debates over welfare provision by examining the use of liberty and equality in those debates, my second aim is to reveal something about liberal conceptions of citizenship by examining the liberal theory—and the central place of liberty and equality in that theory—of public assistance to the nonworking poor.[3]

My examination of the liberal meanings of citizenship is organized in the following way. Before addressing the arguments of the contemporary New Right, I lay out and critically examine the arguments of a theorist who dealt with similar questions over a century and a half ago. In Chapter 1, I begin with an examination of Jeremy Bentham's utilitarian-based recommendations for pauper management. Bentham's political theory as well as his policy recommendations seem to anticipate the contemporary commitment to workfare. Additionally, Bentham's particular *reasons* for providing resources for the poor seem to capture contemporary attitudes in the United States. Few, if any, theorists or politicians advocate an elimination of all benefits. At the least, welfare benefits can be justified by the interests of people whose security is threatened by a predatory underclass. Bentham provides one of the clearest examples of this kind of argument. Analysis of Bentham's political theory thus provides a nice contrast with the position I take in the final part of this book, namely, that public assistance can be justified in terms that take account of the interests of the recipients themselves.

In Chapter 2, I turn to the inegalitarian liberal theory of the contemporary New Right. I identify three major components of this attack on public assistance. First, public assistance hinders the delivery of market benefits (Hayek [1944, 1960]; Friedman [1962]). Second, public assistance undermines the virtues of personal responsibility (Murray [1984, 1986]; Mead [1986, 1992]). Additionally, the virtue of personal responsibility is linked with visions of the ideal sexual division of labor in the family. The provision of welfare benefits encourages single-parent, namely female-headed, families (Novak et al. [1987]; Gilder [1981, 1987]), and this lack of virtue has dire consequences for the social order. Finally, public assistance threatens the exclusive right to private property and coerces taxpayers by forcing them to labor for the benefit of others (Nozick [1974]).

Although these salient distinctions between a range of New Right liberal theorists cannot be ignored, these theorists are nonetheless united in their use of liberty and their emphasis on market-based conceptions of citizenship as ways to delegitimate claims to public assistance. In the first place, the liberty that forms the basis for liberal citizenship is (if only implicitly) identified with economic independence from the state. Clearly, most individuals will attain this status by engaging in paid employment.

Additionally, inegalitarian liberal models of citizenship emphasize the importance of obligations, or contributions, as a necessary corollary to the claims to rights or entitlements. Liberal theorists, especially in this century, have typically identified paid employment in a free market as the liberal contribution par excellence. Thus, whether focusing on liberty as economic independence from the state or on paid employment more directly, inegalitarian liberal theorists of the New Right seem dedicated to articulating a market-based conception of citizenship.

The problem with this conception is that market forces and conventions conspire to prevent some individuals from securing paid employment. As it does so, the market undermines the opportunity for these individuals, according to the terms of liberalism, to secure their liberty— their economic independence—or to make their contribution. In this way, market forces conspire against the opportunity for all people to be full citizens. This market-based conception of citizenship turns out to be more exclusive than New Right liberals are willing to acknowledge.

Moreover, in light of the constraints on women's participation in the labor market, this conception of citizenship illuminates an observation already noted by feminist critics of liberalism. Namely, liberal values and institutions deny women an equal value of citizenship.[4] In conjunction with the claim about the feminization of poverty, a number of feminist critics have already argued that welfare reform in the 1990s in the United States represents an attack specifically on poor *women*.[5] This study broadens that analysis by revealing and examining the liberal theory behind the policy. This book examines the relationship between a theory of citizenship and a public policy that both denigrate women.[6]

Given the weaknesses of the inegalitarian liberal theory of the New Right with respect to citizenship, are there any alternatives within liberal democratic theory for establishing a solid, normative foundation for public assistance to the nonworking poor? Although I have noted that contemporary egalitarian liberal arguments typically leave out any conception of liberty, I begin the second part of the book with an examination of T. H. Green's conception of positive liberty. This conception of liberty led Green and a whole generation of New Liberals to the conclusion that a government's legitimacy depended on its intervention in society for the benefit of the poor. The examination of Green in Chapter 3, however, demonstrates the inadequacy of this celebrated liberal contribution to the question of public assistance, and it serves to clarify the position I take on the relationship between liberty and democratic citizenship in the final section of the book. In Chapter 4, on the other hand, I examine mid- to late-twentieth-century liberal democratic arguments in favor of public assistance, including arguments founded on theories of the social rights of citizenship (T. H. Marshall [1992]), state-funded independence (Reich

[1964]), contract (King and Waldron [1988], Dworkin [1977], Held [1984]), and the duty to provide (Goodin [1988]). Though I share with these egalitarian liberals a commitment to state-funded assistance for the poor, it will become clear that we agree on this broad conclusion for very different reasons.

There are two themes running through this range of arguments that are troubling from the *democratic* perspective that citizenship demands public assistance. In the first place, both Green and Marshall rely on conceptions of citizenship that are never successfully divorced from expectations about paid employment. Although these essentially laborist theories may have represented advances in liberal theory at the time they were articulated, they are now subject to the same charge of exclusivity that can be leveled at the liberal theory of the New Right. Indeed, a plausible line of reasoning may stretch between these theories and the contemporary emphasis on workfare. On the other hand, justifications for public assistance founded on the contractual claim to subsistence, or on the obligation to provide subsistence, fail to address adequately the political status of the nonworking poor. Even if the political or moral status of the nonworking poor justifies public assistance in the first place, there is no sense that this assistance will in turn contribute to a more robust conception of participatory citizenship, rather than simply to the alleviation of destitution.

In the final part of the book, I address in a more constructive way the problems and limitations that I have identified in the liberal treatment of public assistance and its underlying conceptions of citizenship. In Chapter 5, I establish the relationship between freedom, citizenship, and state action in light of a theory of participatory democracy. In the first section, I retrieve the language of freedom from the constraints of inegalitarian liberty and identify freedom with autonomy. In turn, I will define the autonomous person as one who has been enabled to participate in democratic politics. In the subsequent section, I argue that the state must be the guarantor of this autonomy. In Chapter 6, then, I identify an important condition for autonomy. I argue that public assistance to the poor can establish the grounds for autonomy. I conclude this chapter with the argument that the provision of public assistance is an integral component of participatory democratic citizenship. It is because persons ought to be counted as full citizens, even in the absence of having made prepolitical contributions, that persons in a democratic polity ought to receive public assistance. Given that the democratic state must ensure the conditions for the full expression of citizenship, a policy of public assistance to the nonworking poor is a legitimate and necessary function of a democratic state. Public assistance contributes to the constitution of full citizenship, and thereby helps to sustain democracy itself.

I have made it clear that my emphasis is not exclusively on the policy debate about whether the government ought to provide welfare benefits to the nonworking poor but also on a theoretical discussion on the meaning of citizenship. Nevertheless, I hope that the importance of the specific recommendation is not lost. In this sense, too, I believe that the undertaking of this project is of singular importance. The Personal Responsibility and Work Opportunity Reconciliation Act of 1996 represents something of a victory for New Right liberal principles, Mead's frustration with the work requirements notwithstanding. It also represents an admission on the part of people more sympathetic to the poor—witness Clinton's support for the bill—that the particular form that public welfare provision took in the United States was not an unqualified success. That acknowledgment reflects, in part, the failure of a robust conception of freedom and democratic citizenship. At the same time, this victory for the New Right has not meant the end of poverty. The imposition of workfare programs, as studies are already beginning to show, will not draw all recipients into the workforce, much less eliminate poverty. So, as the house of welfare policy lies in ruins, this is an ideal moment to think about rebuilding a policy of public assistance on solid principles. I hope that the following discussion will contribute to such a constructive dialogue.

Notes

1. All of the arguments considered herein can be situated within liberal theory, generally. Furthermore, some of the arguments incorporate distinctively democratic considerations as well. Even among the New Right liberal theorists none is, within its own terms, antidemocratic.

2. For general treatments of conceptions of citizenship, see Barbalet (1988), Heater (1990), Roche (1992), Hindess (1993), and Saunders (1993).

3. My analysis does not discuss at length the distinction between cash and in-kind benefits, such as medical care, housing, and general social services. Undoubtedly, this is an important component of the public debates over welfare provision, and a few of the theorists I discuss below have addressed this distinction. But the distinction has not been especially salient for conceptions of citizenship.

4. See Pateman (1985). Although the question of race is equally salient to an analysis of liberal conceptions of citizenship, my focus will be on gender issues. On the question of race and welfare provision, see, for instance, Pearce (1983), Quadagno (1990), and Roberts (1996). Clearly, New Right liberal theory does not count work in general as a contribution, but only paid employment. If the New Right considered this, then motherhood, for instance, might be considered as an acceptable contribution to society; citizenship might be satisfied by the "work" of childrearing. For the historical argument that in the early welfare state women in fact did maintain that their work in the home constituted service to the state, which entitled them to honorable citizenship benefits, see Orloff (1991) and Lake

(1992). For contemporary normative claims to this effect, see, for instance, Elshtain (1981) and Orloff (1993).

5. See, for instance, Pearce (1990), Roberts (1996), and White (1996). Scholars have offered a number of explanations for public opposition to the poverty-relieving components of the welfare state in the United States, for example, economic self-interest (Cook and Barrett [1992]; Hasenfeld and Rafferty [1989]), the ethic of individualism (Marmor, Mashaw, and Harvey [1990]; Hasenfeld and Rafferty [1989]), the ethic of work (Mead [1992]), and the racial attitudes of white Americans (Gilens [1995]).

6. My investigation of the exclusive nature of the liberal citizenship of the New Right does not turn on assumptions of distinctive male versus female psychologies. I am not pursuing the argument that this liberal conception of citizenship describes a distinctly male psychology. For explorations of these issues, see Gilligan (1982), Jones (1990), and Lloyd (1986).

Liberal Citizenship and the Critique of Welfare

1

Bentham on Utility
and Poverty Relief

In a century ostensibly distinguished by its laissez-faire politics,[1] Jeremy Bentham proposed radically new ideas about the role of the state. Calling natural rights nothing more than "nonsense on stilts," he argued that a democratic state ought not to be restricted to the protection of rights established prior to the foundation of this state; indeed, there were no such rights. Rather, a liberal democratic state, operating on the principles of utility, could play an important role in promoting the conditions for its own development. In particular, this involved promoting the conditions under which individuals hitherto excluded from political participation could become active in the exercise of political power. In this sense, Bentham's theory of state intervention promoted political equality. In other words, against a typical laissez-faire liberal endorsement of limited government, Bentham argued that the state itself could actively contribute to the realization of freedom and could make individuals into citizens. In short, Bentham's theory of state intervention is bound up with distinctive liberal conceptions of liberty and citizenship. Perhaps one of the clearest examples of the relationship between Bentham's utilitarian principles and his specific policy recommendations to Parliament concerned the treatment of the nonworking poor, or the indigent.

Even though Bentham did not explicitly deal with the meaning of citizenship, when he discusses liberty and the four aims of good government, he is discussing terms that liberal theory typically attaches to citizenship. In other words, his distinctive treatment of liberty, along with equality, subsistence, security, and abundance can be seen as a suggestion about the meaning of (utilitarian) liberal citizenship. In turn, his application of these liberal principles to the policy of pauper management further clarifies Bentham's assumptions about citizenship; namely, who counts, and by what means, as a citizen. His application clarifies whether there are limits or qualifications to citizenship.

When examining Bentham's theory in relation to his policy recommendations, it is tempting to read his treatment of the indigent in the workhouse as an unmitigated denial of the individual liberty of the indigent. He would make commitment to the workhouse compulsory for the non-working poor and impose a rigid disciplinary code that regulated every movement of its denizens. In so doing, Bentham would seem to deny a set of civil liberties that are fundamental to liberal citizenship. Indigence would seem to be the forfeiture of citizenship.

This is, however, a too simplistic interpretation of the internal logic of Bentham's political theory. I demonstrate in this chapter that Bentham treats the workhouse not as a denial but as a contribution to the liberal citizenship of the indigent. Although individual freedom from coercion was undoubtedly important for Bentham, he also believed that this individual status could be denied in particular cases in the interest of the free society. In other words, individual liberty might be denied in certain cases without sacrificing the political status attached to freedom conceived more broadly. Whereas the individual freedom of the indigent might be denied by their commitment to the workhouse, their political status as citizens would be served by the protection of the liberty they enjoyed by virtue of their membership in a utilitarian liberal democratic society.

By this interpretation I do not, however, intend to endorse Bentham's proposals. Nor can Bentham be plausibly linked with the set of egalitarian liberals who later argued for the right to welfare. Bentham's proposals for pauper management demonstrate a distinct point about liberal theory. Namely, in the absence of independent financial means, liberal citizenship depends on work. Seen in this way, Bentham's proposals can be viewed as an early-eighteenth-century version of the workfare arguments that have gained such currency in the late twentieth century.

Liberty and the Principle of Utility

As an alternative to the natural rights tradition, Bentham's political theory begins with the principle of utility.[2] "Nature has placed mankind under the governance of two sovereign masters, *pain and pleasure*. It is for them alone to point out what we ought to do, as well as to determine what we shall do" (1973: 66). Thus, pain and pleasure serve two roles. In the first place, they provide an adequate description of the motives for any action. Second, these principles also serve as a standard by which to judge—approve or disapprove—any action. The principle of utility judges any action according to the degree to which it increases or decreases the happiness of people involved. Thus, Bentham defined the value of an action by its empirical consequences, not by its relationship with the first principles of natural rights arguments. This external criterion of judgment enabled a universal application of political principles. The standard of the pleasure/pain ratio was something that all people could understand without instruction in a theory of first principles.

Bentham attached these consequentialist judgments to his arguments about the function of the state. The actions of a "legitimate" government are guided by the principle of utility rather than by a consideration for the protection of natural rights. Its aim is to promote the greatest happiness of the greatest number. In service of this aim the government ought to be guided by four subsidiary goals—security, abundance, subsistence, and equality (1950: 96). Clearly, Bentham believed that security is the most important of these goals. But he meant more than just security of property in defining this aim. Security also stood for Bentham's "disappointment-prevention" principle.[3] That is, despite the critique of custom and tradition that lies in his attack on the language of natural rights, Bentham did place a high value on the *expectations* that individuals would have been likely to form. "From disappointment, as everybody knows and feels, springs pain; magnitude, proportioned to the value set by the individual on the benefit that had been expected" (1843, 5: 414). The principle of utility dictates that these expectations ought not to be disturbed without taking into account a calculus of pleasure and pain. Although Bentham used the principle of utility to defend a certain degree of inequality in property, he used the same principle as an argument against those who wished to abolish all forms of public poor relief. Thus, even insofar as security was promoted in relation to property, security remained in the service of the principle of utility, not in service of a theory of natural (and exclusive) rights to property.

Bentham did not, however, strictly rank these four aims, articulating instead a system in which each reinforced the others. For instance, on the one hand he argued that as society approached absolute equality, society would approach the maximization of happiness. The greater the level of wealth or power possessed by any particular group or individual—the greater the inequality—"the greater the facility and the incitement to the abuse of it" (1973: 200). Thus, in a monarchy, where the distribution of wealth and power are at a minimum, the degree of unhappiness is at a maximum. So a greater equality in the share of the instruments of happiness leads to a greater aggregate mass of happiness. Yet this came with the proviso that "by nothing that is done towards the removal of the inequality, any shock be given to security: security namely in respect of the several subjects of possession above mentioned" (1973: 210–12). In other words, the aim of security competes with the tendency toward equalization implied in the principle of utility.

Still, Bentham did not place an absolute primacy on security over equality. This can be clarified by noting that Bentham worked with two general modes of equality. He considered wealth as one mode of equality (or inequality). But he also considered the mode of power, defined as the capacity to control decision making, to be analytically distinct. Thus, although the interest in *material* equality was subordinated to the aim of security, Bentham reconciled the aims of security and *political* equality by arguing that an increasing equality in the access to power, by the promotion of democratic procedures, would tend to an overall increase in the level of security in society. Although the extension of the suffrage, for instance, may initially disrupt the sense of security felt by the property-owning classes, over the long run political equality becomes the necessary condition for realizing security more broadly. In the long run these two aims could be reconciled.[4]

In addition to the four subsidiary aims of government, Bentham places a conception of liberty at the center of his utilitarian liberal democratic theory. In the first place, Bentham defined liberty negatively; it is the absence of coercion (1973: 175).[5] In this way, liberty may describe a direct relationship between individuals. And in the absence of legal constraint, one individual may exercise his power over another. "You and your neighbour, suppose, have quarrelled: he has bound you hand and foot (or has fastened you to a tree): in this case you are certainly not at liberty as against him: on the contrary he has deprived you of your liberty" (1973: 175). Liberty here describes the physical relationship between two individuals; liberty is denied by an action of the physically superior individual.

Although individual liberty, including the concern for its protection, occupies a central place in Bentham's liberal political theory, he also warned that an unbridled interest in liberty could compete with the principle of utility. In this context, he cautioned against love of liberty as a *principal* cause of action, reasserting the primacy of the maximization of utility as the principle cause of action. He issues this warning in light of the affections that correspond to, or strengthen, the ruling principles. Namely, philanthropy corresponds to utility maximizing. Self-regarding interest, on the other hand, corresponds to the love of liberty (1973: 99–100). In this sense, love of liberty undermines the aims of government; love of liberty represents an "impatience of control." And "control is necessary not only to the well-being but to the *being* of society. Control is necessary to the being of every government: of the best not less so than of the worst. The exercise of control is the essential character of all government" (1973: 100, emphasis added). Thus, the love of liberty, whether exercised against individuals or the law, must remain subordinate to utility.

To be sure, this love of liberty represents a spirit of opposition. Such a spirit, broadly understood, will be necessary for the pursuit of good government; this spirit enabled the replacement of monarchy and aristocracy by democracy. But the spirit of opposition will be effective only as long as it remains subordinate to the principle of utility, as well as utility's corresponding affection—philanthropy. Insofar as the spirit of opposition is not under philanthropy, it tends toward weak or bad government. So, the love of liberty cannot, in fact, be a primary or independent principle. It remains a secondary principle. It is a principle of reaction, not of original action (1973: 100).

The subordination of individual liberty to utility, meaning subordination to the four subsidiary aims of government, demonstrates that Bentham's negative conception of liberty is not the basis for his theory of the state. In sharp contrast to libertarian arguments about a minimalist state, Bentham acknowledged that individual liberty must sometimes give way to the good society; that is, the society in which utility has been maximized. Because he was concerned about the extent to which the protection of negative freedom might stand in the way of a secure society, Bentham did not value individual freedom most highly. Indeed, it can quite properly be said that individual (negative) liberty, as well as self-regarding interest, must give way to the *free society*. The freedom of society as a whole, in contrast to individual freedom, is linked to the promotion of the four aims of government—security, abundance, subsistence, and equality. A free society is under the direction of a free government. And in a free government the distribution of power is among the several ranks of persons (1968, 4: 24).

Pauper Management

Scholars have disagreed on the relationship between Bentham's political theory and his proposals for pauper management, some denying (Manning [1968]), others affirming (Rosen [1983]; Boralevi [1984]) the relationship. This division typically reflects an assessment of the effects of the workhouse on the indigent. Scholars who are more sanguine about the treatment of the indigent tend to see the continuity between Bentham's political theory and his policy proposals. Those who view the workhouse as the curtailment of the civil liberties of the indigent, on the other hand, tend to see a discontinuity. These approaches are each understandable given that Bentham's interest in committing the indigent to the workhouse would seem to contradict his interest in promoting individual (negative) liberty.

I believe, with the former, that these two bodies of Bentham's work are integrally related. In the end, Bentham's proposals for pauper management are both consistent with and related to his utilitarian liberal democratic theory. Pauperism is a practical political problem by which the utilitarian principles of government are tested.[6] But in contrast to others who support this continuity, I do so without denying the conclusion that Bentham's policy proposals would have been draconian in their execution. At the same time, this assessment must remain an external critique of Bentham's political theory and policy recommendations. Viewed through its internal logic, we will see how the workhouse satisfies the four subsidiary aims of government. And in so doing, the workhouse establishes the conditions for a free society. The interest in a free society may sometimes conflict with the interests in individual freedom. But even so, the freedom that is politically salient is protected.

When Bentham began writing about the indigent, most assistance was distributed in the form of "outdoor" relief. Local parish assistance as well as the limited relief mandated by the Elizabethan Poor Laws allowed the recipient to maintain an independent household. In contrast to this, Bentham promoted a more centralized administration of poor relief, by the operation of a network of workhouses. Recipients would not have the option of remaining outside the physical confines of the workhouse. With these proposals, Bentham did not aim to eliminate pauperism as much as he aimed at *controlling* and *capitalizing* on a persistent social phenomenon. Bentham's proposals assumed the continued existence of a permanent secondary labor market. By his proposals, Bentham defined an internal colony, with a distinct economy and administration.

These proposals began with a distinction between the indigent (or paupers) and the poor. The term *poor* was reserved specifically for those who labored for their livelihood. The poor were all individuals who had no real property, but who met their needs for subsistence by working for wages. "Poverty is the state of everyone who, in order to obtain *subsistence*, is forced to have recourse to *labor*. Indigence is the state of him, who, being destitute of property . . . is at the same time, either *unable to labour*, or unable, even *for* labour, to procure the supply of which he happens thus to be in want" (Bentham [UCL, *MSS*, 153: 21]). So the indigent included, for example, the sick who could not work. The indigent also included all the beggars, thieves, and vagabonds who *refused* to work for wages within the free market. The poor, on the other hand, not only had the opportunity to labor for their subsistence, they also played a necessary and distinctive role in the political economy. The labor of the poor was functional for the creation of wealth. Labor made possible the extraction of resources and the manufacture of goods from which wealth was built. Their labor therefore was necessary for the subsidiary aim of abundance. "As labor is the source of wealth, so is poverty of labour. Banish poverty, you banish wealth" (quoted in Zagday [1948: 61]).

In light of this distinction, relief could be provided only under specific terms. In particular, relief should not be provided to the *poor*—those who labor in the free market for their subsistence. Indeed, the poor were able to "keep themselves alive," even if under rather severe conditions. Bentham believed that poverty would always be relative to abundance. Because of this connection, any argument in favor of assisting the (working) poor would make it difficult to establish a permanent ceiling to benefit levels. Advocates for assisting the poor would always push for more. Therefore, Bentham argued, relief for the poor would be driven toward an absolute equality in the distribution of resources in society. Yet such absolute equality would undermine the possibility of wealth—the aim of abundance.[7] Assistance for the indigent is required, among other reasons, by the principle of subsistence. But because the poor, by definition, had secured their subsistence, they had no need of assistance.[8]

Bentham was also troubled by the institutional design of public assistance for the indigent as it stood by the turn of the nineteenth century— the parish system and outdoor forms of relief generally.[9] As a practical matter, this decentralized system of relief undermined the aims of abundance and security. In the first place, it violated the principle of abundance by its economically inefficient administration. It also violated the principle of "less-eligibility"; by providing levels of assistance commensurate with what people would earn in wages, public assistance provided the incentive to the working poor to turn to indigence. As it encouraged the working poor to forsake employment, outdoor relief inhibited the creation of wealth. The workhouse, on the other hand, would prevent this diminution of the nation's wealth by eliminating the incentive to forsake low-wage labor. It would also positively add to the wealth of the nation by contributing to the national food supply by providing a testing ground for new management techniques and by providing military training. Generally, it would reduce the overall tax burden. Additionally, pauper management would promote security insofar as it would protect the real property that might be threatened by paupers not under the control of a central administration. The uncertainty and unevenness of outdoor, decentralized relief encouraged the indigent to take by illegal means that which could not be secured by legal means. So, centralized relief in the workhouse would provide security for the expectations that property owners had developed.

By the promotion of abundance and security, pauper management in the workhouse would seem to serve primarily the interests of the nonindigent. Yet Bentham explicitly argued that pauper management also would promote the interests of the indigent themselves. Centralized relief would serve the subsidiary aims of subsistence and equality. (Of course, as pauper management served the aims of subsistence and equality, it would also serve the interests of the nonindigent. Even the nonindigent have an interest in these two aims, given that subsistence and equality, as much as abundance and security, contribute to the making of a good government and a free society.) He claimed, "their title as indigent is stronger than the title of the proprietor of superfluities as proprietors. For the pain of death, which would presently fall upon the starving poor would be always a more serious evil than the pain of disappointment which falls upon the rich when a portion of this superfluity is taken from him" (1931: 132). Thus, the indigent were owed relief by title, and by the principles of utility, not by sympathy. Relief would also promote Bentham's "disappointment-prevention" principle; that is, pauper management was necessary to protect the expectations to relief that paupers had developed under the parish system and the Elizabethan Poor Laws. Aside from those direct political reasons, Bentham expected the workhouse to provide technical education to the young and a moral education for the whole indigent population. He also believed that the workhouse would contribute to the diminution of the infant mortality rate. Additionally, he suggested that the workhouse could provide an opportunity for the (working) poor who might suffer temporary unemployment.[10]

The aim of equality for the sake of the indigent also informed Bentham's promotion of pauper management as an alternative to outdoor, decentralized relief. Outdoor relief violated the aim of equality by providing inconsistent levels of assistance, and by not providing institutional treatment for the disabled, employment for the indigent, and education for indigent minors. The aim of equality also provided the opportunity for Bentham's critique of private charity (Poynter [1969: 124]).[11] Such assistance was not distributed with equal justice among those in a position to benefit by it. Moreover, benevolence was uncertain and capricious, so that the indigent could not be certain of their subsistence on a consistent basis. Second, private charity did not fall with equal justice among those in a position to give. "The more humane and virtuous give often without any proportion to their means; while the avaricious calumniate the poor, to cover their refusal with a varnish of system and of reason" (quoted in Steintrager [1977: 69]). Even the practice of private charity undermined the aim of equality.

It should be clear that Bentham's articulation of the aim of subsistence in the context of assistance to the indigent can be viewed not only as a practical alternative to the outdoor form of relief, but also as a principled objection to the contemporary natural rights arguments for subsistence. Even in the seventeenth and eighteenth centuries, natural rights arguments for private property were not always couched in terms of an exclusive right to private property. There were equally forceful arguments about inclusive rights to property, namely rights to subsistence. For instance, Thomas Paine defended private property, but he meant by this only property that had been acquired legitimately, namely, property that had been acquired through industry and labor. He also argued that "all accumulation . . . of personal property, beyond what a man's own hands produce, is derived to him by living in society, and he owes on every principle of justice, of gratitude, and of civilization, a part of that accumulation back again to society from whence the whole came" (quoted in Horne [1990: 208]). Thomas Spence emphasized an original common. "The natural right to preservation held by everyone precluded land . . . from becoming the private property of a few" (quoted in Horne [1990: 220]).[12] These were precisely the sorts of arguments against which Bentham directed his own arguments. Although subsistence was one of the four subsidiary aims of government, it could only ever be considered a legal right. Thus it is not a right that could precede the state. There is no natural right to subsistence.

It is clear that Bentham explicitly linked his political theory to his policy proposals by showing how pauper management would satisfy the four subsidiary aims of government. But the question remains whether these two bodies of Bentham's work can be established through the analytic of liberty. Indeed, this connection seems necessary, given the central place of liberty, alongside the four subsidiary aims of government, in Bentham's political theory. If it turns out that the workhouse is consistent with the liberty of the indigent, in addition to serving the aim of subsistence, then we may draw the conclusion that the indigent ought to be considered citizens. If, on the other hand, Bentham considers the workhouse to be a denial of the liberty of the indigent, then their status as citizens is in doubt.

To be sure, Bentham wrote about personal liberty in negative terms, in relation to the liberty of behavior and the liberty of locomotion. Long before writing on the principles of pauper management, Bentham had defined the "liberty of behavior" as either the absence of constraint or the absence of restraint, and the "liberty of locomotion" as either the absence of confinement or the absence of banishment (1973: 176). These definitions of individual liberty do not seem to be consistent with the confinement of the indigent to the workhouse. Indeed, Bentham's collected manuscripts seem to demonstrate quite clearly that pauper management did not respect the liberty of paupers themselves. For instance, "Objection—'liberty infringed.' Answer—'liberty of doing mischief.' As security is increased, liberty is diminished" (Bentham [UCL, *MSS*, 133: 17]). And "That it [the Universal Register for the indigent] would be an infringement upon liberty is not to be denied: for in proportion as security is established, liberty is restricted. To one branch of liberty—the liberty of doing mischief—it would be, not prejudicial only, but destructive" (Bentham [UCL, *MSS*, 154a: 238).[13]

It is difficult to deny that pauper management entailed a sort of control over behavior that was distinct, in Bentham's mind, from the freedom of behavior enjoyed by the poor who were willing and capable of participating in the free labor market. And it was not simply the daily regimen within the panopticon that was a limitation on the civil liberties of the indigent.[14] Bentham also assigned to the management of the poorhouse, "powers of apprehending all persons, able-bodied or otherwise, having neither visible or assignable property, nor honest and sufficient means of livelihood, and detaining and employing them till some responsible person will engage for a certain period of time to find them in employment . . . " (1843, 8: 370). The indigent did not even retain the liberty of choosing to remain outside the workhouse. In fact, Bentham did not consider commitment to the panopticon to be a punishment, but a remedy. There was no crime; therefore, there was no punishment (1843, 3: 404). In this way, Bentham was able to remove "commitment" from the nature of a legal proceeding. This allowed Bentham to remove the issue of commitment to the workhouse from questions of injustice.[15]

To rely on these quotations as evidence of Bentham's contempt for the political status of the indigent, however, is to ignore the larger sense in which he used the term *liberty.* As I discussed in the preceding section, Bentham argued that individual liberty could be denied in the service of the free society—and with no loss to the political status of the person whose individual liberty was denied. The liberty that counts politically may sometimes be the liberty of society, in which all members take part. Thus pauper management provides an example of the way in which individual liberty may legitimately be subsumed under the goal of a free society. The "free" society is the well-ordered society; that is, the society that maximizes utility through the promotion of the four subsidiary aims. In sum, pauper management in general, and the panopticon workhouse in particular, reflect the view that accepts the sacrifice of some amount of freedom from constraint, if done with the aim of serving the free *society,* and along with that, the political status of all citizens.[16]

In addition to suggesting that the liberty of society will be served by the workhouse, and that even the indigent are a "part" of this society, Bentham argues elsewhere that the particular liberty of the indigent will be served and protected by the workhouse. "If security against everything that savours of tyranny be liberty, liberty in the instance of this hitherto luckless class of human beings can scarcely ever have yet existed in anything near so perfect a shape . . . But liberty, in a favourite sense of it, means lawless power: in this sense, it must be confessed, there will not only be little liberty, but in plain truth there will be none" (1843, 8: 436).

In other words, where liberty is understood as lawless power, then Bentham acknowledges that the liberty of the indigent will be denied in the workhouse. Yet where liberty means security against tyranny, then the workhouse will promote the liberty of the "hitherto luckless class of human beings." Bentham's suggestion is that indigence is itself a sort of tyranny—presumably a tyranny of want for subsistence.

The Rationality of the Indigent

Rather than using pauper management to argue that indigence represents the loss of freedom and citizenship, it is more useful to view Bentham's policy recommendations as evidence of the central importance of labor in the meaning of liberal citizenship. Bentham makes this even more clear through his treatment of the agency and rationality of the indigent. In this regard Bentham seems to have assumed on the one hand that the indigent were destitute not only of material goods (and of power), but also of the sort of rationality that is necessary for the procurement of these goods. He contended, "the persons in question are a sort of forward looking children—a set of persons not altogether sound in mind—not altogether possessed of that moral sanity without which a man cannot in justice to himself anymore than to the community be intrusted [*sic*] with the uncontrolled management of his own conduct and affairs" (UCL, *MSS*, 154a: 224, n. 181]).

Ever ready to offer a solution, Bentham viewed pauper management as the means by which this rationality could be inculcated and the agency of the indigent promoted.[17] The daily regimen in the workhouse would instill the liberal value of work. The status of "wardship" within the panopticon need only be temporary. It was necessary only until that time when the pauper "arrived at the prescribed period of intellectual maturity" (UCL, *MSS*, 154a, 224, n. 181]). Thus, however much Bentham might deny the individual liberty of the indigent, he did not treat the indigent permanently merely as "objects of knowledge" and thus permanently devoid of any agency, as Dean (1991) argues. Rather, the significant point is that the workhouse would have provided the opportunity for the indigent to prove their rationality and agency by forced work.

To be sure, on external grounds there is no doubt that Bentham's plans for pauper management severely curtailed the individual liberty of the poor. Undoubtedly, these plans would either offend the sensibilities of those committed to the civil liberties of all individuals, or satisfy those committed to denying civil liberties to individuals who fail to secure their economic standing independently of the state. But either of those positions fails to understand the internal logic of Bentham's position. The point that is missed by ignoring this internal logic is that the route to citi-

zenship, for those without economic means, lies through the action of labor. Thus, this analysis of Bentham's recommendations to Parliament in
the early nineteenth century demonstrates that his plans were more complex, more theoretically informed, and less sinister than might otherwise
be surmised by focusing exclusively on the horrors of the industry house.
As Lea Boralevi has responded to the scholarship of Gertrude Himmelfarb, "it is simply a mistake to look for evidence of humanity and pity in
writings which were to serve as a technical guide for legislation, and had
therefore to be based exclusively on utility. To measure his humanity
from these writings may be the best way of provoking the reader's emotional rejection of Bentham's suggestions, but it is certainly not the best
way to obtain a better understanding of his philosophy" (1984: 103–4).

Citizenship and the
Extension of the Suffrage

Throughout this chapter I have been using liberty and the principles of
utility as a proxy for Bentham's theory of liberal citizenship. His political
theory is largely an articulation and defense of the terms that typically
serve as the elements of liberal models of citizenship. And by using these
terms as proxies, I have concluded that Bentham believes that labor lies
at the foundation of citizenship. In this way, pauper management is just
one part of Bentham's larger project for extending political equality
through state intervention. In this section, I treat Bentham's arguments
for extending the suffrage as another source for his views on liberal citizenship. This will help to illuminate the way in which he attributed a distinctive status to paupers in his model of a free political society.

In his arguments concerning the suffrage, Bentham took direct aim at
the question of property qualifications. Because property rights, according to Bentham, are a legal construct, and not an expression of presocial
claims, ownership of property does not confer the right to be represented
in the law. The right to be represented is a distinct conventional or legal
right.[18] It is based on the notion that any individual has the capacity for
feeling pleasure or pain. That is, any individual counts as a part of the aggregate calculus of happiness in society (see Horne [1990: 148]). From as
early as 1788, Bentham's proposals for reform in England included arguments about extending the franchise (see Steintrager [1977: 57–58]). He
contended that every individual has "an equal right to all the happiness
that he is capable of" (quoted in Steintrager [1977: 57]). Although it
would be difficult to determine the relative amount of happiness derived
from an array of *activities*, it is reasonable, according to Bentham, to assume that this degree will not vary from individual to individual. By con-
tending that the franchise is a source of happiness, Bentham argued that

its extension would be the means of distributing this sort of happiness equally among the people. He did continue to exclude certain groups, for instance, minors and the insane. But in the case of any other exclusions, a heavy burden would fall on those in favor of the exclusion to demonstrate its necessity. Thus, on the eve of the French Revolution, and though critical of the *Declaration of the Rights of Man and the Citizen*, Bentham laid out his first arguments in favor of extending the suffrage. At the time, this would have meant that the working class (which would include the indigent) and women would have the opportunity to be considered citizens by the criterion of the franchise.[19]

By 1809, Bentham had firmly established his reputation as a democrat, based on these arguments for extending the suffrage and on his advocacy of representative government, generally. At this time, he began to focus his attention largely on constitutional questions.[20] In *The Catechism of Parliamentary Reform* (1809)[21], he argued that the extension of the suffrage was consistent with the universal-interest-comprehension principle. He even argued for the inclusion of resident aliens and women (1843, 3: 540–41). He still excluded minors on the grounds that they had not developed the appropriate intellectual aptitude. Although this sort of exclusion did have the advantage of being only temporary; children would mature into adults. His arguments rested on a number of points. Most important, the success of his reforms, in general, depended on the extension of the franchise. The monarchy and the aristocracy on their own would have been unlikely to initiate the broader reforms for which Bentham hoped, and the House of Commons could not have been relied on to spontaneously generate reform. Bentham hoped to make the government dependent on the House of Commons and the House dependent on the interests of the people. Also, considering the four subsidiary aims of government, universal suffrage and representative democracy would advance the goals of security and equality, generally, without thoroughly undermining the security of particular property holders.

Although the suffrage might have had the effect of challenging some *particular* claims for private property, the unhappiness endured by some people would be outweighed by the happiness rendered to others. As we have already seen in his use of liberty, Bentham believed that the consequences of actions must be judged by their effects on society more generally, rather than on particular groups within society. In fact, Bentham had noted that the overthrow of government by revolution was of great importance and only transitory in nature (1843, 1: 311–12). It would ultimately lead to another system of property. He contrasted this change in property relations to the direct attempt to establish a system of equal property. The latter would amount to a permanent shock to security. Where property is redistributed by revolution, however, it amounts to only a temporary shock to security, followed by a more firmly established guarantee of security (see Rosen [1983: 219]). At the same time, Bentham did not envision the complete equalization of property. He simply did not seem concerned, as so many of his contemporaries were, that an extension of the suffrage would lead to the widespread expropriation of property.

Thus, the extension of the suffrage was instrumental to the realization of the reforms Bentham promoted—to the realization of the principle of utility in society.[22] The people as a whole would continue to be excluded from legislative activity. That was never seriously questioned by Bentham. But the people did have an electoral role to play in the reforms that ultimately were for their benefit.[23] A democratic government, defined by Bentham as popular access to that government through the suffrage, could be justified by the expectation that it would consider the interests of more individuals in society and therefore lead to an increase in aggregate happiness.

Additionally, Bentham could find no good argument in favor of the practice of excluding women and the nonpropertied classes. Their happiness was as much a part in the aggregate of happiness in society, so their participation in the suffrage was necessary to increase this aggregate. Political participation through the suffrage contributed to the happiness of individuals. "The happiness and unhappiness of any one member of the community—high or low, rich or poor—what greater or less part is it of the universal happiness and unhappiness, than that of any other?" (1843, 3: 459). Bentham dismissed concerns about the disruptive consequences of the extension of the suffrage. In perfect utilitarian logic, he argued that the mischief that would follow extension of the suffrage (if indeed there was to be any) would be less than the increase of happiness it would bring to those it would henceforth include. He continued to include women in principle and to argue that this inclusion "involved nothing absurd" (1843, 3: 567). In the end, however, Bentham bowed to popular pressure and downplayed the importance of extending the franchise to women (1843, 3: 86).[24]

In *The Radical Reform Bill* (1819)[25] Bentham outlined new qualifications for the suffrage. The age was set at twenty-one (1843, 3: 565), though he was not dogmatic about that (1843, 3: 132). The voter must have occupied a household in the district for four weeks. He must have demonstrated literacy and have signed a declaration certifying honesty and secrecy in the casting of his ballot (1843, 3: 564–67). By this time, Bentham no longer excluded the insane or criminals in principle, although being in prison would have presented a practical—not a principled—obstacle to their voting. Regarding criminals not confined to prison, however, he wrote,

But the most mischievous among criminals, adjudged and denominated such after legal conviction, could not set his foot in either House, without finding himself in company with men in numbers—not to say in a vast majority—more mischievous than himself: men, whose principal differences from himself, consist in impunity derived from situation and confederacy—in impunity derived from situation and confederacy—in impunity added to greater mischievousness: men, whose mischievousness was acting on the largest scale, while his was acting on a petty scale. Exclude criminals? How will you exclude criminals? (1843, 3: 559)

Bentham did not consider the literacy requirement to be much of a hindrance, since literacy could be acquired in a few months of study during rest from work (1843, 3: 560). Although the householder qualification required that the individual had paid both rent and some taxes, Bentham did not use this argument to exclude those who had no real property (1843, 3: 559–60). Indeed, Bentham challenged the argument that property is the "only bond and pledge of attachment to country. . . . Want of property is a much stronger one. He who has property can change the shape of it, and carry it with him to another country. . . . He who has no property can do no such thing" (1843, 3: 560).

In his call for the extension of the suffrage to the nonpropertied, Bentham did not explicitly address the separation of this class into the poor and the pauper. His tracts on pauper management never addressed the question of the paupers' right to vote, although in the *Radical Reform Bill*, Bentham indirectly suggested that the franchise ought not to exclude paupers. Near the beginning of this document, Bentham outlined the merits of a secret ballot. He identified a group of individuals who would benefit from this practice, because they were otherwise dependent on someone else for their livelihood. The secret ballot would allow them to vote according to their preference and not according to the preferences of those upon whom they depended for employment. He also included paupers, as an example of those dependent on the magistrates. The paupers' liberty to vote according to their own preferences would be protected by the secret ballot (1843, 3: 559).[26]

Conclusion

My aim in this chapter has been twofold. In the first place, I have demonstrated the relationship between Bentham's political theory and his recommendations for pauper management. In particular, these proposals are explicable in terms of the principle of utility and the four subsidiary aims of democratic government. Additionally, I have brought to light the relationship between these goals of pauper management and Bentham's conceptions of liberty and citizenship. I have argued that Bentham's model of pauper management takes into account the interests of society generally, as well as the interests of the indigent. Pauper management would promote and protect the conditions for a free society. The freedom of society, in which all members take part, is more politically salient than individual freedom. The latter can be sacrificed without detriment to one's political status.

In more general terms, Bentham contended that the justification for government is not based on its capacity to merely provide a constitution of law—the protection of claims ostensibly made prior to the establishment of government. The state, when it is checked by popular censure, is necessary because it protects that objective in which all people have an interest, most important, the interest in security. A justification for the state intervention in society does not lie with its capacity to protect something in which only a few have an interest, namely, property. So, the reasons for state intervention in society seem to support establishing the conditions for citizenship for the indigent. Bentham's arguments for state intervention are founded on the assumption that, for those without property, citizenship depends on work. Citizenship depends on the rationality and moral development made possible, according to Bentham, by work. The utilitarian liberal democratic state, not constrained by laissez-faire injunctions, becomes the source of this work.

This examination of Bentham's contribution to liberal democratic theory is useful for a number of reasons. First, Bentham's political theory anticipates the contemporary political arguments about workfare, although the latter qualify Bentham's version of workfare by redefining what kind of work, and under what conditions, counts as the grounds for citizenship. In addition, Bentham's reasons for public welfare contrast with the argument I will lay out in Part Three of this book, where I also contend that the distribution of public assistance can be founded on the liberty of the recipient. My argument, however, does not place work at the center, nor does it rely on the conception of liberty used by Bentham. Although I enlist a conception of liberty that does not rely on noncoercion, it is also a conception that *does not contradict* the principle of noncoercion. Finally, my argument for public assistance in Part Three will center around the liberty of the recipient, without Bentham's consideration of the security interests of those ostensibly threatened by a predatory indigent class.

Notes

1. See, for instance, Mises (1985).
2. Bentham was not the first exponent of utilitarianism, but undoubtedly the most famous of them (R. Harrison [1988: xiv]).

3. See, for example, "Bentham on Humphreys' Property Code" (1843, 5: 413–14); "Official Aptitude Maximized: Expense Minimized" (1843, 5: 266); "Pannomial Fragments" (1843, 3: 226).

4. See Rosen (1983: 223f).

5. This suggests that liberty cannot be understood without a theory of power. As I noted above, Bentham seems to equate power with access to, and control over, decision making. The one who has power can make the sorts of decisions that affect others, potentially leading to a coercive relationship.

6. Clearly, Bentham also saw this as a business venture by which he hoped to reap profits, in the form of the National Charity Company, a joint-stock venture. See Roberts (1979: 35), on the reasons for an independent company rather than a government administration, namely, that 1) Parliament could be a watchdog over a private central administration, but a reversal of roles would not be effective, and 2) that in the government there was lack of discipline and a tendency for the promotion of sinister interests. But the *Plan for a National Charity Company for the Management of the Poor all over England* was written before the turn of the nineteenth century, and it does not reflect the democratic principles that he laid out in more detail after 1809. Thus, in the *Constitutional Code*, written later in his life, Bentham included a Ministry for the Relief of Indigence. But I think that even a privatized form of poor relief does not detract from the link I have identified. For an alternative interpretation, see Manning (1968), who argues that there is no relation between Bentham's political theory and his practical policy proposals. Boralevi argues that the shift from a contract system to a state ministry does not indicate a shift in Bentham's mind about the role of the state. Rather, it is a reflection of the shift in Bentham's mind about the capacity of the state to handle the task (1984: 103). See also Poynter (1969: 131, n. 68).

7. See Rosenblum (1978: 49–50); Boralevi (1984: 98–99).

8. See Poynter (1969: 118).

9. See Poynter (1969: 127–28) for this outline.

10. Bentham describes the "Collateral Benefits" of pauper management in Book 3 of "Outline of a Work Entitled Pauper Management Improved" (1843, 8: 397–430).

11. See also Steintrager (1977: 69) and Roberts (1979: 36f).

12. Horne (1990) examines these arguments in detail. Although, Horne's interpretation of Bentham is not entirely similar to the one described here. I return to the findings of Horne in Chapter 4.

13. Both passages quoted in Himmelfarb (1970: 93).

14. For exhaustive descriptions of the thoroughly repressive character of the panopticon poorhouse, see Himmelfarb (1970) and Bahmueller (1981).

15. See Himmelfarb (1970: 91).

16. Some scholars have even suggested that the organization of the workhouse along the lines of a panopticon represented a model for the organization of society at large (Bahmueller [1981: 111]; Wolin [1960: 348]; Foucault [1979]). In that sense, the workhouse is a microcosm of society, so that the free society, in Bentham's mind, was the panopticon society.

17. Dean (1991) has argued that "labour was the objective expression of the adherence of moral subjects, constituted in the act of the exchange of their only

property, that which they held in their own persons, to bio-economic necessity, [and] pauperism was a site outside that act of moral constitution, and the violation of that necessity ... presaged the demoralisation of the individual and the fall of civilisation into the abyss of inertia" (176).

18. The counter position being: 1) Rights to property are grounded in presocial claims. 2) The law exists largely for the purpose of protecting those claims. 3) Therefore, only people with property have a legitimate claim to participate or be represented in the formulation of the law.

19. It has been estimated that in 1831 the size of the English and Welsh electorates was 439,200, which amounted to 3.2 percent of the total population (13,900,000). And the electorate was 14.4 percent of the adult male population. Following the Reform Act of 1832, the size of the electorate jumped to 656,000 (O'Gorman [1989: 179]).

20. See, Steintrager (1977: 78). He notes that there is nothing inherently democratic in the principle of utility. Conservatives, liberals, and even benevolent despots adhered to the principle of utility at the time that Bentham wrote. Still, Steintrager argues, there were potentially democratic elements in Bentham's distinctive formulation of utilitarianism, namely: a) the psychological axiom that each one is the best judge of his own interest, and b) the normative claim that "equality" must be considered among the four subsidiary aims of government.

21. In Bentham (1843, 3: 433–557).

22. He also argued that the importance of universal suffrage to democratic ascendancy would be a restoration of the traditional rights of Englishmen (1843, 3: 469, 471, 475–6, 480–81).

23. Bentham also spoke of the people as a "Constitutive Authority" and the "Public Opinion Tribunal" (1843, 8: 563; 1973: 211–15). The latter was not a specific group designated to make decisions. Rather, it was a fiction, but "one that described the force that lay with the people generally for reform in democratic and non-democratic societies. It represented a judicial body which applied the moral sanction to people and institutions" (Rosen [1983: 28]). Membership in this fictional group extended to all those who were interested in a particular issue (Bentham [1968: 35–36]). Among those activities that loosely constituted this tribunal were, for instance, attending legislative and judicial sittings, attending public meetings, and making public speeches.

24. For the debate over Bentham's views on the role of women in the suffrage, see the exchange between Terrence Ball (1980) and Lea Boralevi (1980).

25. Bentham (1843, 3: 558–97).

26. In an interesting use of language, given the argument of this chapter, Bentham argued, "To look out for grounds for exclusion, is mere *lost labour*" (1843, 3: 559, emphasis added).

2

The New Right and
Market Citizenship

My analysis in this chapter turns to a set of arguments laid out in the context of the post–World War II welfare state, but which clearly bear the marks of a long tradition of liberal democratic theory. The New Right has tried to retrieve, and sometimes refine, a clear statement of the limits of state action, a statement with striking implications for citizenship. And perhaps nowhere can this statement be more fully grasped than in the New Right's critique of public assistance. Relying on a distinction between the public and private spheres, the New Right argues that the conditions for the full expression of citizenship can only be satisfied within the boundaries of the private sphere. Although citizenship in part may designate actions performed in and by virtue of the public sphere, the full status of citizenship depends furthermore on what one is capable of doing in the private sphere. Full citizenship, according to the New Right, will depend upon securing paid employment.[1]

Paid employment is important for the New Right for two reasons. In the first place, paid employment is the foundation for freedom; paid employment signifies one's independence. In particular, it is the mark of *economic* independence. This approach to citizenship demonstrates that the New Right does not define freedom in strictly negative terms. One of my aims in this chapter is to demonstrate that although New Right liberal theorists claim to rely exclusively on a conception of freedom as noninterference or noncoercion in their critique of welfare to the nonworking poor, they also imply a more substantive conception of freedom. Freedom will depend as much on what one does for himself as it does on what others forbear from doing. Freedom will depend on economic independence, a status secured for most individuals by their wages from employment. And, as freedom is central to one's status as a full citizen, paid employment is necessary for full citizenship. Second, paid employment

satisfies a *contributory* condition of citizenship. Citizenship not only entitles one to, for instance, the right to vote and to the protection of civil liberties. The full status of citizenship depends on making a contribution to
the cohesion and progress of society.

In light of this conception of citizenship, the New Right poses two general critiques of welfare provision. On the one hand, since the poor must
rely on the government for assistance, these individuals have not met the
qualifications for full citizenship. Therefore, there is no reason to provide
these benefits in terms of the protection of the interests of the poor. On
the other hand, the actual practice of welfare provision in the United
States has, according to this view, actively inhibited the prospects for full
citizenship. To be sure, the New Right critiques of welfare provision do
not entirely deny the value of the public sphere. The critiques are meant
to define the proper scope of the public sphere. The problem with welfare
provision, according to the New Right, is that it undermines the individual liberty and social order for which the public sphere, or the state, has
its reason in the first place.

Before beginning my detailed examination of the main components of
the New Right,[2] it will be useful to offer a general remark on the distinction between the public and private spheres. On the one hand, the economic liberals, the libertarians, and some moral conservatives set up the
distinction between the private world of the market and the public world
of the state. The familist component of the moral conservatives adds to
this the private world of the family. The point of this chapter is not to focus on a tension between these two different conceptions of the private
sphere. Rather, the two conceptions complement one another in the
philosophical foundations as well as the policy recommendations of the
New Right. To refer to the private sphere, then, in relation to the New
Right is to speak of two private spheres. The aim, generally, of the New
Right is to redistribute the welfare tasks that have fallen to the state over
at least the past fifty years, to either the market or the family.

The Economic Liberals

In this first section, I examine two prominent theorists and apologists of
the free market. F. A. Hayek and Milton Friedman are the two twentieth-
century economists whose statements about the proper limits of state interference are perhaps the most closely identified with a critique of the
welfare state in general, and with specific recommendations for the relief
of poverty in particular. In the end, both Hayek and Friedman accept a
system of welfare provision for the poor. But these benefits are provided
for reasons that have nothing to do with the liberty of the poor. In the end,
Hayek and Friedman deny that welfare recipients are free individuals.

The Limits of Knowledge

Hayek's statement on the distinction between the public and private spheres begins with his epistemology (1960, 1979). Drawing on Hume, Hayek's theory is founded on two premises. First, individuals are capable of mastering only a specific range of knowledge or information.[3] This is especially true of advanced, complex societies. "The more [society] know[s], the smaller the share of all that knowledge becomes that any one mind can absorb" (1960: 26). Moreover, human reason or the mind does not stand outside of nature and is not independent of experience, as Cartesian philosophy would posit. Instead, knowledge is based in experience,[4] and it "exists only dispersed as the separate, partial and sometimes conflicting beliefs of all men" (1960: 25).

These premises, in turn, inform Hayek's interpretation of the development of civilization. "The recognition of our ignorance is the beginning of wisdom . . . for our understanding of society" (1960: 22). Both the *definition*, as well as the *advantage*, of an advanced, modern society or "civilization" is that an individual benefits from more knowledge than he may be aware of. "It might be said that civilization begins when the individual in the pursuit of his ends can make use of more knowledge than he has himself acquired and when he can transcend the boundaries of his ignorance by profiting from knowledge he does not himself possess" (1960: 22). Society, or civilization, is the product of a number of individuals acting on their specific set of information for specific ends. Thus, Hayek's focus in epistemology is not on the measure of individual mental capacity. He does not examine knowledge, or information, in terms of an inventory of facts held by the individual. Rather, Hayek focuses on how the *dispersal* of knowledge is integral to the formation of society. In particular, the growth of knowledge and the growth of civilization go hand in hand, where knowledge "include[s] all the human adaptations to [*sic*] environment in which past experience has been incorporated" (1960: 26). This tacit knowledge, incapable of articulation, refers to all the habits, skills, emotional attitudes, tools, and institutions that constitute society. The history of civilization is the process of the transmission of an accumulated stock of information, even though it is not at the level of conscious decision.

Hayek uses the term *abstraction* to describe the way in which tacit knowledge is communicated among individuals. Abstract concepts "are a means [for] cop[ing] with the complexity of the concrete which our mind is not capable of fully mastering" (1979, 1: 29–30). Furthermore, abstractions allow the capacity for reasoning to develop more fully than would be possible if this capacity depended on mastering particular information. Abstraction enables individuals to benefit from more knowledge than they could possibly be aware of. The communication of abstractions thus leads to the establishment of social institutions. In this way, social institutions are the result of human action. But these institutions are not the result of human design (1979, 1: 21). Given this, Hayek comments on the limits to what humans can achieve purposely.

> Although we must endeavor to make society good in the sense that we shall like to live in it, we cannot make it good in the sense that it will behave morally. It does not make sense to apply the standards of conscious conduct to those unintended consequences of individual action which all the truly social represents except by eliminating the unintended which would mean eliminating all that we call culture. . . . The Great Society and the civilization it has made possible is the product of man's growing capacity to communicate abstract thought. (1979, 1: 33)

Thus, Hayek proposes an evolutionary explanation for the development of these institutions. They are the result of "a process in which practices which had first been adopted for other reasons, or even purely accidentally, were preserved because they enabled the group in which they had arisen to prevail over others" (1979, 1: 9).

Hayek uses the notion of a spontaneous order, or *kosmos,* to describe this development. An order generally refers to "a state of affairs in which a multiplicity of elements of various kinds are so related to each other that we may learn from our acquaintance with some spatial or temporal part of the whole to form correct expectations concerning the rest or at least expectations which have a good chance of proving correct" (1979, 1: 36). A *kosmos*, in particular, describes the growth of civilization. It is the result, not of one mind having imposed his will on society, but of a collection of individuals acting on their own knowledge for their own purposes. In other words, the motor of this evolution of social institutions is the multitudinous actions of individuals pursuing their own ends.

Hayek contrasts his epistemological position and his interpretation of the development of civilization with that of the so-called "rationalist constructivists." He provides an explicit critique of what he sees as "a[n essentially Cartesian] conception which assumes that all social institutions are, and ought to be, the product of deliberate design" (1979, 1: 5). This position is inspired by a tendency to misunderstand the source of order in society; the rational constructivists tend to anthropomorphize this order. As should be clear from the preceding exposition, Hayek considers the rationalist constructivist position to be false in both its empirical description and in its prescriptions for social action. This position aims at controlling all knowledge and at leaving nothing to chance. This objective is implied by Descartes's premise that one ought to reject as false anything for which one has the slightest doubt. It is also implied by the assumption that reason can stand outside of experience and provide the only basis for action. As a critique of society, and as an inspiration for the French Revolution and the "Rights of Man," this epistemological position led to the conclusion that society could be rebuilt from the bottom up.

According to Hayek, however, rational action is typically guided by habit rather than reflection (1960: 65–66). The mark of rationality for Hayek is that an individual is guided in his behavior by the adherence to a set of rules, rather than that his actions are based on something like reason divorced from experience. In other words, rules embody the experience that one is only able to articulate in an abstract manner. This means, again, that social institutions are the product of human action—actions based on a capacity to communicate abstractions, but that are not the product of human design.

In addition to a critique of the rationalist constructivist position on individual grounds, Hayek identifies its limitations for prescribing social action. Taking a consequentialist view, he argues that it would not be possible to make human institutions wholly dependent on design without at the same time restricting the use of individual knowledge. It would involve the imposition of a single will; it would hinder the evolutionary process of connecting particular knowledges. As opposed to a *kosmos*, the rationalist constructivist position appeals to a forced order, or a *taxis*. This sort of order relies on specific commands and is informed by the mistaken belief that an individual or group can foresee all the consequences of a particular decision. The rationalist constructivists err in equating the possibilities of a complex society with the purposefulness of an individual.

Hayek's interpretation of history and his identification of rational possibilities lay the foundation for distinguishing between the public and private spheres, that is, for distinguishing between the state and the free market. More particularly, his epistemology informs his critique of state interference in the market. His defense of the market is not a pure case of the application of neoclassical economics. As a member of the Austrian School, he emphasizes the dynamic tendencies of markets—their equilibrating tendencies—rather than equilibrium as a determinate outcome. And Hayek does not derive his defense of the market from strictly libertarian arguments; he does not deduce his defense from the first principles of the right to private property. Instead, he treats the market as a set of social practices that successfully integrates individuals in society because it is the mechanism most capable of capitalizing on individual knowledge. The price mechanism, in particular, provides signals or conveys information between individuals in an abstract manner. It is an example of individuals drawing inferences about the whole from an acquaintance with a part, thereby enabling them to take action. "The market order in particular will regularly secure only a certain probability that the expected relations will prevail, but it is nevertheless, the only way in which so many activities depending on dispersed knowledge can be effectively integrated into a single order" (1979, 1: 42).

Furthermore, although the market does involve human action, it is not the product of human design. The benefits and burdens of the market are not the result of a deliberate allocation of resources to particular people. The outcomes are neither intended nor foreseen. Thus, Hayek distinguishes his analysis of the market from those who defend the market on the grounds that it rewards the industrious; chance is, according to Hayek, an inherent quality of the market. But neither should it be charged that the market is immoral. Only actions that are the result of the deliberate actions of individuals can be considered moral or not (1979, 2: 31, 74). The market is "just," however, because it relies on a set of rules that apply equally to all people. So the market should not be judged by the relative positions of people producing and consuming within it. The market ought to be judged by its capability for dealing with epistemological limitations. The fact that any particular individual may suffer under the market is not grounds for its indictment. This mechanism is inherently risky with respect to a final distribution of economic resources. Any attempt to eliminate that risk through the imposition of a single will, will have devastating consequences for the cohesion of society and the development of civilization.

It is in light of his epistemology and his theory of the market that Hayek articulates his conception of liberty, or freedom.[5] Accordingly, his view of liberty is empirically based. It is grounded in neither an abstract theory of rights nor in an idealized view of the individual. Still, in his conception of liberty Hayek does focus primarily on the status of an individual rather than on groups as a whole.[6] Liberty refers solely to a relation between individuals. It describes "the state in which a man is not subject to coercion by the arbitrary will of another or others" (1960: 11); the principle of liberty is one of noncoercion. By coercion, Hayek means, "such control of the environment or circumstances of a person by another that, in order to avoid greater evil, he is forced to act not according to a coherent plan of his own, but to serve the ends of another" (1960: 20). In other words, coercion stands in the way of an individual taking advantage of his own specific knowledge in the pursuit of his own plans. "Coercion is evil precisely because it thus eliminates an individual as a thinking and valuing person and makes him a bare tool in the achievement of the ends of another" (1960: 20).[7] Thus Hayek derives his empirical description of liberty from his epistemological theory. The condition of freedom is "a state in which each can use his knowledge for his own purposes" (1979, 1: 55). Interestingly enough, although the status of individual liberty may itself have been merely the unintended consequence of some activity, it has proven itself beneficial. Its protection has provided the basis for social cohesion.

By this conception of liberty, Hayek implies a two-point justification for the *protection* of liberty. On the one hand, liberty is inherently valuable. Liberty ought to be protected because one ought to respect an individual as a "thinking and valuing person." Although Hayek does not use the term *autonomy*, this is obviously the point where he appears to blend a Humean epistemology with a Kantian ethics. Although this suggests that Hayek places the individual at the center of his conception of freedom, he also suggests that freedom is instrumental for another purpose. The protection of liberty also serves the more long run and wider interest of society generally; liberty ought to be protected because of its instrumental value. In particular, the protection of liberty serves two ends. In the first place, the protection of liberty serves the function of integrating society. The imposition of a particular command in place of the evolved Rules of Just Conduct threatens long-run social cohesion. A totalitarian regime may be capable of maintaining some sort of "order." But it will not be a *kosmos*; it will not allow individuals to use their own knowledge under a system of rules applying equally to all persons. Second, liberty is valued because of its role as a motor of progress. The value of freedom rests on the opportunities it provides for unforeseen and unpredictable actions. People will never know what they have lost through a particular restriction of freedom. They will never know the cost of interference. Again, "Freedom means that in some measure we entrust our fate to forces which we do not control; and this seems intolerable to collectivists who believe that man can master his fate—as if civilization and reason itself were of his making" (1979, 2: 30).

Hayek does not define the content of that progress; he makes no predictions about the future. But he is generally sanguine about the prospects for the development of institutions and a standard of living that will be *universally valued*. In fact, he avers that everything people now cherish, all the institutions to which individuals are ready to give their allegiance, are themselves the product of having successfully integrated the individual pursuits of individuals through respect for their ability to do so. This is precisely what the Rule of Law had allowed, as he supposes it to have been practiced in Europe and the United States in the nineteenth century. The task now is to ensure that we all profit from this knowledge. Thus the free market ought to be pursued because it promotes and protects individual liberty. Liberty enables the individual to use his own knowledge in the pursuit of his own goals, and enables the progress of society.

The Misappropriation of
the Democratic Method

Given the constraints of limited and tacit knowledge, the protection of individual liberty is the necessary and central component in the process of
social integration and progress. And the protection and promotion of liberty can be best ensured by limiting the intrusion of the public sphere,
the state, into the private sphere, the market. In turn, the best guarantee
of this limitation is a public sphere that operates on democratic principles. Among the liberal theorists of the New Right, Hayek provides the
most developed analysis of the relation between liberalism and democracy. Thus, understanding his theory of democracy is crucial to understanding his attack on the welfare state.

To be sure, Hayek treats liberty as a distinctly liberal value, not intrinsically related to democracy. But although democracy may not intrinsically
recommend itself, it will contribute to the realization of freedom when
properly conceived and executed.[8] "However strong the general case for
democracy, it is not an ultimate or absolute value and must be judged by
what it will achieve. It is probably the best *method* of achieving certain
ends, but not an end in itself" (1960: 106, emphasis added). The problem
in the postwar era, as Hayek sees it, is that a mistaken view of democracy
has been promulgated. And the state has, in the name of the mistaken
view of democracy, undermined the prospects for freedom and social order. When properly defined, the democratic logic of the public sphere remains subservient to the liberal logic of the private sphere. But in the
postwar era, the public sphere has intruded into the private sphere and
undermined freedom.

Hayek defines and justifies democracy with three arguments.[9] In the
first place, democracy as a procedure of majority rule provides a method
for peaceful change. "[W]henever it is necessary that one of several conflicting *opinions* should prevail and when one would have to be made to
prevail by force if need be, it is less wasteful to determine which has the
stronger support by counting numbers than by fighting" (1960: 107, emphasis added). Second, as I have already indicated, Hayek views democracy as an important safeguard of individual liberty. Democracy is not itself liberty, but "it is more likely than other forms of government to
produce liberty" (1960: 108). He notes that although this argument for
democracy has been most compelling historically, he also warns that we
can no longer be certain of its empirical validity. "The prospects of liberty
[even under a democracy] depend on whether or not the majority makes
it its deliberate object. It would have little chance of surviving if we relied
on the mere existence of democracy to preserve it" (1960: 108). Thus,
Hayek cautions that democracy is a necessary, but not a sufficient, guar-

antee of liberty. Third, the democratic method has an educative effect.[10] Given that democracy involves the process of forming opinions, "its chief advantage lies not in its method of selecting those who govern but in the fact that, because a great part of the population takes an active part in the formation of opinion, a correspondingly wide range of persons is available from which to select" (1960: 108). In other words, democracy can be a means for the development of, and a conduit for the diffusion of, tacit knowledge. This, in turn, is conducive to the goals that he has already specified: the integration and progress of society.[11]

The bulk of Hayek's writings on democracy is devoted to the contention that a mistaken theory of democracy has been put into practice in this century.[12] Hayek identifies three misconceptions about the true nature of democracy.[13] In the first place, democracy was originally, and rightly, grounded in the belief that only that which had been approved by the majority should be binding on society as a whole. From that principle democratic theorists and political activists drew the mistaken conclusion that anything that a majority approves should be binding. It is one thing to argue that only decisions arrived at through procedure X can be binding; that does not necessarily entail that all decisions that have been arrived at through procedure X ought to be binding. In this way, democracy substituted the will of the majority for the Rule of Law. Second, this mistaken view of democracy defined justice in terms of the source from which a decision emanates—the majority. This mistaken conception disregarded the notion that the criterion of justice is identified with its conformity with the rules on which people tacitly agree, namely, the Rule of Law.

Third, and of greatest concern to Hayek, democracy became associated with the pursuit of material equality. Again, Hayek argues that democracy is a "method" for the peaceful change of government; it is a "means" for ensuring stability.[14] Continuing his critique of any society-wide pursuit of substantive ends, Hayek avers that democracy likewise should not aim at a particular distribution of material resources. To be sure, there ought to be equality in the distribution of legal standing; the Rule of Law ought to apply universally. But material equality is an elusive goal, and democracy has mistakenly become associated with this objective. Taking a pluralist view, Hayek regards society as a collection of agents, groups, and institutions that interact for a variety of purposes. In that society, the state is just one of a number of elements. By assuming that democracy involves a particular distributive end, the state has unjustifiably become the most powerful institution among all others. In so doing, it has interfered with the autonomy of the private sphere. In sum, rather than supporting liberty, the mistaken view of democracy, put into practice, has been coercive.

Hayek warns, for instance, that when a democratic society has reached the point at which anything that a majority wills at a particular time has the force of law, the democratic method has become arbitrary. Recall that Hayek describes the Rule of Law as being consistent and universally applied. Consequently, it allows individuals to act on their specific knowledge and to form plans and pursue objectives. In this sense, it respects individual liberty. Therefore, the principle that anything willed at any moment by a majority ought to have force will disappoint the expectations that have been formed in light of evolved social institutions. It will therefore constitute an act of coercion—a restriction of individual liberty. It hinders the individual from using his own specific knowledge for his own ends, and for the good of society. Hayek adds that democracy is not only a condition for freedom. Even more, democracy will not succeed if it is not operating in a society where the Rule of Law applies.

Hayek also discusses the threat to liberty posed by interest-group politics. He argues that political expediency replaces adherence to general rules. When democratic government is nominally omnipotent it becomes the "playball of all the separate interests it has to satisfy to secure majority support" (1979, 3: 99). Universal suffrage leads candidates to pander to the electorate. Whereas Madison argued that factions would maintain a pluralist state of power, Hayek worries that factions have created too large a state. He is not concerned about any particular group or individual gaining too much control. As long as that power remains faithful to and consistent with the Rule of Law, it does not appear to matter if that power is concentrated with a few individuals. Indeed, as long as individuals responsible for maintaining the state remain committed to the Rule of Law, they could never be described as wielding too much power.[15] The concern is that the breadth of influence of the state, generally—the public sphere—has been extended too far. There is a clear distinction between ascertaining the dominant opinion and pandering to particularized interests. Under the mistaken view, and also the mistaken practice, of democracy, legislators have become agents of the interests of constituents, rather than the representatives of public opinion.[16] This has led inexorably to the extension of the public sphere's influence.

Furthermore, the structure of the democratic method for choosing outcomes leads to consequences that the majority might not be willing to accept on principle, but that are nevertheless the result of a process of bargaining.[17] Given the competition among groups pursuing their own interests, democracy induces these groups to vote for particular measures, to which, if they had been asked to vote on principle, they would not agree. "The outcome may indeed be wholly contrary to any principles which the several members of the majority would approve if they ever had an opportunity to vote on them" (1979, 3: 15). Democracy can create false majorities. "It appears that we have unwittingly created a machinery which makes it possible to claim the sanction of an alleged majority for measures which are in fact not desired by a majority, and which may even be disapproved by a majority of the people, and that this machinery produces an aggregate of measures that not only is not wanted by anybody, but that could not, as a whole be approved by any rational mind because it is inherently contradictory" (1979, 3: 6). In other words, these unintended consequences of voting are contrary to the general opinion.

In the end, the use of democracy to pursue substantive ends will, and historically has, hinder(ed) the mechanism of the market. As described earlier, the market is the institution founded upon, and thus most capable of mediating, the limited knowledge of individuals. It therefore respects the liberty of individuals. And it serves as a source of social cohesion and progress. Democracy, when it becomes bargaining democracy, interferes with the market. In this way, it does not simply threaten efficiency. More important for Hayek, it threatens individual liberty, social cohesion, and social progress.

The Limits of the Welfare State

Most significant for Hayek, legislators and citizens ignore the limitations of knowledge when they use democracy to pursue substantive ends. Democracy has become informed by the rationalist constructivist position that one ought to impose some sort of rational order on what had in fact developed spontaneously. This "ideology" has been most clearly manifest in the postwar era, where "a wholesome method of arriving at widely acceptable political decisions has become the pretext for enforcing substantially egalitarian ends" (1978: 152). In particular, the rise of the welfare state (which Hayek clearly distinguishes from socialism)[18] represents the consequence of having promoted the notion that democracy must pursue substantive ends. The political theory in favor of the welfare state, the political theory that permits the provision of public welfare, in particular, can be located in the same rationalist constructivism upon which the architects of the "Rights of Man" had drawn.

So in the first place, welfare policies *in practice* impede the opportunities otherwise provided by the market. Additionally, Hayek *explains* the rise of this "counterproductive" trend in terms of the promulgation of a mistaken view of democracy. That is, Hayek's *critique of the welfare state* is at the same time a *critique of the practice of democracy* in the twentieth century. The policies of the welfare state appeared to represent the will of a specific majority and were therefore considered right and just. These policies may have been expedient for the majority of the society. Nevertheless, they continue to contradict the principle of universal application. The welfare state means that, "since people will differ in many attributes which government cannot alter, to secure for them the same material position . . . require[s] that government treat them very differently" (1979, 2: 82). Thus, the welfare state has created a coercive society—a society that undermines the status of individual liberty. By promoting a welfare state, Western democracies ignored the fact that individual liberty had made all the genuine achievements of Western civilization possible in the first place. So, by way of the welfare state, democracy has threatened the liberty of individuals to use their own knowledge. It has undermined the prospects for liberty to contribute to social cohesion and progress. Where the state is restricted to articulating and enforcing the Rule of Law, the public sphere is consistent with and supportive of the private sphere. Where the state promotes welfare policies, the public sphere undermines the private sphere.

Hayek is no libertarian, though.[19] He in fact embraces the notion that governments actually may have a role to play in providing for the indigent, the aged, and the disabled. In the first place, with jurisprudential logic Hayek relies on the principle of precedent to support these policies. He acknowledges that modern governments do as a matter of fact care for these sorts of groups. Only the coercive activities of government, for example, interference in the market, must be strictly limited in light of the principle of liberty. Thus, Hayek states with approval that "no government in modern times has ever confined itself to the 'individualist minimum'" (1960: 257). He continues,

> All modern government have made provision for the indigent, unfortunate, and disabled and have concerned themselves with questions of health and the dissemination of knowledge. There is no reason why the volume of these pure service activities should not increase with the general growth of wealth. There are common needs that can be satisfied only by collective action and that can be thus provided for without restricting individual liberty. It can hardly be denied that, as we grow richer, that minimum of sustenance that the community has always provided for those not able to look after themselves, and which can be provided *outside the market*, will gradually rise, or that government may, usefully and without doing any harm, assist or even lead in such endeavors. There is little reason why the government should not also play some role, or even take the initiative, in such areas as social insurance and education, or temporarily subsidize certain experimental developments. Our problem here is not so much the aims as the methods of government action. (1960: 257, emphasis added)

Not unlike Bentham, Hayek implies that individual expectations should not be disturbed. Of course, this is not a wholesale argument for the preservation of all government programs; there is plenty that he would eliminate. But programs for specific groups can be executed in a manner that does not contradict the notion of liberty. Hayek also argues for this provision based on a principle of a risk common to all. "The assurance of a certain minimum income for everyone, or a sort of floor below which nobody need fall even when he is unable to provide for himself, appears not only to be a wholly legitimate protection against a risk common to all, but a necessary part of the Great Society in which the individual no longer has specific claims on the members of the particular small group into which he was born" (1979, 3: 55). The risk of destitution respects no distinctions. And the state is an appropriate agent of indemnification in a modern, complex society.

Whenever Hayek mentions this point, he is quick to add that this must be an extra-market provision. He remains critical of policies pursued within the ambit of the marketplace for improving income or maintaining security. "So long as such a minimum income is provided outside the market to all those who, for any reason are unable to earn in the market, an adequate maintenance, this need not lead to a restriction of freedom, nor conflict with the Rule of Law. The problems with which we are here concerned arise only when the remuneration for services rendered is determined by authority and the impersonal mechanism of the market, which guides the direction of individual efforts, is thus suspended" (1979, 2: 87). Labor unions, for instance, represent a monopoly on the supply of labor. This represents an act of coercion against those workers who are consequently denied employment both by the practice of closed shops and by the diminished demand for labor at a higher cost. So Hayek maintains that there is simply no good argument against the state providing resources for specific groups. As long as this provision remains outside of the market, it will neither interfere in the process of integration nor with the progress that is rendered by the coordination of individual knowledge through the mechanism of the market.

Thus, Hayek distinguishes this provision from a principle of liberty. There may be good grounds for providing a minimum income below which nobody need go, but that provision has nothing to do with the liberty of the recipient. Hayek has elaborated a conception of liberty that is intelligible in light of his theory of the market. As public welfare recipients are not participants in the market, Hayek eliminates any sense in which welfare provision could be related to the protection of the recipient's liberty. Welfare provision may, however, have something to do with the liberty of the members of the society at large. Repeating Bentham's warning, Hayek maintains that provision for the poor is "unquestionable, be it only in the interest of those who require protection against acts of desperation on the part of the needy" (1960: 285). Provision for the indigent can satisfy the aim of security for the individual private spheres of those who do participate in the market.

Not only does Hayek divorce his reasons for public assistance from any consideration of the liberty of the poor, he also suggests thereby that the recipients of extra-market welfare provision lack the opportunity to be free at all. As mentioned earlier, Hayek specifically articulates his conception of negative freedom in light of his epistemological theory of the market. An individual is free to the extent that he is not interfered with in the exercise of his prerogatives in the market. But recipients of welfare are not fully market participants since they are dependent on the extra-market provision of welfare. Although they may participate in the market as consumers, they have failed to demonstrate their market prerogatives through the production side of market participation. Hayek suggests, then, that liberty is more than a state of noninterference or noncoercion. Liberty, or freedom, depends on having secured one's economic independence from the state.

The Dispersal of Power

Similarly, Friedman's (1962, 1980) free market theory is explicable in terms of the public/private distinction and has distinct implications for liberal citizenship. His analysis begins with a distinction between freedom and power. Though not defining it with particular precision, Friedman treats freedom in the typical negative fashion. Freedom is a state of noncoercion or noninterference. Power, on the other hand, is the source of coercion or interference. It is the capacity to act in a manner that interferes with another's interests or intentions.[20] Freedom and power exist in an inverse relationship to one another. The analysis proceeds on the assumption that freedom pertains to the individual and that the primary source of antagonism to that freedom is the state. That is, the greater the "power"[21] of the state, the less the "freedom" for the individual. Friedman argues that "the preservation of freedom is the protective reason for limiting and decentralizing governmental power" (1962: 3). At the same time, the preservation of freedom is the reason for any government power. Properly directed, government is an effective guardian of individual threats to freedom. Thus, although the state does have a reason for being—to protect individuals from one another—there is some sphere of individuality that will be threatened by too much state action. The state undermines freedom when decision making becomes too centralized. Still, as for Hayek, Friedman does not describe freedom in purely individual terms. Freedom is a way of judging social relationships (1962: 12).

Friedman's argument relies on the distinction between economic freedom and political freedom. Economic freedom indicates the degree to which the government does not interfere with the activities of individuals within the private sphere or the market. Political freedom indicates the degree to which government does not interfere with an individual in the other areas of social life, for example, the commonly accepted freedoms of expression and association. In turn, Friedman treats economic freedom in two ways. In the first place, it is valued in and of itself. But more important for his analysis, he also places an instrumental value on economic freedom. He relies on the proposition that "freedom is one whole [and] that anything that reduces freedom in one part of our lives is likely to affect freedom in the other parts" (1980: 69). Then, reversing the order in which Bentham and the Philosophical Radicals had stated it, Friedman argues specifically that economic freedom is a means to political freedom. He argues, "Economic freedom is an essential requisite for political freedom. By enabling people to cooperate with one another without coercion or central direction, it reduces the area over which political power is exercised. In addition, by dispersing power, the free market provides an offset to whatever concentration of political power may arise. The combination of economic and political power in the same hands is a sure recipe for tyranny" (1980: 2).[22] And he adds, "Restrictions on economic freedom inevitably affect freedom in general, even in such areas as freedom of speech and press" (1980: 64).

Economic freedom thus can be measured by the degree of the concentration of power in the government. The objective of economic freedom, therefore, is equated with the reduction in the concentration of power. The reduction in the concentration of power, in turn, will lead to an increase in the degree of political freedom. "There is an intimate connection between economics and politics, that only certain combinations of political and economic arrangements are possible, and that in particular, a society which is socialist cannot also be democratic, in the sense of guaranteeing individual freedom" (1962: 8).

Like Hayek, Friedman argues that the market is valued because of its prospects for the protection of freedom. Freedom is a "direct component" of the market. "The basic problem of social organization is how to co-ordinate the economic activities of large numbers of people . . . to reconcile widespread interdependence with individual freedom" (1962: 12–13). This is the problem for which the free market is the solution. The market distributes power away from the state. Any mechanism that contributes to a diminution of the "power" of the state will, by definition, likewise contribute to an increase in the amount of individual freedom in society.

> What the market does is to reduce greatly the range of issues that must be decided through political means, and thereby to minimize the extent to which government need participate directly in the game. The characteristic

feature of action through political channels is that it tends to require or enforce substantial conformity. The great advantage of the market, on the other
hand, is that it permits wide diversity. It is, in political terms, a system of
proportional representation. Each man can vote, as it were, for the color of
tie he wants and get it; he does not have to see what color the majority wants
and then, if he is in the minority submit. (1962: 15)

The political view most damaging to productivity is the idea of economic equality. Economically egalitarian commitments conflict with the
liberal ideal. So, like Hayek, Friedman distrusts making economic equality a matter of policy. He argues that for the Framers of the U.S. Constitution, equality referred to one's standing before God, or at most equality
of opportunity. And a condition of that was limited government. To be
sure, political equality is important. Political equality includes, for instance, equal protection of the law. But that status does not depend on
economic equality; it is perfectly consistent with limited government,
and it does depend on economic freedom. Like Hayek, Friedman argues
that "government measures to achieve 'fair shares for all' reduce liberty"
(1980: 129), where fair shares presumably represent equal shares.[23] Friedman does not entirely exclude the notion of economic equality from his
argument, however. He adds, echoing Bentham's linking of equality and
abundance, that when economic freedom is put first, society ends up
with both more (economic and political) freedom and with greater equality (1980: 148).[24] In short, the limits of state power ought to be defined in
light of economic freedom.

Of course, Friedman's vision of a free society does not depend on the
elimination of the public sphere. As he declares, "the consistent liberal is
not an anarchist" (1962: 34). These intrusions by the public sphere may
come at the cost of some degree of individual freedom. Yet they are nevertheless required by the needs of a free society. The state must act as rule
maker and as an umpire to interpret and enforce the rules decided on, because this is something that the market cannot do for itself (1962: 15,
25–27). "Absolute freedom is impossible. However attractive anarchy
may be as a philosophy, it is not feasible in a world of imperfect men.
Men's freedoms can conflict, and when they do, one man's freedom must
be limited to preserve another's" (1962: 25–26). And perhaps the most
fundamental rule that the state needs to explicitly define and protect is
the right to property. The state also may legitimately engage in enter-
prises that, owing to technical or other conditions, would be too costly or
practically impossible to realize through the market (1962: 27–28). Additionally, the state may engage in paternalistic actions on the grounds that
some individuals cannot be considered responsible. Because "freedom is
a tenable objective only for responsible individuals" (1962: 33), the state

does not contradict its goal of promoting freedom when it acts to protect, for instance, the insane and children.

Given his support for the (dramatically curtailed) public sphere, Friedman, like Hayek, is committed to a carefully designed program of public assistance. Social welfare policies, as Friedman has found them, have had a deleterious effect on the fabric of American society. "They weaken the family; reduce the incentive to work, save and innovate; reduce the accumulation of capital; and limit our freedom" (1980: 127). The use of force, he argues, is at the very heart of the welfare state (1980: 119). As a counter to this widespread coercion, Friedman specifically endorses a negative income tax.[25] "It would provide an assured minimum to all persons in need regardless of the reasons for their need while doing as little harm as possible to their character, their independence, or their incentive to better their own condition" (1980: 120). According to him, there is no contradiction in principle between a free market system and compassion for the less fortunate—as long as provision is made by philanthropy or by some government agency that acts in accordance with the *will of the majority*, for example, when 90 percent of the population agree to impose taxes on themselves to help the bottom 10 percent (1980: 140).

In the first place, a negative income tax, compared with other forms of public assistance, would be consistent with the definition of property articulated by the "umpires" of the liberal tradition. Additionally, when compared with private or market solutions, public assistance in general, and a negative income tax in particular, solves the problem of the "neighborhood effects" of poverty. Friedman reasons, "I am distressed by the sight of poverty; I am benefited by its alleviation; but I am benefited equally whether I or someone else pays for its alleviation; the benefits of other people's charity therefore partly accrue to me" (1962: 191). In the absence of extra-market public assistance, the problem of poverty could never be successfully addressed.

By focusing on the negative income tax as a form of state action consistent with the principles of liberty, Friedman seems to limit his case for public assistance to the working poor. The indigent, to use Bentham's term, have not been considered here. Friedman does, however, endorse cash forms of public assistance for the insane and the physically and mentally disabled. The need for government intervention arises precisely because the market and its voluntary network will fail to provide basic resources for these individuals. Like the negative income tax, this intervention is consistent with his general principles for state intervention and with carefully designed paternalism. The insane and the disabled may not be considered responsible for securing, because they are unable to secure, their livelihood. Reminiscent of Bentham's policies, public assistance to these groups seems to depend on the assumption that these individuals are not free—however much the provision of this assistance may be a condition of the free society.

In another way Friedman shares Hayek's implicit claim that welfare provision to the indigent, aged, and disabled is unrelated to any expectation that these individuals are free. People who rely on the state for basic resources do not have the capacity to be free, because they are not participating, at least not as producers or laborers, in that sphere to which the language and status of liberty pertain. State-funded cash transfers do not conform to the logic of free exchange in the market. To be sure, as I noted already, recipients of public assistance are thereby enabled to participate in the market as consumers, a capacity they share with people of independent economic means. But neither Friedman nor Hayek direct their critiques against other groups who participate in the market only as consumers, but who do not rely on the state for their income, for example, heirs to fortunes or lottery winners. As I elaborate further on, this distinction between two categories of non–labor market participants—the poor and the so-called "independently wealthy"—suggests that liberty is *necessarily* identified with economic independence from the state, and only *contingently* identified with labor market participation. For the poor, however, economic independence from the state will depend on labor market participation. Thus, liberty for the poor will *necessarily* depend on labor market participation. In short, freedom does not simply mean noncoercion or noninterference. Freedom, according to both Friedman and Hayek, additionally means economic independence from the state.

The Libertarian Critique

The market-oriented theories of Hayek and Friedman center on the ways in which the provision of welfare benefits for the poor undermines the prospects for individual freedom. Moreover, insofar as welfare benefits have this consequence, welfare benefits ultimately undermine the conditions for social order. Hayek, for instance, argues for the protection of liberty on consequentialist grounds. The failure to protect liberty will be the failure to respect the limits of knowledge and the failure to establish the conditions for social integration. The limits of state action may be defined in terms of a principle of liberty, but in turn, that principle is valued for its consequences for the social order. Ultimately, liberty and the public/private distinctions have important implications for the liberal meaning of citizenship. But before addressing those implications, I turn to another statement on the limits of state action defined in terms of individual liberty. In this case, however, the protection of liberty is not justified on consequentialist grounds. Individual liberty, according to this view, is not to be valued for the reason that it contributes to the social order. The protection of individual liberty will be its own good and end.

Nozick (1974) defines the limits of state action in terms of a principle of individual rights. Perhaps the most important right, and the one most relevant for this analysis, is the right to property. By the right to property, Nozick means that individuals must be allowed to dispose of their property as they choose. Liberty, in turn, is defined as the capacity to exercise this right. Thus, the principle of liberty is prima facie one of noninterference or noncoercion. The right to property implies that no one ought to interfere with another's prerogative with respect to his property. Any interference with that prerogative necessarily constitutes an act of coercion. Additionally, the justification of this right does not depend on the purported social consequences of protecting it; property rights are justified on principled grounds. Nozick then uses this principle about the sovereignty of individual property rights to define the appropriate limits of state action. Respect for this principle, according to Nozick, requires a "minimalist" state. In a negative and analytical fashion, Nozick argues that the state must not be any larger than is consistent with the respect for the liberty to dispose of one's property as he sees fit. The state should not interfere with one's right to property, nor should it license any other individual to interfere with one's right to property. On the contrary, the state ought to take positive steps to guarantee that one individual does not interfere with another's property rights.

With this in mind, Nozick "backs into" the problem of poverty and the welfare state through his discussion of just and unjust distributions of property holdings. To make this distinction, he begins by denying that there is any central distribution of resources or holdings. No person or group is entitled to control how resources are doled out in society. Thus, whatever one does receive, he receives through exchange or as a gift. "In a free society, diverse persons control different resources, and new holdings arise out of the voluntary exchanges and actions of persons" (1974: 150). This is the foundation for Nozick's "entitlement" theory of justice. In the end, this arrangement is just because it does not require more than a minimal state. In particular,

1. A person who acquires a holding in accordance with the principle of justice in acquisition is entitled to that holding.
2. A person who acquires a holding in accordance with the principle of justice in transfer, from someone else entitled to the holding, is entitled to the holding.
3. No one is entitled to a holding except by (repeated) applications of 1 and 2. (1974: 151)

In other words, a distribution is just if the individuals holding the resources are entitled to those holdings. And an entitlement is defined in accordance with original acquisition or legitimate transfer. Thus, the important thing to identify in any distribution is its underlying generation principle. The resulting pattern is not a consideration in the determination of its justness. That is, "the entitlement theory of justice in distribution is historical: whether a distribution is just depends upon how it came about" (1974: 153). Furthermore, the historical entitlement theory of justice "hold[s] that past circumstances or actions of people can create *differential entitlements* of differential deserts to things" (1974: 155, emphasis added).[26] Nozick is a bit tentative about the details of a theory of just acquisition. He does discuss what he considers to be Locke's theory of acquisition by labor (1974: 174–78).[27] But the point is simply to establish that this is the sort of thing which is necessary in order to define a theory of justice. As he concludes, "From each as they choose, to each as they are chosen" (1974: 160).

Nozick's libertarian critique of public welfare provision is not concerned in the first place with the effect of intervention on the smooth functioning of the market, and it makes no judgments about the long-term consequences for social cohesion or progress. Nozick's critique of public assistance is made in terms of the principles of justice, rights, entitlement, and liberty. Although the resulting pattern of this provision may appear egalitarian, its underlying generation principle is unjust: The beneficiaries are not, by definition, entitled to these resources. He suggests that the impetus for welfare policies has been driven by the sense that distributions under the free market are unfair, because these distributions are unequal. But the defense of welfare policies operates on a current time-slice principle of justice. That principle ignores the distribution's historical genesis. To guarantee a particular end-state principle, "one must either continually interfere to stop people from transferring resources as they wish to, or continually (or periodically) interfere to take from some persons resources that others for some reason chose to transfer to them" (1974: 163). The upshot of this is that the state should not be in the business of providing public assistance. The resources needed to fund such policies depend on coercive takings of private property—taxation. The market, on the other hand, is "neutral among persons' desires, as it reflects and transmits widely scattered information via prices, and coordinates persons' activities" (1974: 163–64). The market operates on the principles of competition and the right to control or dispose of private property according to one's own decisions. The market is conducive to liberty as noncoercion.

Nozick makes no exceptions for people unable to work. There is no separate sphere through which they may be provided for by the state, as there is for Hayek and Friedman. For even under Hayek's extra-market scheme, the provision would still, according to Nozick, violate the principle of noncoercion by taxing people with property to finance projects that are not for the benefit of taxpayers. Even a minimal level of public assistance forces one segment of society—the taxpayer—to labor for the benefit of the welfare recipient. In other words, Nozick does not consider the relief of poverty even as insurance against the desperate actions of indigent individuals; he does not consider the relief of poverty to be a genuine object of collective action, such as the military.[28] If there is to be provision for the poor, it must come from philanthropy or voluntary organizations.

Hayek believes that welfare provision, improperly designed, coerces by interfering with the accumulation and transmission of knowledge. And Friedman emphasizes how welfare coerces by concentrating power with the state, or leaving too many decisions to be made by the state. Nozick, alternatively, argues that welfare provision is coercive for the reason that it unfairly takes property from those entitled to it, and for the reason that it represents a form of servitude for people who work. Despite these important distinctions, Nozick does share the view with Hayek and Friedman that the "problem of welfare" is about more than violations of negative liberty. By limiting the state in this way and by promoting the free market, Nozick leads one to the conclusion that the recipient of public assistance does not have the capacity for freedom. The issue of negative liberty only becomes salient when someone possesses the property upon which the claim for noninterference or noncoercion can be based. And Nozick's entitlement theory of justice eliminates the possibility that this property, or this ground of independence, can be provided by the state. This negative conception of liberty relies on the premise that the language of liberty pertains to those who have secured their economic independence from the state.

Nozick might argue that an individual has property in oneself, and so the "person" can properly be the subject of the claim for noninterference; even the economically destitute can make a claim for negative liberty on the basis of their personhood. But in the context of an argument about the coercive nature of taxation and public assistance, Nozick emphasizes the importance of economic resources as a subject of noninterference. So, although Nozick does not suggest that the state should not recognize the "personhood" of the indigent, he does suggest that the welfare claimant lacks an important basis for recognition (of a claim to noninterference) by the state; the welfare recipient has no liberty to speak of. In short, the minimal state should not address the problem of poverty, because such a policy interferes with the negative liberty of those who hold property to which they are, by Nozick's definition, entitled. Additionally, welfare provision undermines the opportunity that the poor might take to secure their grounds for a claim to the protection of their liberty. Welfare provision undermines their economic independence from the state.

The Moral Conservatives

Like Hayek and Friedman, moral conservatives have criticized the distribution of welfare on a basis of its *consequences*. But rather than complaining directly about the effects of welfare provision on the market, moral conservative critics have focused in the first place on the deleterious effects that welfare has for the well-being of the individual and the traditional family. [29] So their assault on welfare provision extends even to the nonmarket forms of distribution that have been endorsed by both Hayek and Friedman. As it undermines the moral integrity of the individual and the authority of the other private sphere—the family—public assistance undermines the moral fabric of society.

The moral conservative emphasis on personal responsibility, tradition, and authority is not meant to suggest, however, that these theorists are uninterested in the problems of coercion and interference. Bentham, Hayek, and Friedman, in particular, argue that the protection of individual liberty may have direct consequences for the freedom of society generally. And the freedom of society generally is not a state of anarchy. These liberal theorists, at least implicitly, identify a free society with an ordered society. Similarly, the moral conservatives do not view a traditional or ordered society as inimical to individual liberty. They do not recommend a totalitarian state. Instead, they continue to value individual liberty, as it has been defined in a negative way. Thus, their critique of public assistance to the nonworking poor, though immediately concerned with the social order, is equally informed by an appreciation for the value of individual liberty. Citing Tocqueville, a panel of moral conservatives writes,

> Without a populace practicing the habits requisite to their support, free institutions cannot stand. Liberty dwells first in the habits a people acquire in the home and develop throughout the institutions large and small, of society as a whole. Thus, American society is a commonwealth of a special sort, dependent upon the exercise of responsibilities by each and every citizen. It is a society that demands much of individuals, because it expects them to be free. The source of the nation's beauty and of the love its citizens bear it, is that it asks so much of them. (Novak et. al. [1987: xvi])

Dependency and the Welfare Recipient

Charles Murray (1984)[30] does not provide a clear and distinct analytical definition of liberty. Nevertheless, his critique of U.S. social welfare policies implemented in the 1960s is based on an implicit conception of freedom. An examination of this critique will illuminate this conception and its connection with a theory of the limits of state power.[31] Murray's central concern is the so-called problem of "welfare dependency." Why, he asks, would individuals forsake the opportunity to improve their station through paid employment, choosing instead to receive public assistance and to remain mired in poverty? The first explanation Murray offers for what he calls welfare dependency focuses on the incentive structure provided by U.S. social policy. He contends that the New Deal can be fairly well distinguished from the "war on poverty" of the 1960s. Although legislation such as the Work Progress Administration was intended as an emergency measure, social welfare policy in the 1960s signaled that the government was then prepared to take "a continuing responsibility for helping Americans to help themselves" (1984: 23). Having accepted the contention that the poor were merely victims of an economic structure beyond the control of the poor themselves, the policy elite in the United States concluded that the government *could*, and was thus *obligated to*, provide a solution to the problem. The poor, in turn, merely responded rationally to the economic incentives offered to them by social policy. It became perfectly rational to secure one's livelihood through public assistance rather than through a paycheck, even at the cost of welfare dependency and its attendant pathologies. "It became profitable for the poor to behave in the short term in ways that were destructive in the long term" (1984: 9).

In addition to appealing to the rational economic interests of the poor, social policy in the United States effectively removed the moral or normative incentive to choose paid employment over public assistance; U.S. welfare policy failed to shame the nonworking poor out of their indigence. Murray identifies, for instance, what he sees as a softening in attitudes among social workers toward the poor. As it was increasingly accepted that the economic system was to blame for the incidence of poverty,[32] social workers no longer stigmatized the poor. Accordingly, the poor felt less shame in their station and became more willing to seek assistance rather than work. Additionally, because social workers wanted to avoid laying the blame for poverty on the poor themselves, social workers showed an unwillingness to give any credible praise to people who tried to succeed. Without any positive reinforcement, people trying to improve themselves often fell easily back into their so-called indolent ways.

Furthermore, the content of social welfare policy failed to distinguish between the deserving and undeserving poor; welfare policy tended to homogenize the poor. This homogenization failed to distribute the appropriate psychological incentives of both credit and blame. In the urban core, youths were not given any signals that hard work pays off; instead, they saw that social services were provided to the so-called failures. The homogenization also destroyed the status that was historically attached to the low-income independent working family. This in turn affected the quality of life in the urban cores. Similarly, a sense of status was withdrawn from the behaviors that had traditionally engendered escape from poverty. Consequently, the work ethic lost any importance, and "the man who ke[pt] working [wa]s . . . a chump" (1984: 185).

The worst part of this process, according to Murray, was that policy elites and social workers who claimed to be progressive were actually undermining the integrity and responsibility of the poor, especially the African-American urban poor. He argues that social policy in the 1960s was based on a new kind of condescension and racism, namely, that whites owe blacks a debt. By stating that poverty was not the fault of individuals, white society actually sealed off the ghettoes from the rest of society. "Whites began to tolerate and make excuses for behavior among blacks that whites would disdain in themselves or their children" (1984: 223). In light of all this, Murray identifies a new three-point consensus among what he disparagingly refers to as the progressive policy elites: The assumption that inner-city blacks are quite different; the conclusion that it is futile to seek solutions that bring this group into mainstream society; and the conclusion that society ought to give up trying to improve the lot of this group and to simply turn them into permanent wards of the state (see also Murray [1988]).

In other words, a bad situation simply worsened. "My conclusion is that social programs in a democratic society tend to produce net harm in dealing with the most difficult problems. They will inherently tend to have enough of an inducement to produce bad behavior and not enough of a solution to stimulate good behavior; and the more difficult the problem, the more likely it is that this relationship will prevail. The lesson is not that we can do no good at all, but that we must pick our shots" (1984: 218). The so-called law of unintended consequences is not solely to blame for the plight of the poor. That problem could have been addressed with changes in the incentive structure. The really sinister aspect of the history of social policy for Murray is, however, that now the defenders of welfare provision have actually turned their backs on the inner-city poor.

Although the receipt of public assistance represents a rational economic decision on the part of the poor, such that responsibility for the problem of "welfare dependency" can be lodged with the policy elite, Murray does not neglect the culpability of the poor themselves. In this context, Murray relies on the behavioralist assumption that people are neither inherently hardworking nor moral. "In the absence of countervailing influences, people will avoid work *and be immoral*" (1984: 146, emphasis added). He adds to this assumption the prescription that people must be held responsible for their actions (see also Murray [1986]). This attitude of responsibility includes, on the one hand, the belief that one controls one's own destiny. On the other hand, it involves the obligation to bear the consequences of one's actions. Thus, whether these individuals "are responsible in some ultimate philosophical or biochemical sense cannot be the issue *if society is to function*" (1984: 146, emphasis added). A well-functioning society—something not clearly defined by Murray—depends on the individual taking responsibility for her actions. This requires, among other things, that one secure one's livelihood through paid employment rather than through regular Aid to Families with Dependent Children (AFDC) payments. Responsibility means refusing to accept dependence on the state. In other words, although it may have been *economically* rational to accept public assistance, it is *morally* irrational to accept public assistance and to thereby set oneself on the course of welfare dependency. Indeed, in contrast to the attitudes attributed by Murray to policy elites, Murray believes that his own exhortations to responsibility reflect a more profound respect for the poor and their ability to rise above their situation.

Two Views of the Family

Like the economic liberals, the moral conservatives promote a redistribution of the tasks now covered by the state to the private, market sphere. Or they at least promote a modification of the principles by which welfare is provided by the state; namely, by the adoption of market principles. But the moral conservatives additionally promote the redistribution of these "welfare tasks" to the private, family sphere. They have argued that AFDC not only discouraged entry into the labor market, but that it also provided poor women with the incentive to bear children. Although conceding a number of other explanations for why women conceive children, Murray (1984) still maintains that AFDC *enabled* women to keep these children and it *enabled* these women to shun their responsibility to engage in paid employment. Of course, the mother who is married does not have the same obligation to secure her wages in the market. A husband is a legitimate and appropriate source of economic independence from the state. Thus AFDC was pernicious, not only as it discouraged paid employment, but also as it provided an alternative to the family unit. "In 1970, her child provide[d] her with the economic insurance that a husband used to represent" (1984: 161).

Following this theme, others have contended that AFDC discourages women from marrying in the first place or discourages women from remaining married (Novak et al. [1987]; Novak [1979, 1987]; Novak and

Green [1986]). Insofar as welfare benefits discourage the formation of families, welfare benefits interrupt the formation of the social order. "The weakening of family ties, traditions and rules of conduct poses the greatest single threat to our nation's capacity to sustain responsible liberty" (Novak [1979: 5]). Thus, Novak does not value the family unit as an end in itself. The traditional structure of a male-headed household is instrumental to the smooth functioning of society; it is one among many institutions in society upon which the social order is built. With a view toward eliminating poverty, according to Novak, welfare benefits have actually undermined the institution within the private sphere that itself is the most effective resource for eliminating poverty. Instead of making direct payments to welfare claimants, the state ought to address the problem of poverty *indirectly* by fostering the family. "The family is nature's original department of health, education and human services. When things go well in the family, the whole of society reaps many benefits. When families—in one way or another, for one reason or another— fail to accomplish their basic tasks, it is far harder for other social institutions to accomplish theirs" (1987: 16). Within two-parent families with a male breadwinner, an environment conducive to moral development, motivation, organization, and discipline prevails (Novak and Green [1986: 56]). It is therefore incumbent on the state to extend its reach to assist the family in playing its proper role. In this way, it is proposed, the problems of dependency discussed by both Murray and Novak will be overcome.[33]

George Gilder (1981, 1987) also contends that welfare benefits generally undermine the integrity of the family unit. But Gilder is equally critical of workfare proposals, because those policies will themselves undermine the family. Gilder asserts that the woman's primary role as mother is to raise children. In theory, workfare undermines the family, therefore, because it is based on the assumption that the mother's primary role is to earn an income. In practice, workfare undermines the family by removing the mother from her role as caregiver. Because it is clear to Gilder that the abuses of AFDC have been the primary impetus for designing workfare schemes, he infers that these proposals are in fact aimed primarily at women. Workfare is designed to bring women out of the home and into the workforce. In this way, it does not directly contribute to the maintenance of a two-parent family. According to Gilder, only fathers should financially support families, and only fathers are capable of disciplining teenage boys. Therefore, only fathers are really capable of lifting a community from poverty. Female-headed households are a disaster mainly because women cannot tame their teenage boys (1987: 21–25). Thus, although Gilder believes that Novak correctly asserts that the two-parent family is an important institution for breeding moral character and order in society more generally, Gilder thinks Novak errs in his policy recommendation. Workfare places more emphasis on the need for everyone on welfare to work, rather than the need to maintain the traditional division of labor in the two-parent family. Of course, Gilder is not suggesting that when the father is absent, as a matter of fact, that the state should assume the role of the father by providing assistance. The family will not contribute to the cohesion of society if it is not headed by a male breadwinner participating in the free market and complemented by a woman responsible for raising the children.[34]

Although moral conservative approaches to U.S. welfare policy explicitly focus on economic incentives, moral responsibility, and the traditional family unit, they can also be seen as statements on the respect for individual liberty. In the first place, the plea that the state redefine public assistance represents a principle of noninterference or noncoercion. The state should not interfere with the choices that a rational individual (on both economic and moral grounds) would otherwise register. And the state should not interfere with the establishment or the maintenance of the family. At the same time, the emphasis in this moral conservative critique of public assistance is on the problem of dependence, and to be dependent is to be unfree. Conversely, to be independent is to be free. Given that the moral conservatives in fact do lay the blame for "welfare dependency" (at least partially) on the poor themselves, these theorists suggest that the problem is not simply one of coercion or interference from another agent. The status of freedom is also defined in terms of economic independence from the state. People receiving public assistance are not free for the reason that they are not economically independent of the state. Thus the moral conservatives examined here share with the economic liberals and libertarians the belief that one's prospects for freedom depend on noninterference from the public sphere, and they depend on what an individual secures for herself in the private sphere; it depends on securing economic independence.

The Prepolitical Conditions
of Citizenship

In the foregoing analysis I have examined the different ways in which an ideal distinction between the public and private spheres has formed the basis of an inegalitarian liberal critique of welfare provision. The private spheres of the market and the family take priority over the public sphere—the state. By providing public assistance to the nonworking poor, the state has, according to the New Right, failed to respect the integrity and autonomy of the two private spheres. I have also elucidated the relationship between the public/private distinction and a theory of freedom with respect to public assistance. Most significant, there is more to their conceptions of liberty than is typically noted either by the liberal theorists or by critics of liberalism; there is more than the negative idea of noninterference or noncoercion. Liberty, here, is invested with a substantive meaning, identifying it with economic independence from the state. Liberty depends as much on what the individual *does for himself* as it does on what *other individuals refrain* from doing. Liberty is identified with the aim of economic standing, and such standing can only legitimately be secured in the private sphere.[35]

To fully grasp the implications of this more substantive conception of liberty, it will be useful to identify the manner by which, and the conditions under which, individuals actually do secure their economic independence from the state. Most children, for instance, rely on their parents for economic resources, whereas senior parents, in turn, may rely on their children for these means. Furthermore, one spouse, more typically the wife, may depend on the other spouse for market-derived economic resources. Additionally, beneficiaries of unearned income, heirs, lottery winners, and plaintiffs receiving substantial settlements will secure an alternative source of income from the state. And there is nothing in the New Right to suggest that these are not legitimate sources of economic means. Nevertheless, the majority of people will secure this economic independence in the private sphere through wages; that is, paid employment. In short, under contemporary conditions, the substantive conception of liberty for these New Right theorists translates into market participation in the form of *paid employment*.

The exceptions to paid employment noted above help to illustrate the New Right emphasis on economic independence from the state, and, at the same time, they help to illuminate an ambiguity in New Right liberal theory. In this light, two questions suggest themselves with respect to intergenerational transfers of wealth. On the one hand, if an inheritance can establish economic independence, then why not consider public assistance itself to be the ground of independence? Alternatively, if dependence on the public purse indicates a lack of freedom, then why not consider dependence on an inheritance to constitute a lack of freedom? In other words, the New Right never explains why an inheritance is any less destructive to the individual than is public assistance. The New Right's refusal to entertain these questions demonstrates that their emphasis is primarily on curtailing the breadth of the state, rather than on simply trying to encourage self-reliant behavior. This ambiguity helps to illustrate that freedom specifically means economic independence from the state. And for most people this will mean paid employment.

The question of spousal transfers of market-secured economic resources is more problematic. On the one hand, female caregivers may be economically independent of the state. Such independence, like that secured by intergenerational transfers of wealth, does not depend on paid employment. Thus, one would expect that wives and mothers would enjoy the status of freedom, as heirs do, without securing paid employment. On the other hand, the familist component of the New Right specifically recommends that married women assume the role of caregivers in the home. In so doing, Novak and Gilder in fact construct a model of female dependence in contrast to male independence. Although intergenerational transfers of wealth may provide an alternative to paid employment as the grounds for economic independence from the state, husbands and wives are assigned distinct roles that preclude wives from securing true economic independence. Their independence from the state is in fact predicated on their dependence on their husbands. Ideally, the woman does not have the opportunity to ever secure paid employment, at least not any meaningful paid employment. So although it may be true that wives and mothers are economically independent of the state, they are explicitly economically dependent on their breadwinning husbands.[36] Thus, wives and mothers, under the terms of the New Right, still are not free. Freedom here depends on a distinctively male (breadwinner) form of economic independence. Even if the moral conservatives were willing to admit the exception, where the woman is the recipient of intergenerational transfers of wealth and has control over that wealth, the case remains exactly that. It is an exception, and exceptions are hardly the sort of thing upon which one should build a case for freedom.

Citizenship and Paid Employment

Undoubtedly, the conclusion about the relationship between liberty and paid employment is significant in its own right. As I will argue further on, this allows the New Right to assume that the market is capable of distributing the status of freedom to all people who are willing to secure paid employment. Still, of perhaps greater significance is the implication this relationship poses for citizenship. That is, this relationship enables us to recognize the central place of market participation in the New Right's meaning of *full citizenship*. In the main, citizenship is a way of identifying individuals as they stand in relation to the state. To call someone a citizen is to say something distinctly political about that individual. It defines a political status and relationship that is different, from, say, one's relationship with one's family, friends, fellow believers, or coworkers. To call someone a citizen is to have politics or the state in mind at the same time. And to discuss individuals in the context of discussing the state, especially when those individuals are assumed to be "members" of that state, is to suggest that those individuals are citizens.

In elucidating the meaning of liberty advanced by the New Right in relation to the distinction between the public and private spheres—and in relation to their arguments about public assistance—I have laid bare the New Right's description of the *ideal* relationship between the individual and the state. I have shown that for the New Right, the raison d'être of the state is to respect the integrity of the private spheres. Indeed, the state, in the theory of the New Right, exists to serve and protect the interests and institutions pertaining to the private sphere. Therefore, the state ought to protect the status secured independently of the state. Liberty, or economic independence, as it is realized through paid employment, must be protected by the state. In light of this, citizenship is a way of designating individuals who can benefit from the exercise of the state's mandate. That is, citizenship designates individuals whose economic independence from the state needs to be protected. In other words, individuals stand in relation to the state qua citizens because they have secured their liberty as economic independence, and they are now simply in need of the protection of their liberty as noncoercion.

The upshot of all this is that what I have identified as a requirement for liberty will be, in turn, a requirement for citizenship. Where liberty depends on an independent economic status, full citizenship will depend on more than noninterference by the state. Full citizenship will depend moreover on what one is able to accomplish independently of the state. Namely, it will depend on *economic* independence from the state. Full citizenship for the New Right depends on this more substantive conception of liberty. By definition the free individual *is* the citizen, because he is the one who stands in the ideal relation to the state. If individuals were not already free, the liberal conceptions of the state and citizenship would, by definition, be moot. In short, full citizens are those who are economically independent of the state, where this independence is typically secured through paid employment. Thus, recipients of public assistance cannot be counted as full citizens. Moreover, wives, who, according to the moral conservatives, ought to be financially dependent on their husbands rather than workers for paid employment, will not be full citizens.

The Social Obligations of Citizenship

With this implicit conception of citizenship the New Right theorists examined above run straight into a tradition of theorizing about citizenship that begins with the identification of citizenship and work. Judith Shklar (1991)[37] for instance, has argued that citizenship in the United States has been more about *standing* than about active participation. The struggle for citizenship has involved "an effort to break down excluding barriers to recognition, rather than an aspiration to civic participation as a deeply involving activity" (1991: 3). And the primary mode of recognition in the United States has been work. Throughout U.S. history, the opportunity to work has been a buttress against "the fear of being . . . displaced by the social outsider" (1991: 46). Additionally, the American work ethic stood between the equally unacceptable poles of idle elites and unpaid slaves. Protesting against idle elites in particular, Benjamin Franklin had long ago given work a civic meaning. Divorcing it from a religious context, Franklin argued that work alone could make one independent. And it was the independent person who counted as a citizen; the independent (male) individuals had standing (1991: 65ff). "In a polity of interest and rights-claiming individuals, only those who act on their own behalf and are recognized as competent in civil and political society can count as full citizens" (1991: 99). Work is that activity through which one registers this competence.

Similarly, through his attack on public welfare in the late twentieth century, Lawrence Mead (1986) has addressed directly the relationship between citizenship and work, or paid employment. My analyses of the moral conservatives to this point has centered on a distinction between the public and the private spheres. The problem of poverty and public assistance illuminates their theories of the acceptable *extent* of government or the public sphere. Thus, the arguments I have considered, as well as the focus of my analysis, nicely fits what Mead believes is the paradigm of political theory in the United States. He argues that American political theorists have focused almost exclusively on defining the legitimate extent of government. These theorists have analyzed freedom and explored the prospects for and implications of Madisonian pluralism. In this way, Mead contends, political theorists in the United States have neglected an alternative and equally important question about the public sphere, namely, the proper *nature* of government. Thus, Mead tries to draw a sharp distinction between the extent of the state, on the one hand, and the degree to which the state exercises control over the spheres in which it does play a legitimate role, on the other. The latter is an important component of political theory because it allows the theorist to address questions regarding the grounds for social order. By failing to identify and explore the source of *order*, political theorists have neglected to define the *foundations* of society. "Civility is essential to a humane society, but it is not a natural condition, as Americans [and presumably, political theorists] tend to assume. It is something societies must achieve, in part through public *authority*" (1986: ix, emphasis added). In Mead's view, the theoretical focus on freedom and the extent of government, from across the spectrum, has implicitly rejected the notion that authority is necessary to achieve social order.

In this respect, Mead challenges Hayek's emphasis on the free market as the source of social integration. Although Hayek is neither a libertarian nor an anarchist, he does not assign the state a central role in the process of social integration. By the same token, Mead does not reject the contribution of the market to social integration. But he contends that the state complements the market and effects this integration by a more active role in the private sphere. Like Hayek, Mead grounds his analysis in an interpretation of unarticulated social norms. He argues that "the task in social policy is not to invent values supportive of order, but to elevate those that already exist from the social realm into the political order . . . [and] the role of public authority is precisely to make obligatory the norms that people commonly affirm but do not reliably obey" (1986: 12, 87). Hayek contends that only norms that can be discovered in society can legitimately be used in the restriction of freedom. Mead addresses the concept of unarticulated norms for another reason. He emphasizes the way in which the elucidation and imposition of unarticulated norms is necessary itself for social integration.

This emphasis on public authority is the basis for Mead's critique of postwar U.S. welfare policy. He argues that welfare policy for the poor has been driven by the behavioralist assumptions of neoclassical economics. Namely, welfare policy has focused too narrowly on the assumption that individuals will respond in a predictable manner to a set of economic and moral incentives; it assumed that the poor could be induced, in a mechanical sort of way, to rise out of indigence. So, Charles Murray, as we have seen, would ground welfare policy more firmly in the assumption that the poor can be led out of indigence. The problem, as Murray sees it, is that U.S. welfare policy has established a perverse incentive structure, namely one that failed to "shame" the nonworking poor out of their indigence. Mead, on the other hand, argues that it is not enough to rely exclusively on any incentive structure, no matter how well defined. Rather, the poor will need to be *forced* to behave in ways that are necessary for a functional order. In this context, Mead does not refer to Bentham's panopticon workhouse, but he is clearly articulating the Benthamite claim that the indigent can be subject to coercion by the state, when it is done in the interest of social order. So, although he does not dismiss a theory of incentives altogether, Mead contends that individuals respond to more than economic or moral inducements. Individuals are unlikely, in this view, to spring to self-reliant behavior in the absence of a strong government. Many among the nonworking will never be "shamed" out of their indigence. "Some behaviors that government needs from individuals such as tax payment and low-wage work can never be made to serve their personal interests" (1986: 178). Nevertheless, the nonworking poor will respond, by necessity, to authority. The "stick" of forced low-wage work will be more effective than the "carrot" of incentives designed to appeal to the personal (economic and moral) interests of the indigent.

Because the market, in Mead's view, operates on the principle of *free* exchange, rather than by the imposition of a single will, the social order considered broadly cannot be sustained exclusively by the social interactions constituting the market. The social order depends on authority, and the state is the institution most able to impose such authority. By authority, Mead does not suggest complete political centralization, however. He still respects the sovereignty of the market and the family. Thus, he does not advocate a government that reaches into every crevice of the private sphere. But he does advocate a state that operates on a principle of authority in those spheres into which it does legitimately extend. Authority represents "the appeal of some national objectives to political culture. Certain goals come to seem so vital that a consensus forms that centralized powers must be available to pursue them" (1986: 187). Accordingly, he does not advocate a return to the so-called state of nature, as he interprets the economic behavioralists to be doing. Indeed, "a free political culture is the characteristic not of a society still close to the state of nature, as some American philosophers have imagined, but of one already far removed from it by dense, reliable networks of mutual expectations" (1986: 6), and, one should add, by firmly established institutions capable of exerting authority.

So, as a legitimate institution for addressing the problem of poverty, the state must actively require a particular set of behaviors. Unlike the theorists of the New Right considered above, Mead explicitly defines that set of expected behaviors, as well as welfare policy generally, in terms of a conception of citizenship. Although citizenship may be largely a political designation, it has social dimensions as well.

Mead defines political citizenship in terms of a contract between the individual and the state. The citizen has the right to civil liberties such as freedom of speech and equal protection under the law, and the citizen has the right to vote. In return, the citizen owes an obligation to the state. For instance, the citizen may be expected to bear arms for the state. In a negative fashion, the citizen is obligated to forbear from infringing on other citizens' rights; the citizen is obligated to respect the law.[38] In a structurally similar manner, social citizenship involves its own set of *social* rights and *social* obligations. "The structure of benefits and requirements in [welfare programs] constitutes an operational definition of [social] citizenship" (1986: 7). Social citizenship defines a contract between the individual and society, in the sense that by fulfilling the terms of the contract, the social order is maintained. For Mead, state-funded welfare benefits are indeed an appropriate expression of the social rights of citizenship.[39] In turn, the social citizen complements that right through her obligation to secure work. Of course, he does not mean "work" in the abstract. Women's caregiving work, as is clear from Mead's exhortations that single mothers participate in workfare programs, does not satisfy this obligation. Indeed, Mead's analysis on this point suggests a break with Franklin's valorization of the work ethic for its own sake. When Mead says work, he really means paid employment.[40]

In this respect, it undoubtedly is curious why Mead does not suggest that other actions, such as military service, could serve as the obligation corresponding to the rights claim for public economic assistance. Indeed, liberal theorists have long held that rights and obligations are not strictly correlative. I do not, however, think Mead's argument for workfare should indicate a contradiction or his inability to understand liberal theory. Rather, his recommendations demonstrate his attempt to combine (his interpretation of) liberal theory with corporate America's need for low-wage labor (1986: 178). In this sense, Mead seems to view the question of the welfare state not in terms of the problem of poverty, but rather in terms of the problem of ensuring a steady supply of low-wage labor.

According to Mead, then, the failure of social welfare policy in the twentieth century has been the failure to exact obligations on the part of those receiving assistance. The "war on poverty" failed when the arguments about economic incentives for modifying behavior were joined with an assumption about the social rights of citizenship. In an oblique reference to T. H. Marshall's work, Mead believes that policymakers and legislators first became convinced that individuals had a right to welfare benefits. This contention was then joined with the economic behavioralist assumption about the efficacy of incentives. The latter contribution demonstrated how the behavior of individuals could be changed in a nonimposing manner, such that the goods to which they had a right would have their desired long-term effect, namely, to draw them out of poverty. In the process, policymakers and legislators gradually lost the sense of the obligations of social citizenship. By failing to require work in return for benefits, welfare policy neglected the grounds of social order. Contrary to an extreme laissez-faire or libertarian argument, Mead asserts that the state can legitimately provide welfare benefits to the poor. The state should not be limited to enforcing the rule of law. But unless that provision is made on the condition that it requires work, unless that provision is backed up by the *authority* of the state to positively require certain behaviors, the state will undermine the conditions for social order.

It should be noted that Mead does not seem to be arguing that paid employment is the means for developing virtue or rational capacity. Although Mead argues that work ought to have some intrinsic value—it ought to be more than a source of income—he nevertheless suggests that work by welfare recipients primarily represents a debt. Paid employment primarily satisfies the contract between the individual and society. On this point, Mead's theory of workfare differs from Novak's (1987). To be sure, the latter characterizes paid employment as a social duty. Unlike Mead, however, Novak does link paid employment with the capacity for rationality. The ability to secure paid employment does more than satisfy this duty; it indicates the capacity for rational self-governance. "Only those who can govern themselves can fulfill the social duties inherent in a self-governing republic" (Novak et al. [1987: 4]).

As I suggested above, although Mead would extend the hand of the state as far as designing institutions that promote the social order, he does not necessarily support intervention in the free market. His focus on the strength of the state, rather than its extent, does not mean that he is opposed to the autonomy of the market. It is clear that the moral conservatives, as a rule, do in fact promote laissez-faire economic policies when it comes to commerce and industrial regulations. They call for intervention in society more generally when it comes to extra-market social integration. These values of tradition and order do not stymie the objectives of the market. This implies, by the same token, that the market itself does not create the conditions that undermine social order.

Market Citizenship

Despite a number of significant distinctions, the various theorists of the New Right examined herein suggest in common that the full status of citizenship depends on paid employment. With the exception of Mead, these theorists identify freedom or liberty not only with a status of noninterference or noncoercion. They also (at least implicitly) identify freedom with economic independence from the state. And I have argued that such independence will typically depend on paid employment. In turn, given the central place of liberty in a conception of full citizenship, these theorists suggest that people who rely on public assistance for their livelihood are not full citizens. Mead, on the other hand, more directly identifies citizenship with paid employment. Work, by which he specifically means paid employment, is the obligation that serves to balance the citizen's rights-based claim to public assistance.

For these thinkers, then, a citizen is more than an possessor of the franchise and more than the individual who claims the protection of civil liberties. To be sure, these theorists do not suggest, as Bentham's model of the panopticon workhouse does, that if an individual does not work she might forfeit her civil liberties. And neither Bentham nor the contemporary New Right suggest that if an individual does not work she must for-

feit her right to vote. But the upshot of their argument is that the indigent, those dependent on the state for their livelihood, are not full citizens. This also means, for the familist component of the New Right, that
wives—who ought to be financially dependent on their husbands—are
not full citizens.

Another important way to characterize these conclusions of the New
Right is to claim that the state cannot itself make a contribution to the full
expression of citizenship. To be sure, the state can design policies in such
a way that it encourages the status of citizenship. According to the moral
conservatives, welfare provision could be designed in such a way that it
did not provide an incentive to avoid working for wages. Alternatively,
the state could begin to enforce the obligation to work in return for receiving assistance through workfare policies. But the state cannot contribute directly to one's standing as a full citizen. Citizenship may designate the individual's standing before the state. Still, the fullness of that
status will depend on what one is able to do for oneself. That designation
will only apply to individuals who have already secured another status
independently of the state, namely, their economic independence. The
reason for which the state exists is primarily the protection of that economic status. But the state cannot directly sustain the status that it is
meant to protect. It cannot be the source of economic resources; it cannot
be the source of citizenship.

Conditions of Employment

If paid employment has become the necessary condition for the full citizenship of many people in American society, then it becomes necessary
to examine the nature of paid employment itself as a way to understand
more thoroughly the inegalitarian liberal political theory of the New
Right. For the conditions of paid employment, by suggestion, will be the
conditions for full citizenship. The New Right, whether explicitly (economic liberals) or implicitly (libertarians and moral conservatives), argues that the market is the institution in the private sphere that ought to
be the source of economic independence for most citizens. The market is
the source of paid employment. Therefore the market is integrally linked
with the liberal value of freedom. Additionally, however, the New Right
has linked the free market with the liberal value of equality. Thus, it
should be clear that the New Right attack on welfare provision is not
made entirely on the basis of their liberal conception of freedom, with no
regard for a principle of equality. The various theorists of the New Right
seem to share the assumption that the market is defined by the free and
equal exchange between individuals. The market represents the natural
expression of the *equal* liberty of its participants.

Moreover, according to this view, there are ample prospects for the opportunity to participate in the market as producers. Based on his assumption about the availability of jobs in the United States, Mead argues that unemployment is not a necessary feature of a capitalist market. The market does not unequally distribute the opportunity to secure paid employment. Instead, unemployment must be located in the irresponsibility of welfare claimants *as well as* in the failure of the state to enforce the obligation to find paid employment (1986, 1992). Unemployment insurance, for instance, has encouraged holding out for a better or higher-paying job. Mead laments the present-day American work ethic: "We have become a society of job-shoppers rather than job seekers" (1986: 72). Furthermore, he concludes that unemployment may be, for a significant number, a form of social and political protest by inner-city youths. These youths may interpret low-wage jobs that are available as a means through which white society tries to control them. Mead also suggests that a job has come to be seen as nothing more than a source of income, devoid of any intrinsic value. So where the safety net provides a basic source of income, the perception that work is meaningless leads to the conclusion that one should not work. Thus, "we can no longer view most joblessness as strictly involuntary" (1986: 77). In sum, there is nothing inherently unequal, according to the New Right, about the free market.

If the logic of the market is based on the exchange among equals, then by maintaining alternately that freedom and citizenship depend on securing paid employment in the market, the New Right suggests that freedom and citizenship have an aspect of equality. To be sure, the principle of liberty competes with the principle of equality, where the principle of equality refers to an equal distribution of goods. But where liberty is related to the logic of the market, then liberty and citizenship are theoretically available to all. The market provides the *equal opportunity* to secure one's liberty and the conditions for the full expression of citizenship. Even where liberty was conceived as a state of noninterference or noncoercion, the New Right supposes this to be theoretically available to all. As long as the respect of noncoercion is universally recognized, there is no logical limit on its distribution; it need not be a zero-sum distribution. As suggested above, the prospects for liberty and citizenship are equally available to all people because the opportunity for employment is not limited in any way. The failure to achieve one's standing as a full citizen—the failure to achieve an equal market status—will reflect a failure on the part of the individual to secure employment. It will be her responsibility to secure the conditions for this standing. The opportunity to stand before the state as a full citizen, the "right" to request the protection of the state, and the only reason for which the state ought to exist in the first place, depends on the individual's responsibility.

In another way, Mead links his critique of welfare policy with a theory of equal citizenship. Identifying what he considers to be the American ideal, Mead uses equality to refer to the *distribution of obligations and rights* among the citizenry. Equal citizenship means that the obligation to repay the exercise of rights is equally incumbent on all people. That view of citizenship therefore requires not only that everyone has an equal right to relief; it also "requires . . . that everyone discharge the common obligations including social ones like *work*" (1986: 12, emphasis added). Again, according to Mead, given that there are no structural barriers to securing paid employment, the opportunity to repay one's entitlements is equally available.

The Limits of Citizenship

Despite the optimism of the New Right with respect to the market and the opportunity the market provides for respecting the liberty and equality of the liberal citizen, the New Right has ignored some salient characteristics of the market. I want to close this chapter by arguing that the New Right's case for liberty and equality cannot be sustained empirically. When the New Right's conception of citizenship is viewed in light of these aspects of the market, it will become clear that the prospects for liberty, equality, and full citizenship are seriously limited.

In the first place, claims that the market succeeds on a voluntary basis and that the state is an impartial arbiter between competing interests cannot be sustained. Rather, free markets and private property depend on the "coercion" of governments insofar as they depend on the enforcement of contracts. So, not only can the market and private property *not* be sustained in the absence of the state, the manner by which the state must sustain the former is coercive. To be sure, Hayek and Friedman acknowledge that markets depend on the Rule of Law, which must be enforced by the state. And this relies on the assumption that this rule applies equally to all. But it applies equally to all only in the hypothetical situation where everyone actually has equal access to resources. The Rule of Law is in fact more coercive than Hayek or Friedman are willing to admit. Even ideally, it can only really serve to legitimate existing disparities in access to resources, power, and ultimately the conditions for full citizenship.

New Right theorists also underestimate the degree to which firms operating in the market tend to monopolize control of resources and monopolize control of markets within the market, especially, for instance, the labor market. Contrary to the New Right's assertion that the market does not coerce, firms operating on the principles of the market do have the ability to exclude and divide. The logic of the market, for instance, determines acceptable levels of unemployment. Some scholars fear that full employment may undermine the conditions upon which the market depends for its long-term viability. For instance, full employment may contribute to inflation. Alternatively, full employment may depend on surplus production, where the production by the marginal employee will not pay his own wage. In either of these examples, and contrary to the assertions of Murray and Mead, full employment contradicts the priorities of the market. Additionally, the dramatic changes over the past few decades in the labor market have demonstrated its highly uncertain nature. Despite record employment by mid–1999, massive layoffs and the increased use of contractors nevertheless demonstrate that an individual cannot always count on consistent participation in the labor market (Harrison and Bluestone [1982, 1988]). Thus, the logic of the market will necessarily exclude some people from the opportunity for paid employment.

While the New Right fails to understand or acknowledge the coercive nature of the market, they also seem to underestimate the contemporary integration of markets and states. In other words, the public/private distinction upon which their claim for liberty is based cannot be sustained empirically. Namely, the expansion of markets both domestically and abroad, and the growth of capital and private property, have not been entirely private affairs. The U.S. Departments of Commerce and Agriculture, as well as the U.S. Trade Representative, to name just a few, have provided important technical knowledge and facilitated access to foreign markets. Indeed, state-mediated diplomacy cannot be underestimated as a form of knowledge upon which the market operates. The U.S. Export/Import Bank has also assumed the risk of private investors by providing insurance to foreign buyers. And domestically, cities, counties, and states have engaged in virtual fiscal warfare in order to lure or retain firms, often on dubious expectations about the return in the form of individual property or consumer taxes. The expansion of markets and the growth of capital has depended on what James O'Connor (1971) referred to as public risk and private profit. So Hayek, in particular, may explicitly argue against a command economy. But his epistemological theory of the market leaves open the possibility for the state to promote the market in a way that conflicts with his other commitments to a distinction between market and state action. In short, insofar as the existence and growth of markets and property depends on the state, the distinction between the public and private spheres is more problematic than free-market theorists acknowledge.

Furthermore, even among people who are included in the labor market, the market makes divisions and distinctions, thereby belying any claims to equality. For instance, the market was founded specifically upon and presupposes the sexual division of labor (Pateman [1989]).

Thus it was founded at a time when not everyone was able to participate, and when not everyone was considered equally free. From the start, the market has been a patriarchal institution. Free market theory, then, may reinforce differences between participants and nonparticipants, thus perpetuating the social structure upon which it was founded, namely, patriarchy. And the market continues to define employment by gender. This is an objective aspect of the market. Although divisions may be breaking down in some areas, one sex or the other, for instance, continues to be disproportionately represented in a number of employment categories. And on the whole, women continue to be conspicuously underrepresented in the higher-paying professions. Where men and women do perform the same work, women may be compensated at a lower rate than men. Although these objective aspects of the market may, hypothetically, fade with time, the recommendations of moral conservatives will contribute directly to a maintenance of the sexual division of labor. In their view of the family, the moral conservatives place the father and husband in the role of breadwinner and the mother and wife as the primary caregiver (Gilder [1987]). Under these arrangements, whenever a woman is likely to find some work, it will necessarily be part-time, often voluntary, or not well paid, and frequently in positions that are extensions of her caregiver status. Thus, the moral conservatives in particular offer specific recommendations for the way in which the market ought to be divided and how it ought to define the terms of participation. From this it is not clear whether women as mothers ought to be working as citizens in the market or working for their families in the home. If it is the latter, the prospects for the full citizenship of women are foreclosed by their assigned roles as mothers.

Moreover, by insisting that women return to the home to be wives and mothers first, the familist component of the New Right reinforces a significant and long-standing distinction in liberal theory between public justice and family commitment (Pateman [1980]). By their actions in the private world of the market, men develop the sensibility for a public sense of justice. This is the sphere of convention and contract. Women, on the other hand, express their *natural* duties of motherhood through their attention to domestic caregiving. As Pateman has noted, "liberal theory presupposes the opposition between nature and convention" (1980: 32). The implication is that when women participate in the public sphere, they subvert the state, or public justice, because of their competing natural commitment to their families. A commitment to the particular family contrasts with the universalistic commitments of public justice. "Women, according to the liberal tradition, do not have a universalistic standard of justice and are not capable of developing one" (Nelson [1984: 227]). In other words, there is a tension in the liberalism of the New Right between women's commitment to (and responsibility for) families and their full exercise of citizenship.

If the logic and conventions of the market have the power to exclude people from the opportunity to work, then, in the terms laid out by the New Right, the market has the power to determine the opportunity to be free and the opportunity to secure one's standing as a full citizen. Furthermore, people subjected to distinctions in the labor market may still thereby enjoy liberty and citizenship by virtue of their participation in the labor market; the sexual division of labor may imply that women still are included. Nevertheless, under these conditions, the value of this liberty and citizenship will be largely deflated. Given the sexual division of labor, the market does not impartially integrate individuals in society. The market may be a mechanism of integration, but it does not integrate individuals on equal terms, as Hayek's analysis of the market, for instance, would like to claim.

More than any other thinker of the New Right, Mead does suggest an awareness of the power of the market to undermine the prospects for citizenship for the poor, that the private sphere undermines the status pertaining to the public sphere. His recommendations for a policy of workfare seem to challenge the inequalities bred by the market in liberal society. In the terms of his theory of citizenship, he outlines commitments that the state in particular ought to make to correct some disparity in the consequences of the market. In contrast to the other suggestions considered in this chapter, Mead would permit the public sphere to address the consequences of the logic of an institution of the private sphere by *actively* promoting inclusion in the market. Nevertheless, the commitment here is clearly inadequate. As I have demonstrated, he still places conditions on those commitments, namely the *willingness* to secure paid employment. These conditions are under control of the same social practices that are responsible for the inequality that the state is meant to address in the first place. This indicates that, all appeals to equality notwithstanding, the democratic state is powerless in the face of the free market. The market has the power to deny individuals the opportunity to be free citizens because the market has the power to dictate the conditions and the possibility of employment. Again, the conclusion is that liberty will not be distributed equally. And the opportunity for the full expression of citizenship will not be available to all, *at least not on equal terms.*

Even on its own terms, therefore, the New Right has undermined its arguments about the possibility for the equal distribution of liberty and full citizenship. As long as these arguments remain theoretically linked to paid employment, they will not be distributed equally. They will remain dependent on the conventions, practices, and logic of a sphere in which power, generally, continues to be concentrated with capital and the male gender.

Credits

The central argument of Chapter 2 appeared previously as "Citizens of the Market: The Un-Political Theory of the New Right," *Polity* 32, no. 2 (winter 1999, 179–202). I gratefully acknowledge the permission of the editors of *Polity* to reprint it here.

Notes

1. By focusing on the foundations for full citizenship, my analysis in this chapter examines an issue that has not been addressed by the secondary literature on the New Right that has emerged over the past two decades. A group of British scholars, for instance, have typically focused on establishing or challenging the coherence of the distinct strands of the New Right. Desmond King (1987), for one, identifies apparent contradictions in the New Right's public policy, generally, and locates this in the tension between liberal and conservative commitments. The former focuses on individual liberty, whereas the latter focuses on social order and traditional values. King does conclude, however, that the social and moral conservative principles provide a legitimating ideology for the political consequences of liberal economic strategies. Other scholars have suggested that the surface contradictions between liberty and authority may mask more subtle continuities. Andrew Gamble (1986), for instance, argues that the New Right represents a rediscovery of a nineteenth-century liberal political economy linked with the findings of modern positive economics. In a subtle distinction from King, he concludes that the findings of positive economics supports the policies of liberalism. Similarly, Andrew Belsey (1986) argues that there is considerable crossover between neoliberal and moral conservative aspects of the New Right. In particular, the neoliberals are no less concerned with order than the moral conservatives. So the use of the term "liberty" by the former is nothing other than a rhetorical device. Alternatively, David Edgar (1986) emphasizes the tension within contemporary conservatism between the good society, valued by the social authoritarians, and the free society, valued by the economic liberals. Although this scholarship has contributed to our understanding of the New Right, my aim in this chapter is to broaden that understanding by demonstrating that the economic liberals, libertarians, and moral conservatives, by distinct routes, all reach the conclusion that citizenship depends on work, or paid employment.

2. For an alternative taxonomy of the New Right on the issue of welfare benefits, see Roche (1992). He distinguishes the neo- or moral conservatives, on the one hand, from the Austrians, the libertarians, and the monetarists, on the other. He notes that the former do not want to eliminate provision for the poor, only to curtail and reorganize it, whereas the latter are strictly interested in a more radical curtailment, if not total elimination. Gray (1993) ignores the moral conservatives and focuses on three economically concerned schools of thought: the Austrian School of Subjectivism, the Virginia School of Public Choice, and the

Chicago School of Monetarism. For other discussions see, for example, Hoover (1997), King (1988), and Levitas (1986).

3. In the preface to volume 3 of *Law, Legislation, and Liberty* (1979) Hayek revises his use of terms from the previous two volumes. In particular, he replaces the term "knowledge" with the term "information."

4. Gray (1984) dismisses the Humean foundations of Hayek's thought and treats him exclusively as a Kantian. Hayek's philosophy, according to Gray, rejects the empiricist argument that knowledge is constructed only from raw sensory data. Gray focuses on Hayek's conceptual or tacit knowledge. It will become clear below that Hayek relies on both Hume and Kant for his more general theory.

5. Hayek uses these terms interchangeably.

6. Although, as I argue below, there is some ambiguity here.

7. So, the argument about philosophical individualism that complements Hayek's theory of freedom is based on a theory of the limits of knowledge, not upon the assumption of self-interest or egoism (Hayek [1944]: 59).

8. Hayek maintains that in ancient Athens, *isonomy* (a system of equal laws) preceded *demokratia* (a system of equal participation). Hayek relies on this to argue that the principles of liberalism are logically prior to democracy, and therefore more valuable.

9. Hayek concedes that the democratic method may not always place the wisest people in power. He thereby suggests that nondemocratic forms of government might appeal to society's interest in cohesion and progress. But he continues to defend the democratic method among alternative forms of government. "The benefits of democracy will show themselves only in the long run, while its more immediate achievements may well be inferior to those of other forms of government" (Hayek [1960]: 109). That Hayek assumed that someone in the West needed to be assured of the benefits of democracy, in the long run no less, implies a suspicion on his part that democracy does not enjoy the widespread acceptance often attributed to it.

10. In *The Constitution of Liberty* (1960), Hayek regards this argument as the most powerful of the three. In *Law, Legislation, and Liberty* (1979), however, Hayek writes in a footnote that he regrets having called this the most important reason, but was "carried away by de Tocqueville" at the time. "It is very important but of course less important than what I had then mentioned as the first: its function as an instrument of peaceful change" (Hayek [1979, 3: 180, n. 14]). Indeed, he does not mention this reason in the regular text of the three volumes of *Law, Legislation, and Liberty*. And in a lecture delivered in 1976, "Whither Democracy?" (1978), Hayek never once mentions this argument. It ought to be clear that Hayek's argument for the educative effects of democracy are distinct from the educative effects described by theorists of participatory democracy.

11. Alternatively, Bellamy (1994) argues that Hayek articulates two views of democracy: a) the intrinsic view, a deliberative process for elaborating general norms to regulate mutual interaction; and b) the instrumental view, a process for arriving at specific decisions between self-interested agents. He argues that Hayek accepts this two-sided view of democracy in order to resolve the paradox between the arguments that 1) the justification for democratic procedures rest on

liberal assumptions, and 2) liberal institutional arrangements are a necessary constraint on democracy, so that democracy does not undermine itself. I remain convinced, however, that Hayek defines democracy exclusively in instrumental terms.

12. Hayek also suggests, as will become clear in his linking of democracy to the distributive schemes of the welfare state, that his "ideal" of democracy represents the practice of democracy in the laissez-faire climate of nineteenth-century Europe.

13. Hayek never identifies specific democratic theorists who have perpetuated the view. Nevertheless, he implies that the rationalist constructivist and socialist threats to the ideal of individual liberty have both contributed to this mistaken theory of democracy.

14. So, Hayek adds something to the basic argument that democracy is merely a method for choosing elites. It is important as a means for choosing elites, because that ensures a peaceful change in power.

15. Power in this context refers to the force of public opinion and it remains analytically distinct from coercion; coercion is the practice that Hayek is most concerned about when he critically discusses the state.

16. And in a democracy [the Rule of Law] will not prevail unless it forms part of the moral tradition of the community, a common ideal shared and unquestionably accepted by the majority ([1960: 206])

17. Democracy leads, presumably, to all the so-called "games" that social choice theory has identified, for example, vote trading, log rolling, tit-for-tat. But Hayek's attention to these "games" indicates a distinct and peculiar focus in his critique. It is one thing to argue that democracy can undermine an individual's liberty. It is quite another to argue that the democratic method leads to unintended vote outcomes. Oddly, Hayek criticizes democracy even for the outcomes that are likely from the view of democracy as method, which he does accept.

18. Indeed, whereas *The Road to Serfdom* (1944) appears to come down decisively on the relationship between the welfare state and socialism, in *The Constitution of Liberty* (1960) Hayek explicitly distinguishes the two. In fact, he appears to reverse the order of his analysis in the later work by stating that the welfare state only came after the principles of socialism were rejected in favor of a system of state interference that tried to operate within a liberal framework. I suspect that this is a reflection of the timing of the publications. By 1960 it would have been clear to Hayek that countries clearly committed to capitalism had at the same time adopted welfarist policies. In this connection, Hayek remarked in a reference to *The Road to Serfdom:* "I did not, as many misunderstood me, contend that if government interfered at all with economic affairs it was bound to go the whole way to a totalitarian system. I was trying to argue rather what in more homely terms is expressed by saying, "if you don't mend your principles you will go to the devil'" (1973: 7).

19. Clearly, the libertarians will not have him as their own. See, for example, Baumgarth (1978), Dyer and Hickman (1979), Nozick (1974), and Hamowy (1961).

20. As I suggested in my analysis of Hayek's conception of liberty, one can make an analytical distinction between interference and coercion; not all forms of

interference are necessarily coercive. Still, where the negative conception of liberty is articulated as a principle of noninterference, coercion is generally implied in interference.

21. Compare Hayek, for whom "power" refers to the force of public opinion. By his use of the term, the increase in power is a positive thing. Friedman seems to equate power with the centralization of decision making. So, they do seem to be concerned about the same tendencies, but have simply chosen to use different terms and to use the same terms differently. The important distinction, however, is that Hayek provides a much more thorough explanation for why this consequence is undesirable, namely, that it interferes with the exchange of knowledge, upon which society is built. Friedman only argues that power threatens liberty, suggesting that individual (political) liberty is a value in and of itself.

22. It is not clear from this whether Friedman means to say that economic freedom is a necessary or a sufficient condition for political freedom.

23. Friedman shares with Hayek an appreciation for the importance of unintended consequences: "a complex and sophisticated structure arises as an unintended consequence of a large number of individual cooperating while each pursues his own interests" (Friedman and Friedman [1980: 25]). And, borrowing Adam Smith's famous metaphor, "Individuals who intend only to promote the general interest are led by the *invisible political hand* to promote a special interest that they had no intention to promote" (1980: 292, emphasis added).

24. In fact, he argues that greater disparities in wealth can be found in nonmarket economies (1980: 146).

25. So, payment ought to be in cash, rather than in kind, because the former does not interfere with the freedom of the poor individual to choose!

26. There is a similarity between Hayek and Nozick on the distinction between actual patterns of distribution and the process by which distributions occur. But, in contrast to Hayek, end-result principles of justice are not dismissed for the reason that this would be an impossible task epistemologically. Although Nozick asserts this as a principle, he tries to bolster his argument with a brief sociological reference: "*Most people* do not accept current time-slice principles as constituting the whole story about distributive shares. *They* think it relevant in assessing the justice of a situation to consider not only the distribution it embodies, but also how that distribution came about" (1974: 154, emphasis added).

27. Moreover, it seems that the New Right accepts Nozick's theory of property as a contemporary, and correct, explication of Locke's theory.

28. Of course, the maintenance of an army may rely on coercion, namely, conscription.

29. Friedman did note the effects of welfare provision on the family (1980: 127).

30. The place of Murray in a taxonomy of the New Right is not self-evident. Indeed, his focus on economic incentives and rational decision making would seem to place him with the economic liberals. Alternatively, by his own account Murray is a libertarian, and thus perhaps shares more in the way of a theory of the limits of state action with Nozick than he does with Novak and Mead. I have placed Murray in this section, however, because of his moral evaluation of the decisions made by the recipients of public assistance. As we will see, Murray may characterize the receipt of public assistance as a *rational economic* decision, and on

that point he clearly distinguishes himself from Mead. But at the same time he believes that there is something *morally irrational* about that decision—a decision
that cannot be justified on moral grounds. Moreover, viewed in light of the *political* attack on public assistance over the past decade—the attack that focuses on
the dependency of the welfare recipient—it makes the most sense to place Murray with the moral conservatives.

31. Accordingly, the organization of my analysis differs here from my analysis
of Hayek and Friedman. Rather than arriving at this argument about the problems of poverty relief after having defined liberty in the abstract, I will begin directly with his critique of social welfare policy and from that infer a conception of
freedom.

32. Murray as well as Novak suggest that there has been an increasing loosen-
ing of morality, as a distinct explanatory element. But they provide no explanation for the cause of this cause.

33. Novak et al. (1987) also suggest that institutions in society other than the
state, such as church groups, Boy Scouts, and so forth, can assist the family in
playing its proper role.

34. Although my objective in analyzing these arguments is to understand the
political theory that lies behind the critique of welfare, it would be remiss of me
at this point if I did not respond to at least one of the empirical claims of the
moral conservatives. Indeed, "the evidence that the greater availability of welfare
has contributed to marital breakups or reduced the propensity to marry after conception is mostly anecdotal or conjectural. There is little likelihood that AFDC has
influenced the increase in single-parent families" (Levitan [1990: 52]). For instance, since 1975 the proportion of children living with a single parent has risen
from 17 to 24 percent. During the same period, however, the proportion of all
children receiving AFDC dropped from 12 to 11 percent (Levitan [1990: 52]). Additionally, as with nonpoor families generally, the number of children in AFDC
families has steadily declined. The proportion of welfare families with four or
more children dropped from a third to a tenth from 1969 to 1987. Furthermore,
the average AFDC family size declined from four to three persons over the same
period (Levitan [1990: 52]). Even by the early 1980s the modal composition of a
poor household was one adult and two children (Nelson [1984: 211–31]). Lastly,
when states with widely varying welfare payments are compared, there is no
strong correlation between the amount of assistance provided and the incidence
of single-parent families, out-of-wedlock births, or divorces (Ellwood and Summers [1986]).

35. Undoubtedly, my analysis runs up against the limitations of the English
language here. When I call this independence from the state, I do not mean "freedom from the state." This would suggest that we're dealing with the typical negative conception of freedom, where the state is the subject of coercion or interference. I have made it clear that the New Right does make a distinct claim that
public assistance can be an exercise in coercion by the state. But this does not entirely capture the New Right's position.

36. And, of course, given the implicit degradation of care-giving work, husbands are never described as being "dependent" on their wives for that care-giv-

ing. For an extended treatment of the use of male independence and female dependence in liberal theory, see Fraser and Gordon (1992, 1994).

37. I cite Shklar's analysis only as a description of American attitudes toward work. I am not suggesting that Shklar is a partisan of the New Right.

38. This is obviously a thumbnail sketch of political rights and obligations. I only lay it out here in contrast to Mead's theory of social citizenship. Indeed, Mead's analysis does not aim at exploring in detail the terms of political citizenship.

39. This is Marshall's argument, which I analyze in Chapter 4. Although, contrary to Marshall, Mead is a little short on a detailed examination of the meanings of rights. He does not, for instance, explain whether the right to welfare is derived from a more fundamental, and widely acknowledged right, or whether it constitutes a new right, sui generis. Again, his objective is to discuss the failure of U.S. welfare policy, and this he explains in terms of a failure to exact obligations. The bulk of his argument is directed toward defining the content of that obligation.

40. There is an issue here about the limits of paid employment that is worth noting. Namely, just because paid employment is a condition for full citizenship, that does not mean that paid employment automatically confers citizenship. Economic refugees from nearly every continent continue to flood into the United States and work under severe conditions and for less than minimum wage in the fields of Texas and California and the sweatshops of Los Angeles and New York City. These so-called illegal aliens would seem to be the embodiment of hard work, self-reliance, and independence that the New Right cherishes as the foundation for citizenship. Still, this paid employment has not entitled these illegal immigrants to protection by the state. Of course, this really is no contradiction. There are numerous examples where the willingness to satisfy the condition of X does not automatically entitle someone to X. So, there are other conditions that dictate when paid employment will count as the grounds for citizenship and, alternatively, when paid employment will be ignored. When paid employment is performed by illegal immigrants, it will not entitle them to the state's recognition or protection; it will not count for establishing their citizenship at all. It should be noted, additionally, that the demonizing of the illegal immigrant is typically the product of the xenophobia of New Right *political* figures such as presidential candidate Pat Buchanan and former California governor Pete Wilson, and is not an issue directly addressed by the New Right liberal theorists I am considering herein. Still, it is a nice example of what I believe would be a fundamental liberal principle, namely that the willingness to perform an obligation does not automatically grant the corresponding right.

PART TWO

Liberal Citizenship and the Basis of Welfare

3

T. H. Green on Freedom and the Common Good

In the previous two chapters, I have tried to elucidate the conception of citizenship that underlies the contemporary philosophical and political attack on the provision of public welfare benefits to the nonworking poor. I have shown how this conception may preclude the possibility that women and the nonworking poor will be considered full citizens. Bentham and the New Right, however, do not represent the final *liberal* word on these questions. In this chapter I return to the nineteenth century to analyze an alternative liberal conception of citizenship. My aim is to assess this conception and to determine its usefulness for constructing an argument in favor of public welfare provision.

Nearly half a century after Bentham penned his famous description of the panopticon, T. H. Green introduced to liberal democratic theory new and provocative notions of freedom and citizenship, with specific implications for an extension of the power of the state in society. State intervention, generally, could serve the *ideal* as it unfolded in history; that is, the moral development of humanity. The function of the state was not limited to guaranteeing private property or to protecting individuals from acts of coercion by other individuals. The state could also promote *real freedom*.[1] The moral development of the individual in society depended on certain conditions that did not necessarily obtain for all individuals in a purely competitive market society. Therefore, the state could create the circumstances under which the moral development of the individual was made possible. In turn, this development allowed individuals to demonstrate their moral duty, the end of which was the common good. Green used the category of citizenship to describe this capacity for moral development as well as the exercise of moral duty. Thus, the state itself was only justified in terms of, its power only rested on its ability to serve the common good. In other words, the state had the capacity to challenge obstacles to citizenship. This meant, in particular, that the state had the capacity to create citizens out of the poor.

Green provided a new direction in liberal democratic theory by incorporating the poor into the ranks of a newly formulated citizenship, and he developed his theory of state intervention specifically around this attention to the poor. It will become clear, however, that Green's theories of freedom and citizenship specifically addressed the *working* poor. His theory addressed neither women nor the indigent, to follow Bentham's distinction. In terms of specific legislation, Green focused on the importance of factory conditions, education and regulation of the liquor trade. Thus, he did not discount private charity and voluntary organizations for the relief of indigence in the way that Bentham had done. In fact, Green was still concerned about the sense of dependency that cash transfers by the state would have inculcated. This relationship of dependency would have undermined the development of the moral sensibility and the capacity for exercising one's duty toward the realization of the common good.

Green challenged the argument that private property in land was the only sufficient condition for the rights of citizenship. To do so, he relied on a familiar argument that a man had property in his labor. Green failed, however, to examine critically the notion of labor. To be sure, he used his theory of real freedom to challenge the absolute right of the employer to dictate the terms of employment; he was a staunch advocate of the factory legislation of the late nineteenth century. Yet his view of labor was of employment for wages that circulated in the free market. Green did not critically address this free market, and this omission has unfortunate implications for women and the nonworking poor.

Individual Self-Development and the Common Good

The Three Senses of Freedom

Green is perhaps most well known for providing a definition of freedom that went beyond, but did not discard, a sense of negative liberty—a state of noncoercion.[2] Yet he in fact laid out a tripartite structure of freedom, describing a process toward the realization of the moral capacity and duty.[3] The first sense of freedom that Green identified describes the relation of the individual with himself. This is *formal freedom*. He argued that there is no independent agency of the will that determines the nature of the will. The will and the person are identical; "Self-consciousness and its object, will and its object, form a single unity" (1950: 14). A person willing makes an object his own, and that is what determines the will, not something external to it. He furthermore distinguished between *practical reason* and *will*. Practical reason denotes a "consciousness of a possibility of perfection to be realised in and by the subject of consciousness" (1950: 20) "Will," on the other hand, denotes "the effort of a self-conscious subject to satisfy himself" (1950: 20). Accordingly, as the objects of each of these tends to coincide, the individual is free and his will is autonomous.

Green did not conceive of the individual in abstraction from society or conventional morality. The progress of humanity consisted in the perfection of the individual characters of men, but this progress could only be understood in relation to the (collective) expression of this in the organization of life. So the actions of individuals were only the beginning. The process of the reconciliation between practical reason and will in the individual—*the self-realizing principle*—collectively taken, creates a conventional morality—*a system of recognized rules*. It follows that there will be a progressive adjustment of the self-realizing principle to the conventional morality, that is, a progressive sense of what is expected. This system of rules corresponds to the law, and its enforcement is an expression of the negative conception of freedom typically associated with liberalism. Thus Green defines his second sense of freedom in juridical terms.

The distinctive aspect of law is that it looks only to outward actions. The law does not require a moral *disposition*. In other words, by juristic freedom "no reference is made to the nature of the will or preference, of the object willed or preferred" (1950: 9). Instead, this juristic sense of freedom refers exclusively to the relations among men; it exempts men from compulsion by others. To be sure, this exemption involves subjection to the law. Yet that subjection cannot be compared to the subjection of man by man that the law tries to overcome (1950: 2; 1986b: 199).[4] In short, juristic freedom is the legal or social recognition of formal freedom. It is a necessary condition for the development of moral agency; it is a *feeling of possibility*. Juristic freedom is "the first form of self-enjoyment of the joy of the self-conscious spirit in itself as the one object of absolute value" (1950: 17). Where there is no law, an individual is vulnerable to compulsion by another. When that is a lurking possibility, the progressive identification of reason and the will is hindered.

Finally, Green arrived at his third conception of freedom: "positive" or "real freedom." This is not merely freedom from constraint or compulsion. It is not merely the freedom to do as one pleases without consequences. And it is not a freedom which can be enjoyed by one or a few at the cost of freedom for others (1986b: 199). Rather, through a process of reflection, the feeling of what was expected of the individual is increasingly conceived of as that which *should be so universally*. The individual arrives at a conception of the common good. The conventional morality referred to above is reflected back into the individual and accepted as one's own. Until this process is complete, as long as it remains at the level of conventional morality or juristic freedom, the "established morality presents itself as imposed from without" (1950: 24).[5] Real freedom describes the moment at which "the growth of a personal interest in the realization of an idea of what should be, in doing what is believed to contribute to the absolutely desirable, or to human perfection, because it is believed to do so" is realized (1950:25). In a public speech delivered in 1881, "Liberal Legislation and the Freedom of Contract," Green put the matter in less philosophical terms. He argued that real freedom is

> a positive power or capacity of doing or enjoying something worth doing or enjoying, and that, too, something that we do or enjoy in common with others. We mean by it a power which each man exercises through the help or security given him by his fellow-men, and which he in turn helps to secure for them. When we measure the progress of a society by its growth in freedom, we measure it by the increasing development and exercise on the whole of those powers of contributing to social good with which we believe the members of the society to be endowed; in short, by the greater power on the part of the citizens as a body to make the most and best of themselves. Thus, though of course there can be no freedom among men who act not willingly but under compulsion, yet on the other hand the mere removal of compulsion, the mere enabling a man to do as he likes, is in itself no contribution to true freedom. (1986b: 199)

By moving beyond juristic or negative freedom, Green, like Bentham, posed a direct challenge to the natural rights tradition.[6] Green argued that legal rights as citizens enjoy them in modern society are not grounded in prior *natural* rights; they are not grounded in rights existing abstractly or prior to the development of society. In short, there was no state of nature.[7] "The claim or right of the individual to have certain powers secured to him by society, and the counter-claim of society to exercise certain powers over the individual, alike rest on the fact that these powers are *necessary* to the fulfilment of man's vocation as a moral being, to an effectual self-devotion to the work of developing the perfect character in himself and others" (1986a: 23, emphasis added). The foundation of rights rests on the capacity to recognize the common good and the capacity of being determined to action by that conception; it rests on the potential for real freedom. "The person's possession of a body and its exclusive determination by his own will is the condition of exercising any other rights—indeed of all manifestation of personality" (1986a: 117). So, no one has rights except as a member of society, namely, "a society in which some common good is recognized by the members of the society as their own ideal good, as that which should be for each of them" (1986a: 25).

Green further clarified his own interpretation of rights by his distinction between *jus naturae* and moral duty. Although he disputed that rights are predicated on the conjecture of a state of nature, he continued to incorporate a sense of *jus naturae* in his theory. This refers to the entire system of rights and obligations that makes juristic freedom possible, namely, that which should be maintained by law. He argued, however, that these claims are not natural in the sense of a capacity to exist independently of force; natural does not refer to that which exists at birth or for the duration of humanity. Rather, they are natural in the sense that they are "necessary to the end which it is the vocation of human society to realise" (1986a: 17); they are necessary to the development of character in the person, or a moral capacity. What is natural is that which is *necessary to make a person a person*—a necessary (though not sufficient) condition for real freedom.

Additionally, legal rights and obligations pertain only to outward actions. Legal rights, in the first place, involve both claims and recognition. Moreover, legal obligations designate the performance of specified actions, for example, to recognize legal right claims. As correlatives to juristic freedom, legal rights and obligations do not require a moral disposition. The claim of legal rights and the performance of legal obligations do not require the coincidence of *practical reason* and the *will*. So, to reiterate Green's statement on juristic freedom, "no reference is made [by legal rights and obligations] to the nature of the will or preference, of the object willed or preferred" (1950: 7).

Although obligations are a matter of outward action, duties, in particular moral duties, are a matter of internal disposition. Therefore, whereas obligations are legal, duties are not. Duties are moral. By this, Green means they cannot be enforced; they are not the subject of positive law. This does not mean, however, that obligation and duty are unrelated. That which is a matter of legal obligation must be considered *in relation to* a moral end or duty. Those actions should be the matter of legal obligation that are necessary to the realization of the moral end toward which the society is directed. In other words, the law is good because it contributes to the realization of a certain (moral) end, not because it protects some abstract right. Thus, against Hobbes he wrote, "where there are no rights by natural[8] power, no obligatory covenant can be made" (1986a: 42). And of Locke he asked, "how can the consciousness of obligation arise without recognition by the individual of claims on the part of others which may be opposed to his momentary inclinations?" and, "given a society of men capable of such a consciousness of obligation, constituting a law according to which the members of the society are free and equal in what does it differ from a political society" (1986a: 47)?[9] In other words, rights ought to be honored and obligations met only because they are the conditions for, and thereby analytically distinct from, the exercise of one's moral duties.

The distinction between natural and legal rights led Green to contend that "will, not force, is the basis of the ideal state." "It is only as members of a society, as recognizing common interests and objects, that individuals come to have these attributes and rights; and the power, which in a political society they have to obey, is derived from the development and systematization of those institutions for the regulation of a common life without which they would have no rights at all" (1986a: 89–90). The state does not arbitrarily or coercively exercise power. It is an institution through which a consciousness of the common good develops—a consciousness of legal rights. Accordingly, the state was not created out of fear, as Hobbes would have had it: "A habit of subjection founded on fear cannot be the basis for a political or free society" (1986a: 93). Rather, individuals in the context of an established state exercise a habit of obedience out of an increasing consciousness of the moral good.[10] So, for instance, that the common good could be realized in the formation of states is not to be countered by the assertion that the individuals instrumental in the formation of states had had self-serving motives (1986a: 101–2).[11] It was rather the case that the idea had been instrumental in *directing* these selfish motives and actions toward a consciousness of the ideal. "However necessary a factor force may have been in the process by which states have been formed and transformed, it has only been such a factor *as cooperation* with those ideas without which rights could not exist" (1986a: 105–6). A right is real in the sense that the exercise of one is observable and defensible. Yet it is ideal in the sense that its recognition is not dependent on material forces. Rather, it has its being in consciousness, and "it is to these ideal realities that force is subordinate in the creation and development of states" (1986a: 106).

Based on this interpretation of history, Green revealed the error in defining the notion of citizenship in terms simply of rights and obligations. This error limited the range of political questions to, for instance, "what rights can a citizen claim?" and "what obligations does a citizen owe to the state?" With reference to the first question, the liberal democratic tradition had typically assumed that the rights a citizen claimed were aimed *against* the state. That is, in what areas could the citizen claim sovereignty, or noninterference from the state? Green considered, however, that this sort of question arose from the (mistaken) theory of natural rights. Indeed, if an individual owned some rights antecedent to political society in general, or to the democratic state more specifically, then the individual would understandably claim exemptions from state interference. From this negative view of liberty it is possible to argue that the power of the state ought to do no more than is necessary to guarantee civility in society. Given that rights are only recognized in society and only for the purpose of realizing the common good, however, rights should not be the grounds upon which a supposed antagonism between the individual and the state is built.

Green laid out these arguments about the relationship between state intervention and real freedom in his 1881 speech. Countering the position that contracts between individuals were inviolable, Green asserted that contracts should not be viewed as ends in themselves. "We shall see that freedom of contract, freedom in all the forms of doing what one will with one's own, is valuable only as a means to an end. That end is what I call freedom in the positive sense: in other words, the liberation of the powers of all men equally for contributions to a common good" (1986b: 200). Thus, one man's freedom to enjoy and dispose of his possessions as he would like, ought to be secured only as far as it does not interfere with "a like freedom on the part of others" (1986b: 200). Consequently, any contract having such interference as its consequence ought to be made null. Taking the most extreme example, Green argued that "no contract is valid in which human persons, willingly or unwillingly, are dealt with as commodities, because such contracts of necessity defeat the end for which alone society enforces contracts at all" (1986b: 201).

So, by providing more than the mere protection of juristic freedom, the state does not dictate an arbitrary morality; it does not arbitrarily promote a list of rights or obligations. Rather, the state promotes the conditions that are most conducive to the realization of the common good; it promotes a morality based on the common good. Thus, the state must continue to enforce legal obligations. By doing so, it creates conditions for the common good. But at the same time, the burden on the state to create these conditions of moral development will require in some circumstances that the state intervene in ways which, for instance, limit the freedom of contract among individuals. When Green's speech is considered in relation to his more philosophical writings, one sees how much this critique of contracts was not simply aimed at specified agreements such as the labor contract. His critique was also aimed at the supposed contract that lay at the foundation of society—the theoretical nexus between rights and obligations. For the state to merely recognize and enforce the claims to private property as they were expressed by the natural rights tradition would be the equivalent of upholding a contract whereby the majority of "human persons . . . unwillingly . . . are dealt with as commodities" (1986b: 201).

Green also ties this in with his critique of utilitarianism. The end of society is not to establish a set of procedures whereby individuals are free to pursue individual, materially-based wants, without regard to a common good. Again, "the mere enabling a man to do as he likes, is in itself no contribution to true freedom" (1986b: 199). The greatest good to society, measured quantitatively, would not come from the private pursuit of interests. Still, one should also see in these arguments that he was neither absolutely interventionist nor laissez-faire-*ist*.[12] Green did share with the utilitarians an emphasis on the consideration of consequences. He also left it to the particular circumstances to determine the appropriate course of action.[13]

Given that the authority of the state is not derived from some fictitious original covenant, Green reasoned that its authority had not been established once and for all. Therefore, Green offered a teleological interpretation of political society, namely that state authority rested on its *continuing capacity* to maintain the conditions of freedom that are necessary for the moral life. In other words, it is not simply that the state *is allowed to promote* the conditions for the development of a moral capacity. The state *is expected to provide* these conditions when they are wanting and when the state has the capacity to meet them. The true function of government is to "maintain conditions of life in which morality shall be possible" (1986a: 22). To eschew this true function is to undermine the reason upon which the authority of the state rests.

Property in Labor

A review of Green's discussion on property further clarifies the meaning of real freedom and the moral development of the individual.[14] He began with two questions on the origins of property: a) how had men[15] come to appropriate? and b) how had the idea of right come to be associated with this action? Green argued that fundamentally "appropriation is an expression of the will" (1986a: 164). That is, appropriation represents the process through which knowledge is gained and real freedom is realized. Through appropriation, the self distinguishes itself from the material world and that world is reflected back into the self. Acts of appropriation represent

> the individual's effort to give reality to a conception of his own good; of his consciousness of a possible self-satisfaction as an object to be attained. . . . They are not merely a passing employment of such materials as can be laid hands on to satisfy this or that want, present or future, felt or imagined, but reflect the consciousness of a subject which distinguishes itself from its want; which present itself to itself as still there and demanding satisfaction when this or that want, or any number of wants, have been satisfied; which thus not merely uses a thing to fill a want, but says to itself, "This shall be mine to do as I like with, to satisfy my wants and express my emotions as they arise" (1986a: 165).[16]

Not only is there a right of appropriation, the idea of property also implies an obligation by others to recognize that appropriation of property. Green did not analytically separate these two. He contended that within one will is both a) the effort to appropriate, and b) the restraint brought by the customary recognition (1986a: 168). Therefore, the freedom to appropriate is a condition of the growth of free morality, and some institutional force is necessary to ensure a restraint on the part of others, notwithstanding the spiritual principle on which the will, generally, rests. The state does not relinquish its title to providing a framework of law (juristic freedom). Yet juristic freedom could only be understood in terms of facilitating the process toward real freedom; juristic freedom is not an end in itself. Thus the claim to private property and the expectation of its protection by the state is consistent with the conjunction of practical reason and will—with real freedom. In fact, the abrogation of individual property rights would involve "a complete regulation of life incompatible with that highest object of human attainment, a free morality" (1986a: 172).

Seeing the effort to appropriate as an expression of the will meant for Green that property is not merely a contingent condition for real freedom. He did not simply make the argument that property was no hindrance to real freedom, but that property was a necessary condition for real freedom. Given Green's rejection of collectivized property and his revision of a theory of the right to private property, it ought to be clear that Green could not thereby rely on an identification of property with land to make his argument. To challenge that sort of exclusive right to property (and what would logically be the exclusive opportunity to moral development and real freedom) Green argued that labor itself, like property, represents an act of appropriation. Labor is available to those who do not own property in the traditional sense of the term. That is, labor itself represents an expression of the will, a condition for the realization of the common good. In fact, Green came close to questioning the importance of property generally. "Prevent a man from possessing property (in the ordinary sense) and his personality may still remain. Prevent him (if it were possible) from using his body to express a will, and the will itself could not become a reality; he would not be really a person" (1986a: 117). Labor, then, not only acquires the same status as real property. Green accepts the formal equation of labor with real property.

Still, Green recognized that the individual who had nothing but his labor to sell for a bare existence, though he had formal equality under the law, might just as well have been denied the right of appropriation. Property, as well as justly compensated labor, enable one to develop a sense of responsibility. When one's labor brings nothing in exchange but a bare minimum, however, the person in effect has no property through his labor. In other words, labor that brought only a bare minimum does not have the same status as, and could much less be identified with, real property. "To an Athenian slave, who might be used to gratify a master's lust, it would have been a mockery to speak of the state as a realisation of freedom, and perhaps it would not be less to speak of it as such to an un-taught and under-fed denizen of a London yard with gin shops on the right hand and on the left" (1950: 8).

It would seem from the foregoing discussion that Green was prepared to offer a radical critique of capitalism generally, or laissez-faire liberal-ism more particularly. Although critical of laissez-faire liberalism, he did not offer a critique of capitalism generally. "It is not then to the accumula-tion of capital, but to the condition, due to antecedent circumstances un-connected with that accumulation, of the men with whom the capitalist deals and whose labour he buys on the cheapest terms, that we must as-cribe the multiplication in recent times of an impoverished and reckless proletariat" (1986a: 175). The accidents of history—conquest and feudal-ism—had bred the proletariat class. This class had not developed out of any necessary connection with the maintenance of rights generally, or capitalism specifically. Even if the proletariat in the late nineteenth cen-tury had not been trained in habits of serfdom, surely their ancestors had, and those habits had been passed down through the generations. "When we consider all this, we shall see the unfairness of laying on capi-talism or the free development of individual wealth the blame which is really due to the arbitrary and violent manner in which rights over land have been acquired and exercised, and to the failure of the state to fulfil those functions which under a system of unlimited private ownership are necessary to maintain the conditions of a free life" (1986a: 177–78). The protection of property is necessary, but the nature of that protection needs to be reconceptualized. Moreover, capitalism should not be dis-missed because it cannot correct all inequalities. "Considered as repre-senting the conquest of nature by the effort of free and variously gifted individuals, property must be unequal; and no less must it be so if con-sidered as a means by which individuals fulfil social functions. As we may learn from Aristotle, those functions are various and the means re-quired for the fulfilment are various" (1986a: 172).

A New Model of Citizenship

In the preceding section I addressed Green's theory of rationality and self-development, and I identified the role that the state played in this develop-ment. I have shown that for Green the development of the individual and the role of the state in history are integrally bound together. As citizenship is a category invoked to designate the relationship between the individual and the state, the realization of real freedom describes the making of a citizen. More than a mere focus on civil liberties and the suffrage, Green's conception of citizenship is identified with the capacity to realize one's moral duty and to contribute to the common good. Consequently, the process of the realization of real freedom and individual development that I have just outlined describes the full meaning of citizenship for Green.

In the first place, [17] the *citizen* is the morally self-governing individual. This corresponds to Green's first sense of freedom (1950: 14). He is the individual who does not adhere to conventional morality—the morality that is imposed from without (1950: 25). Additionally, the citizen has character, rationality, and self-awareness. Furthermore, the citizen is conscious of a common life and entertains a conception of the common good (1986a: 25–26, 89–90). Moreover, the citizen has *internalized* the fundamental communal norms through self-development; a citizen demonstrates loyalty to the normative ideals embodied in the state. Consequently, the citizen plays a role in the historical process, in the unfolding of the ideal in history. In short, citizenship consists of the realization of real freedom. Therefore, the citizen is not merely a passive recipient of the protection of juristic freedom. The *rights* of citizens do not, as we have seen, protect presocial claims. Rather, the rights of citizens are powers that "are necessary to the fulfilment of man's vocation as a moral being" (1986a: 23). Rights in fact *enable* citizenship.

Although Green invested the category of citizenship with these new meanings, he also addressed traditional questions concerning the prerogatives of citizens, such as the suffrage.[18] Green turned his attention to questions of political participation when he conceded that the administrative agencies and legislative bodies that constitute the state are not without their biases and could be in conflict with the development of the common good.[19] Thus, he asked whether popular control is necessary to protect against these biases. He also asked whether active participation in legislative functions is a necessary condition for an appreciation of the common good (1986a: 93–94). Not surprisingly, he offered no unqualified responses. He considered the answers to both of these questions to be a matter of particular circumstances.

The particular circumstance to which Green pointed was the size of modern states. This characteristic made representative government, rather than direct participation, a matter of practical necessity. Green argued that the political society upon which Rousseau had based his theory of participation was unrealistically small for the case of England. The size of modern states demanded a representative form of government, namely, a representative democracy. For this reason, Green supported universal *male* suffrage. On 15 May 1856, he argued before the Oxford Union "that it is the undoubted right of every English*man* to possess the suffrage" (quoted in Nicholson [1990: 288 n. 78, emphasis added]). At the same time, however, he conceded that the suffrage was no guarantee of active citizenship. A representative government might in fact weaken the active interests of the citizenry.

> But perhaps . . . the lowering of civil [sic] vitality . . . is a temporary loss that we have to bear as the price of having recognised the claim to citizenship as the claim of all men. Certainly all political ideals, which require active and direct participation by the citizens in the function of the sovereign state fail us as soon as we try to conceive their realisation on the wide area even of civilised mankind. It is easy to conceive a better system than that of the great states of modern Europe, with their national jealousies, rival armies, and hostile tariffs; but the condition of any better state of things would seem to be the recognition of some single constraining power, which would be even more remote from the active co-operation of the individual citizen than is the sovereign power of the great states at present. (1986a: 94)

Ironically, the extension of this mark of political citizenship may have had the consequence of destroying an active interest in the institutions of the state.[20] It must be clear, however, that this was only an interest in administration and legislation; Green was not describing the interest in the moral duty or the common good. The two interests remained analytically distinct. The size of modern states does not undermine the new conception of citizenship outlined by Green.

Green's focus on the suffrage can be understood when one sees how he linked the *role* of the citizen in the affairs of government with the *motivation for obedience* that is the foundation of the state. Green distinguished between external forces and internal interests as alternate foundations for the state. He described the loyal subject as the individual who looks to the state only for juristic freedom. In this situation, the "individual's relation to the state is that of a passive recipient of protection in the exercise of his rights of person and property" (1986a: 96–97). The true state, on the other hand, is not founded on the obedience bred by this disposition. The true state is the one in which the citizen feels a spontaneous interest in rendering obedience to the law, "because it . . . present[s] itself to him as the condition of the maintenance of those rights and interests, common to himself with his neighbours, which he understands" (1986a: 96). These citizens are *intelligent patriots* who enjoy real freedom through an active interest in the common good. In other words, it is not enough that one renders obedience to the law. In the true state, obedience is transformed into a moral duty, and this duty is performed out of a recognition that the law is right.[21] This active interest, this higher feeling of political duty, is predicated on participation in the work of the state. The citizen "must have a share, direct or indirect, by himself acting as a member or by voting for the members of supreme or provincial assemblies, in making and maintaining the laws which he obeys. Only thus will he learn to regard the work of the state as a whole, and to transfer to the whole the interest which otherwise his particular experience would lead him to feel only in that part of its work that goes to the maintenance of his own and his neighbour's rights" (1986a: 96–97).

This share is therefore a necessary condition for the realization of real freedom. For Green a representative democracy is necessary (and more realistic than direct democracy) because it guarantees the strength of the state by making intelligent patriots out of mere loyal subjects. Indeed, the common good relies on this strength of the state. A representative democracy is the guarantee that citizens will identify their interests with the common good. This is not, to be sure, the *protective-representative* democracy endorsed by Bentham. Green did not focus exclusively on protecting the interests of the masses against the sinister interests of the ruling few. Bentham's political society remained a collection of separate individual interests, a collection of mere loyal subjects. Green's political society, on the other hand, represents a collection of citizens, a collection of those who have had an internal conversion toward a recognition of the common good. This conversion can be facilitated by some sort of participation in the state. Where Bentham endorsed representative democracy as a means of protecting one group against another, Green endorsed representative democracy as a means of protecting all groups against any alternative to the common good. Therefore an active role in the *administration* of government is not a necessary condition for real freedom or the common good; it is not a necessary condition of citizenship. It is enough to be an intelligent patriot. The suffrage, in particular, is a sufficient means of participation for the realization of this status.

In "Liberal Legislation and the Freedom of Contract" Green countered the objection that biases of the legislative bodies presented an insurmountable threat to the development of the common good. He asserted that the British Parliament had become more democratic by the Parliament of 1868 (see Nicholson [1990: 109–10, 167, 196–7]), both because it had been elected by a more popular suffrage and because it had succeeded in passing, among other things, "the first great education act" (1986b: 197). Thus, Green endorses the position that a state is democratic not simply because it is the consequence of a popular suffrage, but also because the state in turn pursues policies that continue to create or support a democratic society. In his concluding remarks, he maintained that the citizens of England (in 1881) made the laws. There was no longer any danger that legislation was primarily in the interests of a *privileged class* or in the interests of particular religious opinions (1986b: 212, emphasis

added).[22] Again the suffrage was sufficient for protecting against potential biases. It represented an adequate means of control over legislators.

The Objects of State Intervention

Green's theory of the state is teleological. The state is the culmination of
history. The state is not, however, an end in itself. It serves the purpose of
the common good. In the first place, the ideal state *removes* obstacles to
freedom, or the realization of the common good. Additionally, because
the common good is comprised of individual moral characters, the state
more specifically must promote the conditions under which individual
moral characters will be realized. This intervention by the state is predicated on the right of every individual to recognition and the right of
every individual to pursue the development of his moral character. Thus,
by identifying moral development with citizenship, Green identified
state intervention with the *promotion* of citizenship.

This intervention, therefore, is not based simply on the interest in protecting some negative rights of citizenship such as property. It is based on
the development of citizenship itself. When labor contracts, lack of education, and alcoholism, for instance, stand in the way of moral development,
they thereby stand in the way of citizenship. So the objects of state intervention, by claiming protection or education, do not forfeit the status of
citizenship. Instead, the individual has the right to these state programs
for the very reason that he has the potential to become a citizen. In Victo-
rian England, Green meant that the state is able to make citizens out of the
working poor, thereby suggesting a more inclusive sense of citizenship.

At the same time, Green's proposals for state intervention were limited
to addressing labor conditions, compulsory education, sanitation, and
the regulation of the liquor trade. He argued that the state can interfere,
not because the state can *directly* promote moral goodness, but because it
is the business of the state "to maintain the *conditions* without which a
free exercise of the human faculties is impossible" (1986b: 202, emphasis
added). In each of these cases, Green had to counter the argument that
such legislation interfered with a typically juristic sense of freedom. For
instance, a labor contract is a voluntary agreement between two parties;
each party willingly consents to the contract. Green recognized, however,
the possibility that an individual might be forced to consent to sell his labor under conditions by which he would forfeit his opportunity to contribute to the social good; the laborer might be forced to consent to degrading labor conditions. Green addressed the argument that the
enlightened self-interest or benevolence of individuals under a system of
freedom of contract ought to be allowed to bring the degraded individuals into a state of free development. He responded, "ask yourself what

chance there was of a generation, born and bred under such conditions, ever contracting itself out of them" (1986b: 204).

Similarly, Green argued for the regulation of the liquor trade.[23] He considered drinking to be a public act because "the excessive drinking of one man means an injury to others in health, purse and capability, to which no limits can be placed" (1986b: 210). The state ought to prevent something in a person which that person may find to his taste, but which has the consequences of creating a social nuisance. Green agreed that it would be the best possible situation if moderation or abstinence came through the spontaneous actions of individuals. A cure that comes quickly through compulsion might be no cure at all. Nevertheless, Green argued that it would be dangerous to wait. "A drunken population naturally perpetuates and increases itself" (1986b: 211). And there is no need to leave the temptation to drink as a test of one's moral fiber. Green argued that there were a sufficient number of other problems in society to test the moral fiber. He admitted that the moderate drinker might be coerced in a sense. But the moral disposition of the moderate drinker would not thereby be harmed, and the moderate drinker could serve as a witness to the alcoholic. By this action, the moderate drinker would merely be giving up material interests for the moral interests of others, that is, contributing to the common good.

Green provided this theoretical description of the role of the state in promoting real freedom (in "On the Different Sense of 'Freedom' as Applied to Will and to the Moral Progress of Man") at the same time that actual legislation was being passed in the pursuit of, according to Green's interpretation, that real freedom.[24] In "Liberal Legislation and the Freedom of Contract" Green links these two. He noted with approval the transition he observed occurring from voluntary to state action in the area of elementary education. Beyond identifying education as a necessary condition for real freedom, Green demonstrated why it was necessary that the state provide it, especially when it might contradict the interest that working-class parents may have had in sending their children to work in factories rather than to schools. In this case, "the proper substitute is not the casual action of charitable persons, but the collective action of society. The whole body of citizens ought to be called upon to do that as a body which under the conditions of modern life cannot be done if everyone is left to himself" (1911b: 432).

In complex societies, such as the Britain of Green's day, government action had become more effective than voluntary action. Proper (democratically inspired) government action did not stand opposed to individuals in society, but was action taken in the name of the individuals who populate the society. In this way, the democratic state was, according to Nicholson's interpretation of Green, "voluntary action taken to its fullest extent, voluntary action taken collectively by the whole society. State action, on this view, was not government interference with society or with the individual, it was the community acting on its own behalf" (Nicholson [1990: 167]). So democracy as voluntary action meant that the individual now pursued the common good through the state as a citizen, not as a private person (see Nicholson [1990: 196–97]).

Green also brought together arguments about the extension of the suffrage and education. He believed that further democratization depended on extending the franchise to agricultural laborers in the counties in the same way that it had been extended to the working men in the boroughs.[25] "Every means should be taken . . . to bring [the suffrage] about" (quoted in Nicholson [1990: 288 n. 78]). The franchise ought to be extended, and this depended on extending the opportunities for education. Countering the conventions of his day, Green even addressed the status of women when discussing education. He argued in 1868 that the "supply of education [for women] must precede and create a general demand" (quoted in Nicholson [1990: 174]).[26] Notably, however, Green nowhere argues explicitly for the extension of the suffrage to women.

Given what Green has said on these matters, it is tempting to view his arguments for real freedom as the theoretical foundation for the modern welfare state. Indeed, the welfare state, viewed broadly, involves much more than the distribution of basic resources for the indigent. And Green's specific recommendations for education, labor legislation, and temperance would have been aimed at the working poor. Yet it should be clear that the *goods* of state intervention were not direct transfers of cash or tangible goods. In this way, the policies were clearly intended for people who had already satisfied the conditions of bare subsistence through their own labor. To come to the state for subsistence indicated a refusal to do what was in one's power to do, to develop one's moral character.[27] To accept cash outlays would have been the equivalent to entering into a relationship of dependency. "It is enough to point out the directions in which the state may remove obstacles to the realization of the capacity for the beneficial exercise of rights, without defeating its own object by vitiating the spontaneous character of that capacity" (1986a: 162). Provision of cash outlays to the indigent would have been inimical to the development of their moral character. Accepting it would have amounted to the shunning of their moral duty. In short, the state was able to make citizens only out of the working poor.

The Limits of Citizenship

The conclusion to draw from the foregoing is that Green's theory of real freedom was *never intended* as the theoretical foundation for a policy of direct assistance to the nonworking poor. Moreover, the logic of real freedom, or positive liberty, precludes the possibility of even turning it against Green's intentions and using it as the foundation for public assistance in the present day. Contemporary theorists searching for such foundations will not find an ally in Green or his theory of real freedom. Despite a commitment to state intervention, Green remains committed at the same time to labor as a form of property. Public assistance is no substitute for labor in this matter.

At the same time, it must be recognized that this commitment to labor as a form of property upon which the claim for citizenship could be made neglected certain conventions of labor. Although Green was, to be sure, critical of labor contracts, he ignored other aspects of labor that would have important implications for significant numbers of potential citizens. An examination of these implications will illuminate the limits of Green's expansion of citizenship.

The Role of Women

These assumptions about labor in the market indicate that little attention was directed by Green toward the moral development of women. Green's sense of labor contains an implicit distinction between public and private employment. By public labor I mean labor in the free market, while private labor stands for the unpaid, caregiving work performed in the home by women. Green's argument about labor being a condition for citizenship thus only applies to the former. To the extent that women did not participate in paid employment, they did not participate in the realization of the common good. Women could not, in this view, develop the same moral sensibility. The opportunity for this development for women remained permanently precluded by the way Green sets up his argument. This inattention to the status of women's labor in the home is serious in light of Green's arguments for temperance. He defined drinking as a public act, for the reason that it has social consequences. Because it constitutes a public act, drinking could thereby be subject to state intervention. He also employed the same reasoning in his critique of the labor contract. Green does not, however, apply the same logic to women's work. This should not be seen as a contradiction in his theory. Rather, his inattention to the status of women reflects his failure to acknowledge the social consequences of women's work. Green's failure here amounts to an implicit reassertion that women's work is private.

Second, we have seen how Green identified the suffrage as a viable and realistic means of participation. This sort of participation would guarantee that legislation would no longer be an expression of the interests of a privileged class. So, curiously enough, Green does not address the question of women's suffrage. Green's (if only implicit) theory of democracy fails to recognize that the material interests of either sex might not be considered by those in a position to be elected. More specifically, Green's theory fails to appreciate how easily the interests of an entire sex could be, and were, excluded. On the one hand, insofar as the state pursued the common good, the state pursued a *noncompetitive* ideal interest. Theoretically, it might be stated, the pursuit of this interest did not demand that everyone participate. This claim, however, amounts to the antidemocratic claim that a supposed identity of interests obviates the need for universal suffrage. But even if Green did have faith in this sort of arrangement, there does not seem to be any particular reason why women should be denied the suffrage when Green argued for its extension to agricultural laborers.

Additionally, Green did indeed accept that there would continue to be competition for material interests at some level. Green's political theory, therefore, conspicuously omits women from participation in that competition. On top of this, women's suffrage was clearly a speakable issue among political theorists in the latter part of the nineteenth century. As we have seen, Bentham had been an advocate, or a cautious one at least, and J. S. Mill had already published "The Subjection of Women" by 1869.[28] Additionally, the women's suffrage movement was alive and well at the time Green laid out his theories. So, Green's omission cannot be explained by the historical context. Last, Green's silence on women's suffrage is curious given his comments about their educational opportunities. Green is willing to extend an education to women. Yet in other passages he argued that education was a necessary condition for extension of the suffrage to working-class men. So it is not clear why Green does not then join his argument about extending education to women with a justification for that extension, namely, that it would enable them to become a more active and informed electorate.

Green's assumptions about labor as a condition of citizenship were implied in his criticism of cash outlays by the state. He argued on the one hand that if there were to be outlays for bare subsistence, private charity remained a viable form of volunteerism[29] for meeting this aim. He also argued that reliance on the state for this subsistence would contribute to a relationship of dependency. The psychological consequences of this state of dependency would have stood in the way of the development of the moral duty. Once again, women are curiously excluded from this consideration. Having accepted a conventional view of the family, Green appears willing to accept the role of the wife as dependent on the breadwinner—her husband. Consequently, either Green must have been willing to accept that the husband-wife relationship represented a different sort of dependency, or Green is implicitly arguing that women suffer from the same damaging psychological effects of dependency as welfare recipients. In either instance, Green precludes women from the opportunity to become citizens and moral agents.

The Nonworking Poor

Green's theory of citizenship also excluded the nonworking poor of either sex. His arguments in favor of private charity parallel his tacit endorsement of the conventional division of labor within the marriage referred to above. Presumably, private charity would have contributed to a relationship of dependency as well. In this instance, Green did not specify why that sort of dependency is any different for the indigent than dependency on the state. Green might have developed this distinction further by arguing, for instance, that the dependency of the indigent on the state hindered the state from realizing the common good. That is, the relationship would have been detrimental both for the individual indigent as well as for the capacity of the state itself to play the role in history that it ought to play. Whether he accepted this position, the consequence of what he did argue remains that the individual who does not secure his livelihood through wages in the free market[30] will not have the capacity for citizenship and moral agency.

Finally, and this follows from the preceding paragraph, Green did not recognize the power of the market to determine the possibility of employment. When Green argued that an extension of the suffrage meant that there was no longer any danger that legislation would reflect the interests of a privileged class, he betrayed his failure to understand the power of capital to control the conditions and possibility of employment. Green's theory of intervention was based on his critique of a purely juristic sense of freedom and the ensuing inviolability of contract. Still, Green did not extend his critique to the labor contract more generally—the possibility to enter into any labor contract. He did not recognize how that possibility in the first place was controlled by the market. Consequently, he did not recognize how the market, given the logic of his own argument, had the power to hinder the development of moral agency. Green's position is subject to the same critique I mounted against the New Right in the previous chapter.

Conclusion

In this chapter, I have pursued two objectives. In the first place, I have laid out an exposition of Green's theory of citizenship and state intervention. Though not always self-consciously a democrat, Green established an important democratic principle. Namely, the state ought to contribute to the conditions for citizenship. The legitimate state is not simply the state which has been appointed by universal suffrage. That is, the legitimate state also creates and reproduces citizens.

I have also demonstrated the limitations of Green's model of citizenship as well as the limitations inherent to his calls for the extension of the suffrage. In short, according to Green's theory, neither the nonworking poor nor women have access to the goods of citizenship, so neither group can meet the terms of the moral duty for which the new theory of the state has been elaborated in the first place. Neither group will have the capacity to become moral agents. Green's omission of a critique of capitalism and the market reveals a critique of power relationships that is naive at best.

By limiting the sphere of state intervention to the factory acts, education, and temperance, Green ignored the conventions of male-female relationships as well as the power of the market to exclude individuals from the opportunity to labor. Conditions for citizenship for women and the nonworking poor continued to remain outside the control of the state. In a *free* market, those individuals continued to remain under the control of forces that claimed exemption from the state. Any attempt to extend the sphere of the state in the name of equality failed at its task.

Like Bentham, therefore, Green anticipates and shares many of the assumptions of the contemporary theory of workfare. Citizenship depends on rationality, and labor provides the opportunity to prove this rationality. Of course, this method of proving one's rationality is only incumbent on the poor. Persons of independent financial means are not suddenly stripped of their citizenship. This demonstrates that citizens must be workers only when the alternative for these workers would be economic dependence on the state. By labor the working classes prove their rationality as well as their economic independence. In short, citizenship is identified alternately with the moral consequences of labor and with economic independence. In the final part of the book, I will draw some inspiration from Green as I articulate a conception of autonomy and its relationship to welfare provision. One of the important implications of that chapter will be that the democratic state must guarantee the conditions for citizenship. For this, Green has provided an important theoretical foundation. But to make that argument, I will not follow Green through his theory of real freedom. As I have tried to show here, that conception of liberty remains integrally related to the notion that labor for wages in the market is the only satisfactory alternative to the control of property when it comes to the conditions for citizenship.

Notes

1. Following Nicholson (1990: 120—21), I will use the language of real freedom, rather than positive freedom. As Nicholson has pointed out, Green himself used the latter term less often than the secondary literature on Green would indicate.

2. I have found Nicholson (1990, chap. 7) especially useful in this explication of Green's theory of freedom. Other discussions include Wempe (1986, chaps. 3, 5) and Norman (1987, chaps. 2, 3). For critiques of Green's theory of freedom, see Berlin (1969), MacCallum (1967), and Weinstein (1965).

3. Such a discussion of Green's supposed Idealist philosophy begs for a comparison with Hegel. For many years, there seemed to be a consensus that Green was significant for having introduced Hegelian thought to Britain. Unfortunately, such an argument seems to have led uncritically to the position that Green's entire system was Hegelian in structure and substance. Scholarship over the last twenty-five years or so, however, has challenged the idea of a complete identification of Green's thought with Hegel. Nicholson (1990) identifies specific points on which Green followed Hegel, for example, on the importance of mutual recognition to self-consciousness (244, n. 15) and that no person was free unless all were free (246, n. 42). He also argues that Green's tripartite structure of freedom corresponded to Hegel's three moments of the will, though Green did not expressly acknowledge it (120). In general, Nicholson argues that Hegel's main contribution to Green's thought was the historical dimension, that is, that ideas are continually changing (2). Thomas (1987) takes one of the strongest positions against identifying Green with Hegel. He argues that Green is clearly an independent thinker. According to Thomas, Green rejected or omitted much of what was central to Hegel, and many of Green's important arguments were unconnected or antagonistic to Hegel's philosophy (2). Jenks (1977) argues that Green made an important departure from Hegel insofar as Green's theory of the common good may have called for disobedience to the state (482). More generally, though, Jenks argues that Green's theory of the common good was much more of an elucidation of a Kantian ethics of duty and that on points that separated Kant and Hegel, Green regularly sided with Kant. Jenks concludes that, "although Green tends to express his ethics in Hegelian jargon, the ethics itself is a Kantian philosophy of duty" (484). Alternatively, Paul Harris and John Morrow (1986) argue that many apparently Kantian and Hegelian themes that ran through Green could also be found in earlier English writers such as S. T. Coleridge and F. D. Maurice. According to Harris and Morrow, these writers "expounded a form of Platonic immanentist incarnationalism" that undoubtedly prepared Green for accepting German theology. "His [Green's] work must not be seen as merely an anglicised version of Hegel's philosophy but as successfully overcoming the mid-century view that it had theologically suspect implications" (5). Indeed, it is reported that Green himself claimed about Hegel's work that it "must all be done over again." Green felt that Hegel had only encapsulated one aspect of human thought (Vincent [1986: 7–10]).

4. Compare Bentham's third notion of liberty (1973: 175).

5. Thus, Green seems to be up to something similar to Bentham insofar as he outlines the way in which what pertains to the individual is aggregated in society

toward the common good. But where Bentham describes this in terms of the aggregation of individual interests, Green describes it in terms of the aggregation of the self-realizing principles. And of course, for Bentham there is no reflection back into the self.

6. Martin (1986) argues that Green's theory of rights is a logical development of the natural rights tradition, not an entirely new theory. Similarly, Vincent and Plant (1984) contend that Green provides an internal reform of the liberal tradition. For a different focus, see Greengarten (1981), who argues that Green remained a possessive individualist and merely injected liberal capitalism with democratic principles.

7. However, according to Green, rights do predate the development of modern institutions of government. Rights exist in the society of families. The modern state is the institution, developed by the ideal in history, which guarantees these rights.

8. See supra (1986a: 16—17) for Green's sense of natural.

9. In other words, Locke's state of nature is really a political society.

10. Compare Bentham's definition of political society as that situation in which individuals are in the habit of obedience (1973: 128).

11. Among others, Napoleon furnished this sort of example for Green.

12. However, Green would argue these positions over political and social issues, not economic issues. See Nicholson (1990), who argues that although Green may repudiate the epistemological empiricism and psychological hedonism of utilitarianism, he did embrace their consideration of consequences. "They both think that the limits to state action must be established according to what is in the public interest, or socially expedient; and they both think that investigation of the facts must decide whether government interference in a particular case is expedient or not" (190).

13. Green seems to have approved of J. S. Mill's revision of utilitarianism, namely, that some kinds of pleasure are more desirable and valuable than others. Still, Green ultimately found Mill's position to be inadequate, despite the revision, because Mill remained committed to the doctrine that all desire is for pleasure. See Greengarten (1981, chap. 7).

14. MacPherson (1973), Hansen (1977), and Greengarten (1981) treat Green as a possessive individualist. (Although Hansen, as distinguished from Greengarten, bases his argument on the position that Green had a sophisticated understanding of capitalism.) In a slight variation, Lawless (1978) counters Hansen by arguing that Green clearly misunderstood the nature of capitalism by claiming that wages and profit were of the same nature; that property was all of one type. He argues that Green used metaphysics to justify capitalism a priori—that Green had no real understanding of political economy. In a critique of MacPherson, Morrow (1983) argues that for Green, the mere possession of property has no moral significance. He sees Green as distinguishing among types of property and attaching ethical significance only to property when it allowed the individual to contribute to the common good through socially responsible, self-determined action.

15. Indeed, Green was not critical of the point that men in the specific sense had been the appropriators for the most part. In fact, he described the family as a

unit wherein the man was motivated to acquire property in the interests of providing for the wants of the wife (1986a: 181).

16. Green elaborates here on his critique of empiricist epistemology. Resources are not consumed merely for the satisfaction of basic needs. Appropriation and consumption are part of the process by which a further purpose is realized, namely, the common good. In making this observation, I have admittedly overlooked the important distinction between property as real assets, that is, as capital, and property as consumable goods. This is done only in the spirit of Green himself. Although Green did provide some important distinctions in the nature of property (see Morrow [1983]), there are other important distinctions that he glossed over but that were a part of the language of political economy of Green's time.

17. Vincent (1986: 49) provides a clear outline of this. He argues that Green's theory cannot be understood without considering Green's theological presuppositions. See also Richter (1964) and Vincent and Plant (1984). Richter sees Green's theory of citizenship as a surrogate faith, as a response to the attacks on Christianity by natural science and new biblical interpretation. Greengarten (1981), on the other hand, treats Green's philosophy independently of his theology.

18. Nicholson (1990) suggests that Green did not write extensively on democratic theory. However, as Nicholson notes, more than one of his contemporaries identified Green as a democratic theorist. John Addington Symonds, Green's brother-in-law, wrote that Green recognized that democracy, implying political and social advantages on equal terms, and socialism, implying an equal distribution of wealth, were active elements in modern politics and the cardinal questions of the modern world (Symonds [1967, 3: 176—77]). In his well-known memoir of Green, Nettleship cites a speech given by Green before the Oxford Reform League in 1867. Green argued at length about the need for reform. But it was no longer a struggle between the House of Lords and the House of Commons; it was now between the Commons and the masses (Green [1911, vol. 3: cx–cxi]). And Caird (1883) argued that Green was a democrat because of Green's belief in the essential equality of man and because "his sympathies were always with the many rather than with the few." He also attributes to Green the belief that there is an "instinct of reason in the movement of popular sentiment which may be wiser than the opinions of the educated classes" (1883: 4).

19. As we have seen, these potential biases or self-serving motives do not contradict the notion that the state is the realization of the ideal in history.

20. Hegel makes a similar argument: "As for popular suffrage, it may be further remarked that especially in large states it leads inevitably to electoral indifference, since the casting of a single vote is of no significance where there is a multitude of electors" (1967: §311). Compare Avineri (1972: 161–67).

21. It is not rendered out of fear. Also, the true state is the one in which the law is not administered in the interests of a particular class. Yet even where the administration of the law is applied equally to all, there may be a distinction between the "loyal subject" and the "intelligent patriot."

22. Harris and Morrow (1986) point out that at the time of this speech, there were 3 million qualified voters out of an adult male population of roughly three

times that many (347, n. 38). In the last section of this chapter I challenge Green's assumption that the exclusion of women from the suffrage did not imply that men were a privileged class.

23. For a detailed examination of Green's specific proposals for the latter, see Nicholson (1986).

24. Greengarten (1981) treats Green's theories as a purposeful justification for the legislation.

25. *Oxford Chronicle*, 29 February 1868, 27 January 1870, cited in Nicholson (1990: 110).

26. See also Nicholson (1990: 162).

27. Vincent and Plant (1984) argue that Green equivocated on whether the state ought to provide basic physical sustenance (60, 62). Although later in their book (107–8) they describe how Green relied on Kantian ethics to demonstrate that individual morality is the keystone to the morality of the state, that "self-discipline and reliance are the source of morality and the good will." The inference they draw from this is "that self-maintenance by the individual in nearly all aspects of his life was the key to morality and the real will."

28. Although it had been written during the winter of 1860—1861.

29. Though this is distinct from the new sort of "democratic volunteerism" Green discussed.

30. Again, the argument is not directed against those who control property even if they don't participate in the labor market, for example, a rentier class.

4

Citizenship and the Right to Welfare

Although New Right theorists seem to have captured the leading role in the contemporary public debates over welfare policy, they certainly do not represent the entirety of liberal theory on this issue. In the face of Nozick's articulation of the right to private property, for instance, egalitarian liberal theorists articulate the right to subsistence, or the right to the satisfaction of basic needs. Despite the exhortations to the indigent to independence and responsibility heard from the New Right, the theorists examined in this chapter emphasize the claims on, or the entitlement to, a range of basic resources. These arguments are important for challenging the near hegemony of the New Right in the debates over welfare reform. By emphasizing the right to welfare these egalitarian liberal theorists have sought to remove welfare provision from the more contingent status of policy choice; the decision to make welfare provision should not be left to the vicissitudes of electoral politics. These theorists have sought firmer ground by identifying the provision of welfare benefits with what it means to be a person or, alternately, a citizen. Indeed, the right to welfare can be a politically powerful argument. It is the language of contemporary democratic states and movements.

Despite the important theoretical contribution of egalitarian liberals to the welfare debate, a number of their arguments are still unsatisfactory. To be clear, the problem is not one of internal inconsistency, nor is the problem with the language of rights in general. The problem lies with the conception of citizenship suggested by these normative claims for public assistance. In this chapter, I address three major limitations. In the first place, the right to welfare argument often does not transcend—indeed, it often relies on—the independent/dependent dichotomy that feminist scholars have shown is suspect. Second, the right to welfare argument can lead in the direction of an argument for the right to work; that is, citizens are still expected to be workers. Finally, many arguments about the right to welfare draw on political language in order to address the economic standing of the poor; these arguments amount to nothing more than a justification for the "alleviation of destitution." In so doing, many arguments on the right to welfare miss the opportunity to address the political status of the poor. They fail to recognize the potential that public assistance itself has for the making of democratic citizens.

The Nature of Rights

Although each of the theorists examined below relate the provision of welfare benefits to the language of rights in different ways, there is a common conception of "rights" among these theorists.[1] Before examining the distinctive arguments in detail it will be useful to identify and address this fundamental, shared conception.

Rights are typically conceived of as *claims*. Dworkin (1977) captures this when he argues that rights are claims that have political priority. "Individual rights are political trumps held by individuals. Individuals have rights when, for some reason, a collective goal is not a sufficient justification for denying them what they wish, as individuals, to have or to do, or not a sufficient justification for imposing some loss or injury upon them" (Dworkin [1977: xi]). Similarly, Jones (1994) defines rights as "entitlements which it is incumbent upon others to acknowledge and respect" (1).[2]

As a claim or entitlement, there are at least two significant and distinct senses in which the language of rights can be related to the provision of welfare benefits. On the one hand, it can be argued that there is a recognized claim to welfare, *simpliciter:* there is a direct link between the concept of a right and the specific goods of public policy, for example, cash, housing, or food. This sort of argument is exclusively conceptual. On the other hand, it can be argued that there is a final status or good to which an individual can make a claim, for example, equality and basic needs. In turn, public welfare is cited as an intermediate good; that is, the particular institutional means through which that final good is provided. In this way, the concept of a right, a claim, can be joined with any number of goods.[3] This sort of argument then joins a conceptual with an empirical analysis. In this case, the argument proceeds by first establishing the various final claims that individuals can make, in view of their entitlements, as citizens. Then, one can assess whether the state as an institution is capable of guaranteeing the satisfaction of those claims. This is similar to the way in which it is argued that the justice system is capable of guaranteeing the claim to private property. In the arguments that follow, welfare benefits are indirect claims.

As I have already suggested, to conceive of a right as a claim implies at least two agents: the individual or group making the claim, as well as a second-party guarantor. To make a claim for some good implies the performance of a duty by this second party.[4] As it implies a duty, or social guarantee, a right can be *in personam* or *in rem*. A right *in personam* is held against a specific person or group of persons, whereas a right *in rem* is held against people at large. As a citizenship right, the claim to welfare benefits is a right *in personam*. To be sure, the duty falls on society in general. In contrast to a human right, however, a right of citizenship is directed against a specific government. In fact, therein lies one of the major attractions to rights claims as a form of political argument. This may beg the question for the moment, but if something can be established as a right of the citizen, the state must be the guarantor. And this is, in many countries, a matter of good strategy for the reason that the state is the institution in society most capable of delivering that social guarantee. The state has the muscle to guarantee the claim or entitlement.

Property Rights in Welfare Benefits

Among the set of arguments for welfare provision, I turn first to a tradition of liberalism that more directly challenges the New Right on its definitions of property and independence. This tradition is not, to be sure, only a product of the welfare debates of the twentieth century. Liberal theorists since the eighteenth and nineteenth centuries have questioned an emphasis on *exclusive* property rights and have drawn on the natural law tradition to articulate an *inclusive* conception of property rights.[5] Around the turn of the nineteenth century, these "defenders of the poor" began to promote the argument that labor, rather than some historical acquisition by *fiat* or *might*, provided the only legitimate title to property. The significance of retrieving these early liberal arguments, according to Horne, is that "the [contemporary] liberal welfare state's legal recognition of rights to welfare is the realization of aspirations long held and of moral values deeply ingrained and that so far from being at odds with the liberal tradition of private property rights, it is instead the fulfillment of that tradition" (Horne [1990: 8]). More specifically, if welfare benefits are identified with property rights, then liberalism itself provides an answer to the New Right's claim for the central place of independence in their conception of citizenship. Armed with an inclusive conception of property, one may be able to reassert that the provision of welfare benefits represents a contribution to citizenship, not its denial. As much as wages from employment, state-funded welfare benefits can make a person independent.

As Horne has shown, Adam Smith, for one, may have objected to the Elizabethan Poor Laws, but not for the reason that the taxes necessary to fund this program violated the (exclusive) property rights of people already holding property—the Nozickian critique of public welfare in the twentieth century. Rather, the Elizabethan Poor Laws inhibited the mobility of the poor, and these laws distorted the wages structure. The poor laws violated the rights of the poor to freedom of movement[6] and they violated the *property* rights of the poor to a fair wage.[7] Similarly, Thomas Paine defended private property, but he meant by this only the property that had been acquired legitimately, namely, property that had been acquired through industry and labor. Additionally, he argued that "all accumulation . . . of personal property, beyond what a man's own hands produce, is derived to him by living in society, and he owes on every principle of justice, of gratitude, and of civilization, a part of that accumulation back again to society from whence the whole came" (quoted in Horne [1990: 208]).

Furthermore, Thomas Spence focused on the idea of an original common. "The natural right to preservation held by everyone precluded land . . . from becoming the private property of a few" (quoted in Horne [1990: 220]). Thomas Skidmore, an American agrarian, agreed with Spence, arguing that the right to be included was required by common ownership of the earth. William Cobbett provided perhaps one of the strongest justifications for including the interests of the poor in a discussion of property rights. He used the natural law discourse to condemn large landholdings. Cobbett did not blame the poor for their station, and he opposed the workhouses. He considered poor relief to be neither a gift nor a favor. He averred that a right to relief would have been insisted upon at the social contract. Accordingly, "the poor . . . did not receive alms but what they [had] a right to by the laws of nature" (quoted in Horne [1990: 231]). The only absolute and inalienable right to property was, according to Cobbett, the inclusive right to subsistence. Horne notes about these liberal arguments in general, as if to address a concern of the contemporary New Right, "there seems to have been no sense that any substantial group existed that was destitute by choice" (Horne [1990: 233]).

This attempt to link welfare provision with the notion of property was forcefully articulated by Charles Reich (1964) in the twentieth century in an attempt to constitutionalize welfare benefits under the auspices of the Fifth and Fourteenth Amendments. Reich[8] begins his argument by noting the tremendous growth in this century in government largess. Pointing to federal and state employment, licenses, subsidies, cash transfers, and contracts, Reich argues that the creation of wealth increasingly depends on government actions. With this trend, not only is the government a basic source of income or tangible goods for more and more people and in newer ways, but additionally "more and more of [a nation's wealth] takes the form of rights or status" (1964: 738). Just as liberals in the eighteenth and nineteenth centuries challenged conventional conceptions of property by maintaining that only by labor and industry could property be created, Reich challenges contemporary variants of exclusive, private forms of property by claiming that as government largess creates wealth, so it creates property.

In conventional liberal language, Reich argues that property "performs the function of maintaining independence, dignity and pluralism in society by creating zones within which the majority has to yield to the owner" (1964: 771). Furthermore, "political rights presuppose that individuals and private groups have the will and the means to act independently. But so long as individuals are motivated largely by self-interest, their well-being must first be independent. Civil liberties must have a basis in property, or bills of rights will not preserve them" (1964: 771).

Reich notes that when this liberal argument was being formulated in the eighteenth and nineteenth centuries, property rights and personal liberty were complementary.[9] The argument for property by industry and in labor was directed against feudal restraints; the protection of this new conception of property was instrumental to the protection of personal liberty. In time, however, the antifeudal conception of property was increasingly used to the advantage of the bourgeois class at the expense of those who ought to have had, as a part of the antifeudal conception, property in their labor. Moreover, the property of the bourgeoisie and the liberty of the laboring man were increasingly set at odds. Increasingly, in practice, a bourgeois system of property became as exclusive as the old feudal system of property. In short, "the defense of private property was [now] almost entirely a defense of its abuses" (1964: 773).

As a remedy to the abuse of private property, according to Reich, governments began to dispense welfare to the poor. Reforms took some of the power away from private corporations to determine one's livelihood. But the early efforts to redistribute wealth on the basis of a perceived need did not restore the individual person in poverty to his personal domain. Governments handed out this wealth on the theory that it was handing out gratuities. Governments were not, in theory, handing out property.

The important point for Reich is that despite the abuse of private property in practice, property—the means of independence—must be restored to the individual, even property in the form of government largess. "More than ever the individual needs to possess, in whatever form, a small but sovereign island of his own" (1964: 774). Given the increasingly central position of government largess in the distribution of wealth, this largess must "begin to do the work of property" (1964: 778).

This interest that the individual has in his private domain must be vested; it must be protected as a matter of right.

> The aim of [welfare] benefits is to preserve the self-sufficiency of the individual, to rehabilitate him where necessary, and to allow him to be a valuable member of a family and a community; in theory they represent part of the individual's rightful share in the commonwealth. Only by making such benefits into rights can the welfare state achieve its goal of providing a secure minimum basis for individual well-being and dignity in a society where each man cannot be wholly master of his own destiny (1964: 785–86).

Remaining firmly within a liberal framework, Reich takes seriously the contention, forcefully stated by the New Right, that citizens must be independent. There ought to be some private sphere or boundary into which no one else can venture. But although using the same terms, Reich challenges the conclusion that the *source* of that independence must be from some private activity. The New Right theorists argue that this independence can only logically be built from property related to some original acquisition (Nozick), or from wages garnered in the labor market (Hayek). Reich's description of government largess gives the lie to the claim that wealth today is created in any truly private or nongovernmental way. Where even the spheres of independence of people who earn wages in the market or who support themselves through accumulated capital depends on government largess, there is no compelling reason to deny that government largess can also legitimately be distributed through the provision of public welfare benefits.

Although Reich draws upon liberal arguments from the eighteenth- and nineteenth-centuries, he advances those arguments by identifying welfare provision with property. Earlier theorists may have been important for establishing a principle of inclusive property rights, but the principle was made in the context of pitting labor against feudal holdings. The principle was supportive of the powerless in a specific historical context. To rely on the same principle in the context of the twentieth century, however, is to endorse the arguments of the New Right. Indeed, this principle has been incorporated in the language that the New Right now deploys in its attack on state-funded welfare provision. It is precisely because the New Right theorists think that citizens ought to be workers that they condemn this provision. If everyone accepted the responsibility of paid employment, there would be no need for direct cash outlays. Reich advances the argument about the right to welfare by arguing that welfare provision constitutes a form of property itself as well as a source of citizenship.

In spite of this important immanent critique of New Right liberalism, as well as a critique of the eighteenth- and nineteenth-century liberals

considered above, Reich's argument remains unsatisfactory more generally because this argument remains linked to an expectation that citizens
must be *independent*. He solved one problem, but left another untouched.
Although Reich remains sympathetic to the poor, he ultimately does a
disservice to them by failing to acknowledge the highly *inter*dependent
nature of social, economic, and political relationships. The conception of
citizenship articulated in this justification for welfare provision reinforces
the notion of essential separateness. Why is it that "political rights must
presuppose that individuals and private groups have the will and the
means to act independently"? It is equally possible that political rights
presuppose that individuals and groups can overcome separateness and
move toward solidarity (see Fraser and Gordon [1992]).

Additionally, the independence/dependence dichotomy must be tran-
scended because it has been constructed along gendered lines. Masculine
independence has been constructed in contradistinction to feminine dependence (see, for example, Fraser and Gordon [1994]). Given the essential interdependence of social, economic, and political relationships, what
one should seek is a conception of freedom as autonomy. As I will argue
in the final chapter, this expectation becomes more possible when freedom as autonomy is made central to democracy itself, and not just made
an element of liberalism.

The Social Rights of Citizenship

T. H. Marshall's main contribution to the set of arguments attempting to
establish welfare provision in citizenship is not so much a normative argument in favor of welfare rights as it is a description of how welfare
benefits have come to be conceived in terms of a right. He also offers an
interpretation of the meaning of social citizenship.[10] Perhaps Marshall is
most well known for his cursory description of the three successive conceptions of citizenship that emerged over three centuries in England
(1992). The first stage, roughly corresponding to the eighteenth century,
was marked by the development of civil citizenship. This conception denoted a series of rights that were deemed necessary for the protection of
individual freedom, for example, freedom of contract or freedom of
speech. The courts were the institution through which these rights were
expressed and enforced. In the nineteenth century, the practice of political citizenship was extended to working-class men. This denoted the
right to participate in the exercise of political power. Individually, the citizen expressed this right through the vote. Collectively, the assembly expressed the meaning of this conception of citizenship through legislation.
Finally, in the twentieth century, the social conception of citizenship
emerged. This represented for Marshall "the whole range from the right

to a modicum of economic welfare and security to the right to share to the full in the social heritage and to live the life of a civilized being according to the standards prevailing in the society. The institutions most closely connected with it are the educational system and the social services" (1992: 8). That is, the twentieth-century welfare state was the institutional realization of the conception of social citizenship.

According to Marshall, the social conception of citizenship is qualitatively distinct from the previous two conceptions. Additionally, it transformed the way we look at citizenship generally. Citizenship is no longer simply an inventory of natural rights. The social rights of citizenship are not a list of claims that exist prior to the community. Rather, the importance of citizenship now lies in the way in which it signifies full membership in a community (1963a: 230). To be sure, the earlier language of rights is not abandoned entirely. Still, as citizenship is an expression of community, and as citizenship does refer to a bundle of rights, rights are an expression of, and only make sense within the context of, a community. Rights are no longer expressions of presocial interests. The rights of individuals must be "defined and limited so as to fit a complex and balanced pattern of the welfare of the community" (1963b: 246). Marshall illustrates this new relationship when he maintains that the factory represents a microcosm of citizenship. Membership here means more than the mere fulfillment of the wage contract—the respect for (an eighteenth-century conception of) civil rights (1963d: 280). Marshall adds that one of the primary aims of citizenship, one of the marks of inclusion in a community, is security. A (social) right is a claim "exercised with a view toward security in the enjoyment of the means to life and happiness" (1963d: 235).[11] In his short history of the stages of citizenship, Marshall has tried to demonstrate that a communitarian conception of rights now complements a liberal conception of rights.

For Marshall, the major achievement of the twentieth century has been the change in the nature of social stratification. The gradual extension of the social, or democratic,[12] conception of citizenship has made equality the primary characteristic of the social structure. But this is not the sort of equality that would come with the elimination of class from the social structure altogether. The equality described by Marshall pertains to social *status*.[13] He means by this *equal inclusion in the community*. Thus, democracy in the twentieth century has meant that social status has replaced a class-based status as the major element of the social structure. To be sure, class distinctions and income inequalities do remain.[14] So, in a sense, democracy has legitimized these two minor characteristics. But these distinctions and inequalities have become meaningless for social stratification. They are irrelevant to being considered a citizen, that is, a member of the community.[15]

In relation to the establishment of social citizenship, Marshall describes the roles of the agents involved in the institutional expression of this new model of citizenship. In the first place, the *state* can ensure citizenship by considering welfare benefits a legal right. As with the rights of social citizenship more generally, the right to welfare benefits for the poor are not the expression of a natural right. "They are part of the mechanism by which the individual is absorbed into society and simultaneously draws upon and contributes to its collective welfare" (1981b: 91). This mechanism implies the obligation on the part of the state—the community—to relieve destitution (1965). Marshall notes that programs for relief that can be enforced by statute, namely, legal rights, are distinct from philanthropy, or voluntary schemes.[16] The agents of philanthropy do not consider themselves responsible to members of the community who are in need. Voluntary schemes do not lend themselves to the same expression of community. It is not simply that legal rights imply a mechanism for enforcement. More important and fundamental, a legal right implies the expression of a sense of community.

In turn, the *individual* in need, the beneficiary of this conception of citizenship, expresses his membership in the community by claiming the provision as a right. Yet Marshall adds to this by defining the *duty* that the citizen in need is required to perform. The social right to cash disbursements is correlated with *the duty of the citizen to avoid destitution* (1981b: 90). To argue that someone has a duty to do X includes the presumption that it is *possible* to do X. Marshall does not mean here that one satisfies this obligation to avoid destitution by applying for welfare benefits; that would be begging the question. He does imply, however, that work is the most plausible means by which most people will perform this duty. In other words, Marshall prefaces his description of the claim to welfare by stating that the individual expresses his citizenship first and foremost through paid employment. What appeared at first as an unconditional claim of social citizenship is instead a residual expression of social citizenship. The expression of social citizenship applies only after one has not been capable of expressing one's membership in the community through the activity of work.

One begins to see how beneath Marshall's discussion of social citizenship is a theory of citizenship that remains tied to work, or paid employment. In other words, Marshall's theory, like the theorists discussed in the previous chapter, emphasizes the *contributions* that citizens must make. In addition to implying this much in his theory of rights to welfare benefits, Marshall more directly describes how work signifies community and the marks of membership in that community. He argues that citizens recognize that work is a function of social life. It is an attribute of membership (1963a).[17] In this light, it should come as no surprise that

Marshall used the factory as an example of a microcosm of citizenship. In the twentieth century, the state—community—no longer performs any of the ceremonies that can stand as "visible expression[s] of the truth that work is a function of social life, an attribute of the membership of society" (1963a: 220). Instead, abstract ideas must deputize for ceremony. In particular, according to Marshall, the social-democratic conception of citizenship deputizes for that ceremony. "Today all workers are citizens, and we have come to expect that *all citizens should be workers*. Service to the community is an obligation which can be freely recognized by those who enjoy full rights as members of the community, rights which include, not only the vote, but equal justice, freedom of speech and social security" (1963a: 220–21, emphasis added).

Because a job signifies one's membership in the community, Marshall recognizes that the opportunity to work cannot remain a contingent matter. The conditions for this obligation must be available to all people. The opportunity to perform one's duties must not be precluded by any other economic decisions or social forces. For this purpose, Marshall argues that the obligation to work, as well as the "security in a particular job[,] can be supplemented by the general 'right to work'" (1963a: 231). In short, the citizen has both a right and a duty to secure paid employment. Through a labyrinth of arguments, Marshall has thus led, strangely enough, from the right to welfare benefits to the right to work.

In one sense, this conclusion should not be too unexpected. Marshall's analysis of citizenship is informed throughout by a class perspective. Marshall's rough sketch of the successive stages of citizenship does not mention groups that were not included, or were included in a different manner, in the extension of citizenship. For instance, the civil rights of the eighteenth century were not distributed evenly between the sexes (Pateman [1988]). And to attribute the extension of political citizenship—the suffrage—to the nineteenth century entirely overlooks the exclusion of women and specific ethnic groups. This omission clearly is a reflection of Marshall's focus on class stratification. The achievements of social citizenship that he describes have been the achievements of working-class males. Marshall's analysis of citizenship is oriented around describing how the working classes have been integrated into society through the annulment of class as the primary element of the social structure. To make his point, Marshall remains focused on work as the contribution to the community, in place of, for instance, virtue or tangible property. Thus, even his description of the poverty-relieving aspects of the social conception of citizenship will only make sense in light of an expectation that the indigent, too, must contribute to the community through work.

But of course, by work, Marshall does not mean labor in the abstract. He specifically equates work in the context of social citizenship with paid employment in the market. His conception of work for this purpose does not extend to labor—usually female labor—in the home. This means that the most that the (residual) right to cash disbursements, such as an AFDC program, can now do for the indigent is to relieve her destitution.[18] This reading of Marshall demonstrates, therefore, that his account of the social rights of citizenship does not greatly advance the argument from the New Right's position. Marshall's account fails to consider the place of women, and he fails to consider the nonworking poor. Of course, Marshall wrote his essay on social citizenship at a time when Britain promoted a policy of full employment. But even if such a lacuna was not significant at the time, it certainly is significant at a time when governments no longer make this a matter of policy. To be sure, Marshall can be clearly distinguished from the eighteenth- and nineteenth-century liberals whom I considered briefly in this chapter. Where they had linked civil and political citizenship with labor, Marshall conceives of a new and distinctive model of citizenship. But even this new model, which ushers in a new substantial right, remains linked to the performance of the same activity stipulated by the theorists of exclusive property. Even people who would receive benefits must labor for wages.[19]

J. Donald Moon (1988) reaches a similar conclusion about the value of work through his analysis of a tension inherent to poverty relief—a tension first noted by Hegel (Avineri [1972: 151–54]). To be sure, morality dictates that the state ought to provide for the poor. Yet, as the state makes this provision, it undermines the liberty of the poor; provision inculcates dependency.[20] On the one hand, Moon does argue for the right to welfare benefits, and he is committed to a policy of providing them. The guarantee implied in the language of rights is far superior to, for instance, the contingent nature of charity. On the other hand, he believes that state aid to the poor has disturbing psychological consequences. Although the leading principle of distribution is exchange in a market-dominated society, welfare benefits are distributed on the principle of outright transfers to the poor. Given this clash of principles, welfare benefits as poor relief "undermine [the] status or membership [of the poor] in civil society, and with that their dignity and self respect" (Moon [1988: 29]). One may have a right to welfare benefits, but the benefits do nothing for the development of self-respect. One develops this attitude only through the performance of the duties of citizens. Self-respect is a matter of what the individual does for herself, not what society does for her.

The individual must confront the expectation, which Moon maintains is widely held in the United States, that citizens will be economically independent; that is, that they will receive wages in the labor market. Only by accommodating oneself to these expectations can the individual develop the self-respect that is necessary for citizenship. Furthermore, only by accommodating oneself to these expectations will society accept poor individuals as members in society. Whatever is gained by an appeal to rights will in turn undermine the conditions for citizenship when there is a failure to exercise one's correlative duty. In short, Moon believes that there is an unresolvable dilemma between the dictates of morality and the conditions for self-respect and citizenship.

Moon's argument is problematic for at least two reasons. First, it is odd that Moon identifies self-respect with accommodation. Self-respect is often identified instead with self-confidence. And surely self-confidence suggests that an individual does not easily accommodate prevailing expectations, at least not without good reason. Thus, although self-respect is a personality trait generally admired, that is usually so in conjunction with self-confidence, rather than accommodation. Second, Moon does not explicitly identify the duty of citizenship that contributes to self-respect, but he clearly implies that participating in a network of exchange is one of them. For instance, he does welcome a number of the income maintenance programs of the welfare state, generally, for example, social security and unemployment insurance, precisely because they rely on anteing up one's "fair shares." A citizen performs her duties of citizenship by contributing to the "pot." And she is able to contribute because of the wages she received from work. So these programs do not evoke the same stigma as poverty relief; they are not really considered "welfare."

Moon's conclusion on the duties and conditions of citizenship look much like Marshall's conclusion. They both rely on a theory of citizenship similar to the one that lies at the foundation of the New Right's critique of welfare benefits. Namely, citizens must be workers; citizens must secure paid employment. So Marshall's social rights of citizenship and Moon's dictates of morality are inadequate foundations upon which one might hope to build a satisfactory justification for the provision of welfare benefits by the state. Perhaps unwittingly, Marshall and Moon share the New Right's conclusion that citizenship depends on prepolitical conditions. Yet, as mentioned in Chapter 2, it is important to consider the contemporary context within which paid employment takes place. The market excludes and divides and is no sure foundation for the equal distribution of the opportunity for full citizenship. Full employment contradicts the priorities of the market, and the market also creates a division of labor between the sexes. By some accounts, women are excluded altogether from this opportunity for the full expression of citizenship. Even if women may participate in the paid labor market, they do so under conditions different from men, such that the opportunity for the full expression of citizenship may not be available *on equal terms* for all.

Furthermore, like Reich, Moon remains bound to the sense of liberty informed by the independence/dependence dichotomy. Moon does not

acknowledge the fact of interdependence or the possibility of more solidaristic modes of social interaction. As Fraser and Gordon (1994) have
shown, dependency is a distinctly modern construct, and its negative
connotations are typically associated with women. If the capacity for self-
respect is based on perceptions of values that may in fact change with
conditions, then there is hope that self-respect could equally be built
upon, or at least not contradicted by, the receipt of welfare benefits. Indeed, if the recipients of welfare provision feel stigmatized by their position, this may be testimony to the hegemony of the ideology of the New
Right. And that morally upstanding, hardworking taxpayers find it easy
to apply this stigma is further testimony to this hegemony. The challenge
is to overcome that hegemony and to recognize interdependence and to
promote solidarity. In this case, even people receiving benefits might find
the source for building self-respect.

Marshall's and Moon's theories of welfare provision are inadequate
because of the implicit claims about the meaning of citizenship that underlie these theories. Additionally, these theories betray a limited understanding of the full meaning of poverty. Poverty is viewed primarily, if
not exclusively, as a problem of inequality or economic destitution. To be
sure, the political status of the poor is not denied, as it is by Nozick. Indeed, these egalitarian liberals use the political status of the poor to justify public assistance—to address the problem of poverty. Even the poor
have at least one political claim: Because they are citizens, they can make
a claim for the right to welfare. Still, the political component is operative
here only as a response to the problem of poverty. So, poverty is not itself
defined in political terms. There may a political *solution* to the problem of
poverty, but poverty itself remains simply a problem of economic inequality and economic destitution. In the following chapter, I explore the
way in which poverty poses a threat to the freedom of the poor. Seen in
this light, public assistance becomes a means for addressing more than
economic inequality and economic destitution. Public assistance will address the political status of the poor; it will remedy the lack of freedom
caused by indigence.

Contracting to Welfare Provision

The Right to Equal Respect

Where Marshall described the emergence of a bundle of social rights in
the twentieth century, Ronald Dworkin (1977) identifies the fundamental
right on which other rights are based and by which social policies must
be judged. Equality is that fundamental right, namely, the right to equal
concern and respect. This substantive definition suggests that a right is a

sort of political attitude that enforces the ontological assumptions humans are said to hold about each other. Collective goals, or public policies, that conflict with an attitude of equal respect can never be justified.[21]

From this, Dworkin turns to the Rawlsian hypothetical to help identify the political and sociological expression of this ontological assumption. Covering well-trod ground, Dworkin maintains that if individuals are rational and act only in their *self-interest*, they will choose the two principles of justice, namely, 1) that each should have the largest political liberty compatible with a like liberty for all,[22] and 2) that inequalities of resources ought to be permitted only insofar as they work for the benefit of the worst off individuals. Although tentatively accepting this statement, Dworkin adds the following proviso: "just because someone might have agreed to something in advance, if asked, this is no reason to use that as a criterion for justice in a situation where she has not in fact consented." Thus, the point of laying out the Rawlsian hypothetical is not to argue that there was a once-and-for-all agreement that ought to be morally binding on future situations. "The fact, therefore, that a particular choice is in my interest at a particular time, under conditions of great uncertainty, is not a good argument for the fairness of enforcing that choice against me later under conditions of much greater knowledge" (1977: 153).[23]

The original position is not, according to Dworkin, the foundation of Rawls's general argument; neither is it an expository device for Rawls's technique of reflective equilibrium. Instead, it is one of the major substantive products of his theory as a whole. "The original position is therefore a schematic representation of a particular mental process of at least some, and perhaps most, human beings . . . " (1977: 158). Thus, the contract "must be seen as a kind of halfway point in a larger argument as itself the product of a deeper political theory that argues for the two principles through rather than from the contract" (1977: 169). Thus, Rawls's use of the contract makes sense in light of a deontological theory, which takes the right to equal respect seriously.

On the one hand, Dworkin challenges Nozick's deontological theory of rights with a deontological theory of his own. On the other hand, and as with Nozick, the contract is not teleological. "An individual has a right to a particular political act, within a political theory, if the failure to provide that act when he calls for it, would be unjustified within that theory even if the goals of the theory would, on the balance, be disserviced by that act" (1977: 169). Goals can never "trump" rights. Furthermore, in this interpretation of Rawls, Dworkin clearly distinguishes himself from those who view the contract as an aggregation of rational, calculating decisions designed to indemnify oneself against the uncertainty of the future. Individuals in society contract, so to speak, because of their mutual belief in equality, not because of their mutual distrust of one another.

In sum, Dworkin interprets Rawls's use of the original position as a representation of a methodology for establishing a fundamentally rights-based theory, one that is at odds with Nozick's. In other words, contract theory follows from a theory of rights, not vice versa. "It seems natural . . . to try to identify the institutions an individual would veto in the exercise of whatever rights are taken as fundamental" (1977: 176). The argument for rights is not "nonsense on stilts." "It requires no more than the hypothesis that the best political program, within the sense of that model, is one that takes the protection of certain individual choices as fundamental, and not properly subordinated to any goal or duty or combination of these" (1977: 176–77). The inequalities implied in Rawls's second principle are politically acceptable only because of a more basic sense of equality itself, namely, equality of respect. Accordingly, the contract implies a more abstract conception of equality than is associated with a number of political theories, and thus represents an important strategy for guaranteeing respect for all. "Men who do not know to which class they belong cannot design institutions, consciously or unconsciously, to favor their own class. Men who have no idea of their own conception of the good cannot act to favor those who hold one ideal over those who hold another. The original position is well designed to enforce the abstract right to equal concern and respect, which must be understood to be the fundamental concept of Rawls' deep theory" (1977: 181). This right does not emerge from the contract. It is assumed in its design. Women and men possess this simply as "human beings with a capacity to make plans and give justice" (1977: 182).

Despite the primary focus on equality, Dworkin does not dismiss a conception of freedom. He connects these two political values through the language of rights. People have rights to distinct liberties. But those rights are derived from the fundamental right to equality. Individual rights to distinct liberties must be recognized only when (and because) the fundamental right to treatment as an equal requires it. An individual political liberty "allows us to enjoy the institutions of political democracy, which enforce overall or unrefined utilitarianism, and yet protect the fundamental right of citizens to equal concern and respect by prohibiting decisions that seem, antecedently, likely to have been reached by virtue of the external components of the preferences democracy reveals" (1977: 277). Therefore, he challenges the conventional argument that in liberal democratic theory there is a basic tension between equality and rights, on the one hand, and freedom, on the other. One of the conclusions he draws is that it is not inconsistent to argue for some liberties while denying others. Liberties are independent of each other, and dependent individually on the right to treatment as an equal.[24]

From this conception of rights, it may be argued[25] that state-funded, nonmarket mechanisms for distributing welfare benefits are consistent with and an expression of the right to equal concern and respect. To anticipate the New Right's response, this does not mean that the state must treat all individuals equally,[26] that it must tax them all equally, or provide exact parity in services for all individuals. It would be quite a stretch to say that Dworkin is implicitly arguing for an absolute equality of income throughout society. Equality of respect is compatible with an unequal distribution of goods, in accordance with Rawls's second principle. Nevertheless, when particular individuals, for a number of individual reasons, are not able to draw their income from wages in the market, Dworkin's "postulate of political morality" would expect that an *attitude of concern* by the government be expressed through the provision of resources. "Government must treat those whom it governs with concern, that is, as human beings who are capable of forming and acting on intelligent conceptions of how their lives should be lived. Government must not only treat people with concern and respect, but with equal concern and respect" (1977: 272–73). People who are due equal respect and concern are also those one expects to be free, not merely "capable" of acting, but who are "allowed" to act as well. To be treated with equal concern and respect means that the government ought to guarantee the conditions under which individuals continue to be "capable of forming and acting on intelligent conceptions of how their lives should be lived." The right to welfare benefits is an expression of the right to equal concern and respect.

Dworkin's analysis of contract theory is useful for addressing Nozick's arguments about the inviolability of private property rights. Even the right to property must be subordinate to the right to equal concern and respect (1977: 277–78). Dworkin provides an alternative conception of the relationship between contract and welfare benefits. Namely, where the contract is the expression of concern or equal respect for individuals, the contract is perfectly consistent with the provision of welfare benefits. To clarify further, welfare benefits here are not viewed as the outcome of a series of individual rational decisions for self-preservation. As the contract is not a means of protecting society from a war of all against each other, welfare benefits here are not a rational indemnification against future economic uncertainties, a guarantee without which society could not function. Welfare benefits are the expression of equal concern and respect.

Consenting to Subsistence

Desmond King and Jeremy Waldron (1988) also derive an argument for the right to welfare benefits from an interpretation of Rawlsian contract theory. In contrast to the analysis offered by Dworkin, however, King and

Waldron treat the contract directly in relation to an original position. And they do not base their argument on an assumption of equal concern and respect. Furthermore, King and Waldron seem to rely on more atomistic and egoistic assumptions about individuals. Additionally, they explicitly develop their argument in relation to a theory of citizenship.

Based on their interpretation of Rawls's principles of justice, they set out to determine the sort of society to which individuals would be likely to consent. That is, they set out to determine the list of rights that citizens would be likely to enforce. Among this inventory of rights, the important right this book considers is the right to subsistence. This right is "a necessary condition for a genuine and meaningful consent to social and political arrangements" (1988: 442). Individuals would only reasonably consent to the sort of society that promised these rights of subsistence prior to claims for exclusive private property. The provision of welfare benefits by the state, they argue in turn, is the most effective institutional arrangement for guaranteeing this right.

Additionally, citizens are likely to consent to the sort of society in which certain expectations are satisfied. Over a number of years, governments have established the convention of providing welfare benefits to the poor. Accordingly, citizens have developed the reasonable expectation that this provision will always be available. Citizens may even have taken appropriate risks in light of this expectation. Echoing Bentham's concern, to curtail or eliminate welfare provision for the poor would be to disappoint the expectations of the poor.[27] This priority must be established, given the likelihood that claims for private property will at some point conflict with the fundamental right to subsistence.

Facing the contemporary assault on welfare provision, King and Waldron argue that a theory of citizenship must remain at the center of the debate. By centering the debate in citizenship, the authors seem to believe that the right to subsistence will be taken seriously. In other words, they think their argument is on firm ground, because they assume that citizenship is primarily about rights. King and Waldron define welfare benefits as *collective* resources transferred to individual citizens in need. Welfare benefits signify a sense of belonging for some individuals; they are an expression of the social sense of the self.

Promise, Trust, and Equal Liberty

Virginia Held (1984) offers an alternative conception of the "right to welfare benefits" that, although contractual in terms, does not draw on Rawls's two principles and his conception of the original contract. She takes a decidedly teleological perspective, arguing that through the political process, society ought to strive to do what can be justified on consequentialist grounds. With respect to welfare provision, she brings together two arguments, one based on social cooperation and trust, the other based on a respect for equal liberty.

The primary goal or purpose of a political society, she argues, is cooperation. Like Dworkin, she expresses the grounds of this cooperation in the abstract terms of the social contract. Held then explores one of the attitudes that lies behind the consent of the social contract and the behavior of social cooperation. That attitude is trust. In a general sense, trust refers to an expectation of performance by some second party, following that party's promise to do X.[28] If you trust me, that means that you have a good reason, and have presumably accepted that reason, to believe that I will fulfill that promise. Trust in this context, therefore, also implies obligations.[29]

Now, exactly what promises are made with a view toward social cooperation? One such promise is to respect a variety of rights. One of the rights that constitutes the social contract is the right to equal liberty. Held challenges the conventional focus on negative liberty and declares that "rights to freedom are rights to *the enablements to be free* and not only rights to freedom from interference" (1984: 128, emphasis added). In the spirit of Dworkin's postulate of political morality, Held argues that liberty must be understood as the freedom to live, to work, and to develop one's potential generally. In other words, although it is helpful to think of liberty as independence, that need not be independence as it is defined by the New Right. She does not restrict the term to economic independence or the earning of wages in the market. Rather, independence refers to the capacity to do a specified range of things. For those purposes, it does not matter whether the source of that capacity is from wages, inheritance, or the state. Freedom as a principle of noninterference, however, still has a role to play in Held's theory. As corporate power is as much a threat to the principle of noninterference as the New Right maintains the state to be, a minimum guarantee of income can ensure the liberty to do a range of things—the liberty not to be interfered with in the pursuit of these goals.[30] Thus, independence in Held's sense of the term can be extended to everyone through the provision of welfare benefits. It is through a right to economic subsistence that society protects the right to liberty.

Accordingly, the provision of welfare benefits satisfies one of the rights that would have been agreed to in the social contract. Just as cooperation requires the expectation that promises will be kept, cooperation demands in particular that the promise to protect the right to liberty will be kept. And in many cases, the right to liberty will not be met in the free market. So welfare benefits are required to satisfy the *right to liberty*. In this way, the provision of welfare benefits satisfies the conditions for social cooperation for the individual recipient in question.

Although welfare benefits in general contribute to social cooperation, they address in particular one's basic needs. "A contemporary developed society would have to guarantee that when the society had the resources to do so, it would meet the basic needs of all its members. The means to acquire enough to eat, to obtain medical care, education, housing, and employment would have to be assured" (1984: 75–76). By society, Held means the state, for she recognizes that the market as well as private forms of charity are institutions in society that have proven incapable of providing for everyone's basic needs. Thus, Held points to a fundamental conceptual distinction between rights and charity. Charity typically denotes a form of provision that remains at the prerogative of the provider. If this provision for basic needs remains a matter of mere private charity, it will be in danger of being provided in a manner contrary to the interests of people who stand to benefit by such provision. Being the prerogative of the rich, it "can dry up at [their] whim" (Held [1984: 76]). Even the welfare benefits that ought to be forthcoming from the state should not be characterized as a form of government charity. To conceive of welfare benefits in this way is to imply that they can be withdrawn on the prerogative of the majority of the electorate. Charity is not a component of the social contract. Through its ability to levy taxes, the state does in fact command the resources necessary to meet these needs. But the provision must then be provided on terms that guarantee it, to use Dworkin's term, antecedently; that is, antecedently to the vagaries of electoral politics. In this context, when welfare benefits are not forthcoming as a matter of rights, individuals will have no grounds on which to trust one another.

To be sure, much of Held's argument is compelling. In the following chapter, I too maintain that it is important to recognize the one-sidedness of the typical use of the principle of noninterference. And her claim that welfare benefits can contribute to the liberty to do a range of things establishes the sort of principle that I will find useful in describing the relationship between welfare benefits and freedom as autonomy. As far as this goes, Dworkin's "postulate of political morality" is also useful. Nevertheless, the sense in which both Held and Dworkin discuss the right to liberty as the right to do something does not specify its relationship with citizenship. Although neither explicitly use the term *citizenship,* they both seem to assume that as citizens, individuals are entitled to these benefits. These benefits may in turn enable recipients to do a variety of things. But they do not specify that these benefits enable recipients to be active citizens; they do not specify that these benefits may enable recipients to participate in the democratic process. [31]

King and Waldron, on the other hand, explicitly use the language of citizenship. Yet they then fail to appreciate the central place of liberty or freedom in a theory of citizenship and public assistance. They share with Marshall and Moon a blindness to the full extent of the problem of poverty, viewing it primarily as a problem of economic inequality or economic destitution. Like Marshall and Moon, King and Waldron appeal to the political status of the poor as a remedy—a justification for public assistance. Still, they fail to appreciate that poverty itself is a political problem, that poverty represents a lack of freedom for the poor, rather than simply a dearth of economic resources.

The Duty to Provide

Although rights must necessarily imply duties, Dworkin has noted that rights and duties are not necessarily correlative. There could be a duty to do X that does not correspond to any particular right, X. There could be, for instance, an obligation to provide welfare benefits that does not correspond to any right to welfare benefits. This represents an account of welfare provision that is not simply a complement to the preceding arguments. Thus, in this section I turn to an argument for provision based on the principle of nonexploitation and an obligation toward dependent others. The argument about duties that follows is made on its own terms. It specifically avoids linking this to a right to welfare benefits. Nonetheless, from this argument one can glean the implications for the citizenship of women and the nonworking poor.

If, despite the critique already registered, one maintains for a moment the dichotomy between freedom as independence and dependence, Robert Goodin's argument (1988) is a welcome response to Moon's concern about dependency and the provision of public welfare. For Goodin, the object of public policy is not to eliminate dependency. Rather, the object must be to ensure that dependent individuals are not exploited. Although Goodin does not address the question of citizenship directly, the implications of his position for a theory of citizenship are striking. One may no longer expect citizens to be independent, but simply expect that they not be exploited. In other words, any contribution that the state makes to prevent exploitation contributes to the conditions for citizenship.

In addition to his positive argument for welfare benefits, Goodin maintains that the typical "new left" arguments for welfare provision, namely, those based on needs, equality, or community, all lack "real moral support." The argument based on need, for instance, usually gives priority to needs over desires. Yet Goodin does not understand how meeting needs makes any greater contribution to a person's welfare than does satisfying desires. It may be that needs are given priority because they are the necessary condition for pursuing all particular ends; they are the conditions for personal autonomy. Still, he argues, there is no good reason to say that providing the conditions for autonomy is morally more important than exercising it. Furthermore, he argues that empirical studies have shown that the provision of welfare benefits is not egalitarian. What often passes for an argument about equality is really an argument about sympathy. Although Goodin accepts the value of the communitarian ideal, he doubts the extent to which the provision of welfare benefits actually makes a contribution to that ideal. Empirically, there is no sufficient link between community attachments and welfare provision.

Goodin defines the state, as it assumes the role of welfare provider, as an institution that intervenes in a market economy to meet certain basic needs through relatively direct means. It is a system of compulsory, collective, and largely nondiscretionary provision. Its defining characteristic is its attempt to relieve distress. The provision of welfare benefits thus satisfies the obligation to protect and not to exploit individuals who are dependent on others for their basic needs. "The welfare state thus construed is not so much a grand plan for social reorganization writ small as it is a modest principle of interpersonal ethics writ large" (1988: 121). Goodin challenges the contention that policies such as AFDC encourage a psychologically debilitating relationship of dependency. He argues, on the contrary, that particular forms of welfare can positively address the status of dependency. In the first place, welfare benefits do not necessarily inculcate debilitating dependencies. Additionally, welfare benefits can protect people who are already, or who might otherwise be, in dependent relationships. Goodin does not attach the same sort of moral opprobrium to dependency, per se, and he does not linger on arguments about poverty as a problem of personal responsibility. Dependency simply indicates a situation in which one individual relies on another for basic needs. For Goodin, that in itself is unproblematic, and has no implications for one's political status. The problem, however, is that this sort of relationship is liable to exploitation. The solution to dependency, therefore, is not the freeing up of latent psychological power through getting people "off of the dole." The solution is rather to ensure that those who are dependent are not exploited in their dependent condition.

By exploitation, Goodin means the taking of an unfair advantage over another. Exploitation is "a violation of the norms governing certain social interactions" (1988: 143). It is "playing for advantage where it is inappropriate to do so . . . [it is] an abuse of power" (1988: 144). Exploitation violates the obligation to protect the vulnerable. Although much has been written about exploitation in the labor market, Goodin does not limit his analysis to this sphere. Individuals who do not participate in ordinary labor markets can be exploited as well. Goodin's concern in this respect is for those who typically receive welfare benefits.

The obligation to protect the vulnerable has two parts. First this obligation involves a suspension of ordinary competitive rules; it means not pressing one's advantage against the vulnerable. Second, the obligation involves taking *positive* measures to ensure that an individual is not exploited. It is not simply incumbent on X not to exploit Y. X ought to take measures to ensure that Z also does not exploit Y.

The provision of welfare benefits by the state can prevent exploitation of dependent individuals. "The task [of providing welfare benefits] is not to eliminate dependencies and not even to make them mutual, but merely to make them unexploitable" (1988: 368). [32] Goodin cites four instances in which dependencies are likely to be exploited: 1) in an asymmetrical relationship, 2) where the subordinate absolutely requires the resources that another supplies, 3) where the subordinate must rely on some particular superior, and 4) where the superior enjoys discretionary control over the resources that the subordinate needs. When the only option available to individuals in need is reliance on family, friends, or voluntary organizations—private charity—individuals are liable to exploitation. All four of the specified conditions are likely to obtain in those relationships. Taking direct aim at the neoconservatives, Goodin argues that the greatest likelihood of exploitation lies with the discretion permitted by these relationships. Although the neoconservatives assert that the family is the best guarantee of inculcating values, Goodin argues that familial discretion can be the source of manipulation, arbitrariness, uncertainty, and intrusiveness. Moreover, these relationships permit no mechanism for guaranteeing that they will not become abusive. Alternatively, whereas the first two conditions—asymmetry and dire need—may still obtain when the state provides welfare, it is only through this institution that the third and fourth conditions can be eliminated. It is possible to design the distribution of public welfare such that a) the dependent individual need not rely on any particular individual or family member for her income, and such that b) the providing agency does not exercise discretionary control over that income provision.

To guarantee the elimination of this last contingency, however, the state must not set conditions on the receipt of income assistance. Means-tested assistance, for example, the procedure by which the state tries to single out the truly needy and deserving, lends itself to discretion, and therefore to the exploitation of dependent individuals. As it is difficult to guarantee that discretion will not be abused, the risk of exploitation can only really be overcome by eliminating discretion itself. "By guaranteeing that everyone's basic needs will be met through the impersonal and non-discretionary agency of the state, we render otherwise dependent people substantially less dependent upon (and hence less vulnerable to) the actions and choices of particular others, who might otherwise have taken unfair advantage of those dependencies and vulnerabilities to exploit them" (1988: 125).[33] Accordingly, fully funding welfare programs is a necessary condition for eliminating discretion. By erring on the side of generosity, these problems can be largely avoided.

In general, there are typically two alternatives to a regime of discretionary power, according to Goodin. On the one hand, one could appeal to a regime of rights, what Goodin calls "control from below." In fact, Goodin does recognize the political significance of a rights-based strategy. But any reference to rights by Goodin is more pragmatic than foundational. The language of rights is only a first approximation. The most significant limitation of this strategy is that the indigent are often in a poor position to press their case for rights.[34] Alternatively, an obligations-based strategy represents "control from above." Goodin's conception of an obligation includes two notions. In the first place, an obligation implies a duty. In turn, a duty stipulates particular actions. Second, an obligation implies responsibility. This in turn stipulates particular outcomes. That is, an obligations-based strategy is superior to a rights-based strategy, because it is only through the performance of obligations that one implies not only specific actions, but specific outcomes as well, namely, the outcome that dependent individuals will not be exploited. Furthermore, by specifying that bureaucrats are required to discharge their duties, as a practical matter that obligation can be enforced by the courts. The individual bureaucrats can be required to stand in court themselves as defendants. This represents an improvement in oversight when compared with a strictly rights-based strategy, under which only the poor would stand in court to press their case for relief.

As I mentioned above, Goodin views the policy of public welfare distribution as an intervention in the market. But this does not mean that the state and the market are two institutions that stand at odds with one another. On the contrary, Goodin considers both of these institutions to be mechanisms for the promotion of public welfare. In this less adversarial relationship, the state corrects for market failure by providing welfare benefits. And more fundamentally, the state, as it provides a guarantee of basic needs, actually plays a role in safeguarding the *preconditions* of the market.

In the first place, the state secures the property rights in basic needs that the market presupposes. If individuals have the right to take other people's private property for self-preservation—as Goodin interprets Grotius and Hobbes—then the title to that property is morally less than completely secure for the first titleholder. To make one's property morally secure for the first, it would be prudent to protect that property from claims of necessity by others. This can be done by ensuring that the claim never arises unexpectedly. The provision for basic needs by the state, although drawing on the private property of others through taxation, in the main protects private property against *unexpected and uncoordinated claims*. On this point, Goodin's argument for welfare benefits moves away from any interest in the dependents themselves. Like Bentham, Goodin addresses the interests of those with property in his justification for state-funded welfare benefits. And like King and Waldron, Goodin provides a sort of rational choice account of a policy to which individuals would be likely to agree.

Furthermore, Goodin maintains that the logic of the market presupposes extra-market institutions. The courts and the police, for instance, must be independent of the market, otherwise it would undermine the system of property rights upon which the market depends. The system of property rights needs an external guarantee, an arbiter. This need for extra-market institutions provides a model for the provision of welfare. Those resources most necessary for people's dignity—those things necessary to guarantee that a dependent relationship will not be exploited—ought to be made available outside of the market. Undoubtedly, most individuals do receive basic resources through the market or through the private distribution of the family. But given the potential for market failure to provide these resources for everyone, and given the potential for exploitation of people who are dependent on their families, Goodin believes that the state can make a guarantee of nonexploitation.

Finally, welfare benefits secure a level of economic independence for its beneficiaries. The market, according to Goodin, presupposes independent agents. By providing for basic needs, the state ensures that people are qualified to participate (as consumers) in the market.[35] And Goodin addresses the concern that people receiving welfare benefits gain some economic independence at the expense of political dependence. When "assistance is placed as far beyond the discretionary control of those charged with its dispensation as it is possible to place it" (Goodin [1988: 172]), recipients of welfare benefits will *not* be unduly influenced in their political decisions, in the way they vote. Without this distance, this nondiscretion, the poor will remain dependent on the charity and beneficence of the electorate and the legislators. "In the welfare state, the poor [need not be] dependent on the arbitrary will of any other person. They are no less free to vote independently than is the oil tycoon who depends upon the government's policy of oil depletion tax allowances for his profit" (1988: 177, n. 39). The state thus secures the minimal independence that is required to participate in other market and quasi-market sectors of society. Thus, "by giving to people who would otherwise be in fairly desperate circumstances the wherewithal of an independent existence, the welfare state protects them against the allures of fundamentally coercive offers that the market [or that candidates for office] might throw up" (1988: 133).

As I indicated at the beginning of this section, Goodin's argument provides a welcome response to Moon's uncertainties about the provision of welfare. Dependency may not be a problem in and of itself. Indeed, the complex nature of the economy indicates that, perhaps with the exception of ascetics and hermits, humans are all interdependent, and our survival depends on it. The implication for a revised theory of citizenship in light of actual sociological possibilities sounds promising. No longer expecting citizens to be independent, one may instead expect only that citizens not be exploited.

Still, the problem of poverty poses more of a problem than exploitation. Like those theorists examined already in this chapter, Goodin misses the opportunity to define the provision of public welfare more directly in terms of an individual's political status. Although it is undoubtedly important that these individuals not be exploited, it is equally important that these benefits enable the poor to challenge a range of unfair advantages exercised over them, and not simply the unfair advantage inherent to the provision of welfare benefits. To be sure, Goodin does articulate the principle that welfare benefits *enable individuals,* in the sense that beneficiaries are able to participate in the market. And he approaches the issue of political autonomy when he argues that nondiscriminatory provision will not interfere with independent voting. But surely that is distinct from an argument about how welfare benefits positively enable individuals to participate as citizens more generally.

Additionally, Goodin's discussion of the family in relation to the possibility of exploitation suggests, but does not explore, another important familial dynamic. I mentioned above how Goodin recommends the state as a source of welfare benefits over reliance on the family. Among the "needy," those relying on their family for support are more likely to be subject to exploitation: The relationship between the benefactor and beneficiary is direct and observable, and the benefactor maintains discretionary control over the resources. His example of the family does not address the relationships, however, between husband, wife, and nonadult children. His example is meant to describe family members who might otherwise be expected to provide for themselves, for example, elderly parents or adult children. So in his reference to the family, Goodin does not acknowledge that they are often structured along gendered lines, with the husband and wife assuming different roles. Where the male is husband and breadwinner and the woman is wife and caregiver, the woman is typically dependent on the male for her financial resources. If this indeed constitutes a dependent relationship, then how can one be certain that the woman will not be exploited? To follow the logic of

Goodin's argument, should the state pay female caregivers in the home a wage for their work?

Conclusion

Justifications for the right to welfare suffer from a number of limitations. As articulated by Marshall and Moon, the right to welfare provision is predicated on the assumption that citizens must be workers, meaning that citizens must secure paid employment. By identifying citizenship with labor in general and paid employment in particular, these arguments do not take into account gendered structures; they amount, therefore, to an exclusive conception of citizenship. Alternatively, Reich has accepted the contention that citizens must be independent. And in contradistinction to the New Right, he argues that the state, by providing welfare benefits, can contribute to the independence of citizens. Independence is not defined exclusively by securing one's livelihood independently of the state. As such, this argument remains wedded to a conception of citizenship as independence, rather than one of interdependence and solidarity. Finally, egalitarian liberals in general address little more than the economic status of the indigent. Failing to recognize that the problem of poverty is one of unfreedom, rather than simply inequality, these theorists contend that welfare provision contributes primarily to the alleviation of destitution. Welfare provision, according to these theorists, does not address the *political* status of recipients.

To be sure, rights-based arguments have been an important source of gains for groups and individuals, and the language of rights carries great political currency. The language of rights can be important for establishing that the state has a role to play and for ensuring that the state will in practice continue to play this role in the relief of poverty. Faced with the arguments from the New Right about the naturalness of the market, that it is somehow immune from political critique, perhaps the most significant implication to draw from this range of arguments for welfare benefits is precisely that the social consequences of the free market are not "off limits" to public policy. If only implicitly, these arguments support the view that unjustifiable power relations do not obtain only between the state, on the one hand, and individuals or the market on the other. These arguments point to the uneven and unjustifiable gender-based and class-based power relationships made possible by the exercise of free market relationships. Rights to inclusion, rights to equal respect, rights to subsistence, or rights to equal liberty must "trump" the consequences of the free market. So it follows that the contemporary liberal state can intervene to address the consequences of this disparity in power. In short, this conception of citizenship amounts to a challenge to the sovereignty of the private sphere. Put this way, it sounds as if the place of welfare benefits might be more directly related to freedom—enabling individuals in the face of unequal power relationships.[36]

But even if that is the implication of these theorists' arguments, their analyses then fail to take the next logical step. If there are illegitimate exercises of power in society other than those pertaining strictly to economic relationships, can theorists' conception of a right "trump" the consequences of those practices or institutions as well? If so, can state institutions play a role here as well? If, in principle, the state can play such a positive role, is it possible that welfare benefits in particular can be given with a view toward addressing the consequences of these relationships? In particular, is it possible that welfare benefits could enable citizens to participate in the democratic process, with the long-term consequence of being enabled to challenge any number of power relationships?

Given this important implication, it is surprising indeed that these justifications do not use the language of freedom, at least not more directly. It is surprising that scholars in favor of benefits have allowed the New Right to take the lead, especially given the predominant place of (a negative view of) freedom in the political discourse in the United States.[37] By defining citizenship primarily by rights, and failing to emphasize the importance of freedom, these arguments are placed at a strategic disadvantage vis-à-vis the New Right in the political debates over the provision of welfare benefits. This silence on the question of freedom means that these justifications have failed to get to the heart of the New Right's argument, namely that freedom as the willingness to work is either a condition for or a duty of citizenship.

Notes

1. For a good analytic overview of the language of rights, see Jones (1994). To the historian of political thought, the suggestion that there can be an ahistorical analytic definition of rights is highly suspect. See, for instance, Shapiro (1986).

2. According to Hohfeld (1919), claim rights are just one of four distinct relationships captured by the term "right." The others are liberty rights, powers, and immunities. Jones (1994) follows Hohfeld's analysis and uses the term "entitlement" to capture the commonality between the four distinct conceptions. Jones himself cites the right to welfare benefits as an example of a claim right. My point in noting this is to clarify that claims and entitlements are complementary, if not similar, terms. Some attempt to analytically distinguish claims and entitlements undoubtedly stems from their distinct predicative forms. An individual can *actively* claim X, versus, she is only *passively* entitled to X. But the terms are related, and the Xs are the same in the sense that she can legitimately *claim* X, for the reason that she is entitled to X. Or she can claim welfare benefits because she is entitled to them *as* she is entitled to property, equality, or basic needs.

3. Thus, it is even possible to claim that one has a right to freedom.

4. Again, in terms of Hohfeld's analysis, the place of a second-party guarantor is not implied by all four "rights" defined relationships. But it is implied by the sort of right that is related to the provision of welfare benefits.

5. These arguments have been collected and analyzed in Horne (1990).

6. For a contemporary response to this question, see *Shapiro v. Thompson*, 394 U.S. 618 (1969), where the U.S. Supreme Court held that a state's one-year residency requirement for AFDC eligibility was unconstitutional on the grounds that it had a chilling effect on the right to travel. See *U.S. v. Guest*, 383 U.S. 745 (1966) for the principle that the right to travel from state to state is a fundamental right protected by the Constitution.

7. By implication, what is fair is what the market delivers when it is unencumbered by public law. The point here is obviously made without reference to the encumbrances posed by the structure of wage labor.

8. Reich did not have the benefit of Horne's scholarship, so he does not acknowledge the arguments noted briefly in the preceding paragraph.

9. Like Marshall, who follows in the next section, Reich does not explicitly state this, but he is clearly referring to the Anglo-American context.

10. In his later writings, Marshall makes some clearly normative arguments about welfare. "Welfare decisions, then, are essentially *altruistic* and they must draw on *standards of value* embodied in an autonomous ethical system which, though an intrinsic part of the contemporary civilizations, is not the product of either the summation of individual preferences [as in the market] or of a hypothetical majority vote" (1981b: 109, emphasis added).

11. Marshall concludes in that same article that the desire for security does not necessarily demand satisfaction through tangible property. Cash payments, for example, social security or means-tested benefits, are ways by which the desire for security are met without tangible property. "In our society, [tangible] property is becoming less and less important in this respect as more and more is added to the status of citizenship, or to the status of wage-earners" (1963d: 239).

12. Marshall is not always explicit on the point, but he does seem to talk about citizenship and democracy in the same breath. Although he uses the term democracy sparingly, he presumably has that in mind when he discusses citizenship. In this light, it is not clear whether he considers political and civil citizenship to be a democratic conception of citizenship, or if he specifically equates democracy with social citizenship.

13. Marshall defines status as that which "emphasizes the position [rather than the role], as conceived by the group or society that sustains it. . . . [Status] emphasizes the fact that expectations [of a normative kind] exist in the relevant social groups" (1963e: 211).

14. Of course, a strict correspondence between income and class does not necessarily obtain.

15. According to Marshall (1965), by the 1960s the welfare *state* had been replaced by the welfare *society*. Economic planning had transformed capitalism, and social legislation had altered the structure of society. In particular, the working class had realized full membership; the working class had been given the full status of citizenship.

16. Note that Marshall specifically equates voluntary schemes with philanthropy, where the decision to provide resources amounts to a private decision. This use of the term voluntary is distinct from those analyses that equate voluntary activities with the expression of a community.

17. Compare Shklar (1991) as this applies to the United States in the nineteenth century.

18. Marshall does claim that a welfare society "recognizes its collective responsibility to seek to achieve welfare and not only to relieve destitution or eradicate penury" (1981b: 88). But this amounts to an argument for the "duty to provide," and is distinct from Marshall's conception of social citizenship.

19. Additionally, see Fraser and Gordon (1992), who argue that Marshall's account of social citizenship is modeled on civic citizenship, namely, a contractarian ideal that historically meant the exclusion of women and that continues to emphasize separateness and independence.

20. Although this is precisely the concern of the neoconservatives, Moon's commitment to welfare rights places him in this section.

21. Dworkin seems to accept the conventional assumption that a *justification* for a right is implicit in the *nature* of a right. That is, Dworkin's theory of rights is strictly deontological. Alternatively, Wellman (1982) distinguishes between the nature of a right and its justification. In other words, the nature of a right is deontological, but a right must in turn be justified in terms of teleological considerations.

22. Dworkin seems to mean by this a negative conception of liberty.

23. Presumably, this is aimed against a number of ideological uses of Rawls's theory. Dworkin's treatment of Rawls is meant to be an exposition and clarification of Rawls's intended meaning; this is not a critique of his theory.

24. Again, Dworkin seems to have a negative conception of liberty in mind. By speaking of liberties (in the plural), Dworkin presumably means distinct "spheres of noninterference."

25. What follows is not Dworkin's argument, but a plausible application of his principles.

26. In Chapter 2, I identified this as one of Nozick's critiques of the welfare state.

27. Thus, they actually join a number of possibly distinct arguments—those about human needs, wrongful harm, and the social contract.

28. The infinitive "to do" implies both the sense of engaging in a particular action as well as forbearing from specified actions. I can also promise to entertain such and such an attitude, though for practical purposes, that sort of promise is not enforceable in the way that the previous two promises are.

29. By discussing trust in connection with her theory or rights, Held at least implicitly links rights and obligation in a way that Dworkin does not.

30. In some respects, Held and I share some of the same conclusions about the inability of the market to deliver the sort of liberty its proponents would have us believe.

31. There are a number of other arguments about the right to welfare that I will not consider at length here, but that are equally problematic from the perspective of democratic citizenship: for instance, that there is a primary positive right to a

fair share of the community's resources (Fried [1978]); that a welfare right is a claim to one of the "goods" of life (Golding [1968]); that welfare is an entitlement to the efforts of others (McCloskey [1965]); that welfare is justified in terms of a right to the goods needed to survive and have a worthwhile life (Peffer [1978]); and that a "right to life" implies an ethical claim against society for sustenance in an emergency (Bedau [1968]).

32. In fact, he argues that it might actually be desirable to create new dependencies, new needs, and new vulnerabilities.

33. Additionally, attaching a number of conditions on the receipt of aid has meant that there has been little difference between state aid and private charity. Practically speaking, Goodin recommends the elimination of the caseworker. Even that person is capable of exploiting the dependent individual. Further, in his critique of the existing policies, Goodin asks why it is that a higher standard of conduct is imposed on welfare recipients than on the public at large.

34. Goodin argues against social control theorists who view the welfare state's redistributive policies as a payoff to the disgruntled. Goodin contends that people most in need will be the least able to cause social unrest if they are denied benefits. This does seems to be a particularly apt description of the rolling back of AFDC in the United States in 1996.

35. Note that Reich's linking of welfare and independence was made in terms of political rights, not in terms of access to the market.

36. Because I am interested in exploring the meaning of citizenship in relation to arguments concerning public assistance, I have deliberately ignored a justification for assistance that could be grounded in a theory of human rights. For a general treatment of the literature on welfare provision as human rights versus citizens' rights, see Jones (1994: 157–69). For a specifically human rights argument, see Shue (1996).

37. By not addressing the problem of freedom generally, the arguments in this chapter miss the opportunity to address the claim by the New Right that the market in particular is the instrument for the realization of freedom.

PART THREE

Freedom, Poverty, and Democratic Citizenship

5

Autonomy and Participation

Through an examination of the liberal theory that lies at the foundation of a range of normative claims concerning the distribution of public assistance to the nonworking poor, I have offered in the preceding chapters a critique of typical liberal conceptions of citizenship. In the first place, the New Right attack on the distribution of public welfare is informed by more than a negative view of freedom. Freedom will not simply depend on noncoercion by the state (or any other agent), but will also depend on what one does prior to the state; freedom will depend on economic independence from the state. For most people, this will mean that freedom depends on paid employment. By placing the grounds for freedom within the private labor market, the New Right effectively limits the possibilities that women and the nonworking poor can be considered completely free. Consequently, this limits the possibilities that these individuals might realize the full expression of citizenship.

The New Right's conclusions are thus disturbing on two counts. Not only does the logic of their political theory exclude particular groups from full citizenship, the New Right also would seriously curtail, if not abandon altogether, a practical commitment to ensuring the economic and political standing of the nonworking poor. In this context, egalitarian liberals initially seem to offer an important counter to the New Right. Indeed, these liberals are committed to the rights of the poor, suggesting moreover an important alternative to the inegalitarian model of liberal citizenship. Yet these arguments turn out to be equally unsatisfactory. The models of citizenship upon which the rights to welfare are built rest on assumptions about paid employment or independence, and they typically address merely the economic standing of the claimants.

Having elucidated and questioned the conceptions of liberal citizenship that underlie the debate over welfare provision to the poor, in this chapter I address these limitations more constructively by outlining an alternative, distinctly democratic, model of citizenship. In contrast to the egalitarian liberal language of the right to welfare, such a model necessarily begins with and relies upon a conception of freedom. Still, a democratic model of citizenship does not mean a return to the language of inegalitarian liberalism. The language of freedom has been held captive too long by liberal theory. My aim in this chapter is to deploy a *democratic* conception of freedom. Furthermore, this model of citizenship draws on a distinctively participatory democratic theory. Starting with the assumptions and commitments of participatory democracy, the following model of citizenship addresses the limitations that I have noted in the preceding chapters. The model of citizenship that follows does not depend on prepolitical contributions and is not identified with independence. Moreover, this democratic model of citizenship assumes the potential for the political agency of the poor.[1]

Freedom and Democratic Citizenship

Before defining the democratic conception of freedom, it will be useful to establish analytically the relationship between freedom and citizenship. At this point, the relationship will necessarily be preliminary, because without a clear understanding of exactly what is meant by freedom, the meaning of the relationship between the two will not be thoroughly intelligible. Nevertheless, it is fruitful to begin here, as a way for guiding the elaboration of the meaning of freedom.

The idea of citizenship typically designates the two related notions of membership and equality. People who are *members* are *equal* with respect to the rights and duties associated with membership. Whether this status is identified with Aristotle's property-owning male, Machiavelli's soldier, Rousseau's man of public conscience, or the contemporary New Right's wage-earner, that is, aside from the question of who qualifies for this status, citizenship typically designates membership and equality. But citizenship is also about freedom. The idea of citizenship is a way of designating people who are, or who ought to be, politically free. Citizenship indicates a distinctly political relationship that is different from, say, romantic, familial, or professional relationships; it is a formal recognition of an individual's claim or entitlement to the status of political freedom. Indeed, the Marshallian models of political (the protection of civil rights) and legal (the right to the suffrage) citizenship are predicated on notions of individual freedom. And given the relationship between citizenship and formal political institutions, howsoever it is that we define the status of freedom, citizenship is the *state-mediated* avenue for guaranteeing that status. Therefore, to call someone a citizen means, among other things, that this individual is free. Or, one expects that such a person ought to be free. The promise of membership and equality is the promise to guarantee that status of freedom. Thus, in order to know exactly what is meant by calling someone a citizen, the content of that freedom must be defined. To such a definition I now turn.

Because I am ultimately aiming to elaborate a *democratic* conception of freedom, it will be useful not only to contrast this conception of freedom with liberal conceptions. It will also be useful to examine how liberal theory, armed with its conception of freedom, has accommodated democratic theory. That is, it will be instructive to contrast liberalism's *tension* between liberty and democracy with my own *integration* of the two.

Typically, a (liberal) conception of freedom has been linked with democratic theory through arguments aimed at justifying the practice of democracy. Freedom, which even for many democratic theorists has meant the absence of constraint or coercion—the typical liberal and negative conception of freedom (or liberty)—has been held to be valuable in and of itself. This much was taken as self-evident. Democratic theory can be incorporated into liberalism, then, by arguing that a democracy is the best political arrangement among a range of alternatives set for the protection of liberty.[2] Because a democratic state is designed in the first place to protect this prepolitical condition of liberty, the democratic state could not legitimately abridge that freedom; that would represent a contradiction of its purpose. Of course, all but the most extreme anarchists have recognized that in a society with conflicting interests, exceptions to this ideal of this democratic practice were inevitable. Nevertheless, the primary function of the democratic state, it has typically been argued, is to serve the interest of protecting that liberty. And the state's actions generally can be expected to answer to that standard.

The point to be emphasized is that although the status of individual liberty and the institutions of democracy can accommodate each other, the two remain distinct in liberal theory. In their ideal relationship the practice of democracy must remain subordinate to the status of individual freedom. Indeed, the fear of some liberal theorists, most notably Hayek, is that too much democracy, because of its emphasis on equality, threatens the fundamental liberal commitment to freedom. In this way, not only must democratic values and institutions remain subordinate to the values of liberalism, there is also a constant tension between these two sets of values.

As I discussed in Chapter 3, however, liberal democratic theorists have also articulated a positive conception of liberty, holding out the promise of easing the tension between freedom and democracy. Freedom may also consist in the ability to do a range of things. Green, for one, used this conception in order to justify a more positive role for the state. The democratic state, in this view, need not be restricted to enforcing a constitution of law or to enforcing contracts. A democratic state could legitimately provide funds for public education as well as limited forms of public assistance. In the first place, this function of the state did not contradict the role of the state as the guarantor of negative freedom. Green did not countenance the argument made nearly a hundred years later by Nozick about the coercive nature of taxation. Additionally, a new, positive conception of liberty in fact required that the state perform this function; a government's legitimacy was conditional upon performing this function.

With a view toward articulating a distinctively democratic conception of freedom—and ultimately viewing that as the grounds for the provision of welfare benefits—I must begin to move away from the discussion laid out in terms of positive versus negative freedom. To be sure, I have shown the impossibility of an exclusively negative conception of liberty. In my analysis of the New Right, most notably the libertarian arguments of Nozick, I demonstrated that a negative conception of liberty requires a substantive conception as well. In terms laid out by the New Right noncoercion depends upon economic independence. So, deconstructing the negative conception of liberty is still an important first step in constructing a democratic alternative.

To be sure, moreover, the introduction of a positive conception of liberty does provide some important inspiration for challenging the former position. Still, Green remained too much of a liberal at the expense of his democratic commitments. There was nothing in this description of positive liberty, for instance, that led Green to endorse the suffrage for women. The foundation for this exclusion of women lies with the connection between positive liberty and the expectation that citizens must be workers. The positive conception of liberty was meant to address the conditions specifically of the *working* poor. The positive conception of liberty was explicitly not aimed at those who, for a number of reasons, did not work for wages.

There is, moreover, little if any sense in Green's writings that the things to which citizenship entitles the individual will constitute the conditions for participation in a democracy. Positive liberty denotes a range of things that citizens ought to be able to do, but it does not of itself reinforce democracy. There is no link between "being able to do something" and the viability of democracy more generally. Alternatively stated, the notion of positive liberty legitimizes positive actions on the part of the democratic state, and it goes further by conditioning the legitimacy of the state upon taking these positive actions to ensure that citizens can do a range of things. Still, this notion does not suggest that the state's actions can contribute to the conditions for participation.

In sum, the most prominent alternative in liberal democratic thought for easing the tension between freedom and democracy still does not integrate the two components as an organic whole, and this turns out to be a disappointment for ensuring the categorical application of the status of citizenship. A model of democratic citizenship, on the other hand, will include the assumption that the conditions for participation as a citizen will be categorically available, and this assumption is more plausible in the context of a theory that does indeed organically relate freedom and democracy.

Autonomy

Alternative Conceptions

As an alternative to viewing liberty in terms of noncoercion or economic independence and as an alternative to a positive conception of liberty, I will identify freedom with *autonomy*. Because the idea of autonomy is no less subject to a variety of interpretations than is liberty, I turn first, however, to distinguishing the meaning of autonomy, which is integral to a theory of participatory democracy from a number of alternative (liberal) conceptions. Among these alternatives are conceptions of moral and personal autonomy. Kant (1964) provides one of the more well-known accounts of "moral" autonomy, identifying it with the capacity to be fully rational. Rationality, in turn, depends on subjecting the *natural* self of sense and desire to the control of the *true* self of practical reason. Autonomy is identified with rational scrutiny. Only in this way can the individual be *self-determining*. Furthermore, this self-determination depends on acting in accordance with principles that can be universalized. Autonomy describes the disposition of governing oneself in accordance with universally valid moral principles. In this sense, moral autonomy can be defined as *self-legislation* or *self-regulation* (Benn [1976]; Kuflik [1984]). The "morally" autonomous individual determines her actions in accordance with principles that she has not mindlessly borrowed from others. This person does not do simply what she wants to do. "The morally autonomous person subscribes to principles that have either been formed or (more to the point) ratified, by his own moral scrutiny" (Kuflik [1984: 272]; compare Wolff [1970: 13]). Although this conception of autonomy defines a definite process of moral deliberation, this does not require that the autonomous individual submit herself to a life of ceaseless reflection. It only requires periodic rational scrutiny. Furthermore, this conception need not suggest that what is morally "right" is a matter of purely subjective preferences. "The morally autonomous person forms his every day judgments about right and wrong in light of considerations that can bear the weight of his own critically reflective moral scrutiny. . . . [The morally autonomous individual] must be able to justify, on morally rational grounds, the direction he has taken" (Kuflik [1984: 273]). This suggests that moral autonomy is related to a principle of noninterference and to the value of choice.

The emphasis on choice is also the characteristic of typical conceptions of personal autonomy (Benn [1976, 1988]; Raz [1989]). An individual is personally autonomous when she is not interfered with in the exercise of her choice. In turn, individuals must have the opportunity to exercise an actual choice; the individual must have options. Single-candidate elections that do not allow for the option of formally rejecting the candidate, for instance, are shams because the options for a voter are limited to not-voting or voting, but the option of voting is itself constrained to simply voting "yes" for the single candidate. So a meaningful election includes the options of not-voting and voting, where voting, in turn, must include more than one option.[3] "To be autonomous and to have an autonomous life, a person must have options which enable him to sustain throughout his life activities which, taken together, exercise all the capacities human beings have an innate drive to exercise, as well as to decline to develop any of these" (Raz [1989: 375]). In short, autonomy depends on *number*.

Additionally, autonomy may not simply indicate the ability to make *any* decisions. Rather, autonomy pertains to the *quality* of the decision. Choices are autonomously made when, or the individual is autonomous only to the extent that, the decisions she makes are derived from norms that are distinctly her own. Here, the opportunity to choose is joined to the Kantian description of moral autonomy. As opposed to an autonomous chooser, the heteronomous chooser "assesses situations, adapts means to ends, and so on, but always by norms of propriety and success absorbed unreflectively from parents, teachers, or workmates" (Benn [1976: 123–24]). The autonomous individual makes her *own* decisions. Additionally, autonomy is not just evaluative or reflective. It also involves the ability to alter one's preferences, in order to make them effective. "Autonomy is conceived of as a second order capacity of persons to reflect critically upon their first order preferences, desires, wishes and so forth, and the capacity to accept or attempt to change these in light of higher order preferences and values. By exercising such a capacity, persons define their nature, give meaning and coherence to their lives, and take responsibility for the kind of person they are" (Dworkin [1988: 20]). Drawing on these notions, liberalism has invested the term autonomy with a distinctly political meaning. Within liberal discourse, autonomy is often defined as the state of having the opportunity to choose a lifestyle, rather than to have one thrust upon the individual (Berlin [1969]). Alternatively, the individual is politically autonomous when he is treated as an end, and never as a means (Callahan [1984]; compare Nozick [1974]).

Personal autonomy has also been articulated as *self-direction* rather than *self-determination*. (Sher [1997]). Self-direction is understood here as "exercising one's will on the basis of *good reasons*." In this view, autonomy does not obtain simply because an agent's goals, plans, and decisions originate in his own will. Building on the notion of self-direction, autonomous action is that which "is motivated by an agent's appreciation of *reasons* provided by his situation" (Sher [1997: 57]). Personal autonomy can also be conceived as the exposition of moral autonomy I provided above (see, for example, Lindley [1986]). In this light, personal autonomy has been identified with *self-mastery*. The developed self has control of his immediate passions. It involves the consciousness of oneself as a being who acts for reasons "whose behavior can be explained by reference to one's own goals and purposes" (Lindley [1986: 6]). The language is similar to Kant's, but autonomy here is not related to universalizable moral principles.[4]

The conceptions of autonomy outlined above all have a conventional *liberal* ring to them. These conceptions are individualistic or self-oriented. The idea of autonomy here typically applies to individuals whose "decisions, plans of life, and moral and other principles are exclusively their own. Autonomy is to have beliefs and values and to make decisions that are all one's own and *are by that token not anyone else's*. Thereby one comes to be one's own person" (Schmitt [1995: 5]). Autonomy signifies something like exclusive ownership. Additionally, these conceptions of autonomy are typically associated with *independence;* the terms used to describe autonomy are the same terms used to describe independence. Given the identification of liberty with independence in liberalism, the distinction between autonomy and liberty in liberal theory begs for clarification.

Even a self-oriented theory of autonomy has been distinguished from conceptions of independence. In other words, autonomy is not strictly identified with liberty in liberal thought. Young (1986), for instance, argues that "the autonomous person . . . must not be subject to external interference or control but must rather, freely direct and govern the course of his (or her) own life. The autonomous person's capacities, beliefs and values will be identifiable as integral to him and be the source from which his actions spring" (Young [1986: 1]). Still, this definition of personal autonomy is not reduced to independence. This is an impossibility, in Young's view, given the social nature of existence. In other words, one can be free from external interference or control at the same time that one is bound within a social network of mutual assistance and exchange.

Dworkin (1988) also questions a simple identification between autonomy and independence by arguing that his conception of autonomy insists on procedural independence, as distinct from substantive independence. Autonomy, according to Dworkin, must not be inconsistent with other values, such as loyalty and commitment. Yet the pursuit of substantive independence—the actions of a "selfish person"—prevents the realization of these values. Procedural independence, on the other hand, does not undermine these values. Procedural independence, the standard for autonomy, only insists that one is independent of the *influences* that prevent an individual from making decisions and performing actions that are truly her own.

Autonomy also appears to be linked to the idea of liberty through the notion of noncoercion. Conceptions of *self-legislation, self-mastery,* or *self-control* imply the possibility of both internal and external impediments to the realization of autonomy, and the identification of impediments sounds much like a discussion of (negative) liberty or freedom. Indeed, it is plausible to speak of being at liberty to execute our *rationally chosen goals,* or of being at liberty to tend to our *self-determination,* and I have already noted the connection between moral and personal autonomy as a principle of *noninterference*—the typical liberal conception of freedom. Nevertheless, liberal theorists have explicitly made a distinction between autonomy and liberty, with respect to noncoercion. The distinction here may be founded on the principle that the abridgment of liberty is a periodic or occurrent event, affecting specific choices. Autonomy, on the other hand, refers to a *disposition* that is part of a long process of development. Thus, it may be possible to hinder the exercise of one's options at a *particular moment*—abridge one's liberty—while not affecting one's ability to choose one's preferred mode of life (Dworkin [1988]; Kuflik [1984]; Rosenbaum [1986]; Young [1986]).

Autonomy and Freedom

To sum up thus far, within liberal theory there is, first of all, typically a tension between democracy and liberty, with the former subordinate to the latter. Additionally, conceptions of autonomy as *self-mastery, self-determination* or *control over decisions* can be distinguished from liberty. The distinction between autonomy and liberty is based on a conception of liberty in strictly negative terms—the absence of coercion or interference. All of this stands in contrast to a conception of freedom (or liberty) as autonomy that lies at the center of a theory of democratic citizenship.

To address the long-standing concern of liberalism with negative freedom, I do not reject outright the value of respecting spheres of liberty. Some principle of noninterference, carefully explicated, is integral to a vision of participatory democracy. Indeed, democratic commitments bring to the table the demand that one should extend that principle to acknowledge when the conventions and logic of the free market interfere with the opportunity of individuals to be full citizens; the principle of noninterference must discipline the state as well as the market. This is precisely the sort of acknowledgment that the liberal theorists of the New Right refuse to make. Still, in contrast to liberal theory, a model of citizenship that accounts for women and the nonworking poor will identify freedom with autonomy.[5] And, again in contrast to liberal theory, it will rely on freedom qua autonomy in relation to *political participation*.

Thus, the conception of autonomy that I relate to participatory democracy and that defines the content of citizenship therein does not depend on overcoming a bifurcation between the "natural self" and practical reason. It does not depend on the self-mastery associated with either moral or personal autonomy, and this conception of autonomy is not related to universalizable moral principles. In more general terms, the conception of autonomy I rely upon does not depend on the sense of ownership or independence implied by the conceptions of autonomy as disposition, mental reflection, or choice.

Contemporary philosophers have already begun to discuss autonomy in a way that is useful for overcoming the distinction and tension between the guarantee of liberty and the practice of democracy—for articulating a distinctively democratic, and participatory democratic, conception of liberty. Schmitt (1995), for instance, has argued that the test of autonomy is whether an individual *contributes actively*, by engaging others in discussion, and whether that individual's contributions are valued (Schmitt [1995: 6, emphasis added]). In this view, the typical liberal conceptions of autonomy suffer from a fundamental assumption of social separateness. Liberal conceptions are rooted in the notion that each person has her own beliefs and desires. As an alternative to that, Schmitt defines autonomy in light of his conception of "being-in-relation." The latter refers to joint acts that are neither one person's nor the other's. "Two or more persons constitute an agent insofar as they have a shared understanding with respect to some more or less specific matter" (Schmitt [1995: 58]). Rosenbaum (1986), too, defines autonomy in *relational* terms. Autonomy is not a preformed or static sphere carried into and throughout one's relationship with others. Rather, autonomy signifies "the range of *control* the participants in a particular social situation have with respect to each other over their own private actions and over the exercise of their respective processes of decision making, valuing and willing. Autonomy is thus a relational notion because the actual range of a participant's social autonomy is mostly a function of his *role* relatedness to the other participants" (Rosenbaum [1986: 107]).

Inspired by this relational notion, one can begin to emphasize autonomy as a form of *enablement*. Moreover, it is important to eschew an abstract formulation of this conception and to locate it directly in the context of a participatory theory of democracy. Autonomy here will refer to *the status of having been enabled to participate (in some way) in the governing of the state, and/or in an ongoing democratic dialogue.* The individual is free, or autonomous, when that individual has the capacity—has been enabled—to participate in political decision making or to contribute to the democratic dialogue. The individual is free when she has the capacity to contribute actively, by engaging others, in this discussion. And the individual is free when she has the capacity for "role relatedness" to other participants in a political dialogue. In contrast to liberal theory's emphasis on freedom as noncoercion or independence and its emphasis on autonomy as self-determination, self-mastery, and so forth, freedom in this sense refers to "the autonomy that allows all citizens to participate fully in all aspects of social and political life" (Pateman [1995: 26]).

In light of my analysis generally, this emphasis on autonomy is of singular importance for those who have not been accounted for in models of liberal citizenship, namely, women and the nonworking poor. As I established at the beginning of this section, a conception of freedom, whether as independence or as autonomy, is integral to models of both liberal and democratic citizenship. Freedom is a way of describing the status of those who are citizens, and the promise of citizenship is the promise to guarantee that status of freedom. Thus, by identifying freedom with autonomy—with the capacity for participation—I mean that democratic citizenship indicates the capacity for participation. Thus, I am challenging the liberal position that the full expression of citizenship depends on independence. To reiterate my conclusions in Chapter 2, the full expression of citizenship must not depend on making a prepolitical contribution, especially where the opportunity to make that contribution is foreclosed by the conventions and logic of the sphere within which that contribution is possible—the market. In short, democratic citizenship does not condition full citizenship on paid employment.

Additionally, rather than substituting one kind of contribution for another, I am moving away from a contributory model altogether. There is an inherent problem for the equal distribution of the conditions of full citizenship when those conditions, whether landownership, military service, or labor market participation, are identified with the notion of prior contributions. Prepolitical contributions can always be defined in such a way to exclude people who are unable to make that contribution. By focusing on freedom as autonomy, one can begin to focus on the conditions for full citizenship in a participatory model of democracy, conditions whose equal distribution can be guaranteed.

Finally, the identification of freedom with autonomy contrasts sharply with Green's theory of positive liberty. To be sure, Green laid the groundwork for an important claim on the state, namely, that the state itself could contribute to the constitution of citizenship. Still, the substantive conception of that citizenship is a long way from the democratic model described above. As I have already noted, Green articulated a conception of freedom that was useful for incorporating the working class into political society and for supporting a list of social reforms. Yet Green was self-consciously opposed to the incorporation of the nonworking poor. Also, despite his commitment to the political inclusion of the working poor, Green's theory of positive liberty is not integrally related to political *participation*. Finally, Green makes no claim that positive liberty is necessary for sustaining democracy itself.

Participatory Democracy

A complete explication of this conception of autonomy depends on a general exposition of a theory of participatory democracy. To expand on my claim that autonomy indicates the capacity to participate in decision making and in a democratic dialogue, I turn to exploring these forms of political participation in more detail. To anticipate my normative justification, the principle of public welfare provision for the poor must be founded on a view of democracy that is different from the view of democracy informing the New Right critique of public welfare benefits, namely, the minimalist, representative model of democracy described by Hayek (1960, 1979).

A theory of participatory democracy includes at least three major components. First, such a theory must include a precise definition of participation. Second, a theory of participatory democracy will identify the benefits thought to follow from participation; it will explain why participation is necessary. Finally, such a theory will articulate the conditions that are required for participation. Additionally, in light of much criticism from the New Right on the prospects for more than a minimalist model of democracy, a participatory democracy must be justified on empirical grounds. It must be possible to show not only that a participatory democracy is desirable, but that it is also possible. Although the primary aim of this chapter is to explore one of the *conditions* for a participatory democracy, I will say something briefly on the other three components of a general theory.

The Meaning of Participation

In the first place, participation means involvement in both decision making as well as in the construction of a democratic dialogue. Rousseau, of course, provides the model of direct participation in decision making. The benefits of participation that he identifies can only be understood in light of this meaning of democracy. It is a well-worn observation by this point that direct participation in decision making in a national or federal government is simply impossible for everyone. Still, mechanisms exist for dealing with this problem. On the one hand, participation as decision making, even in this larger context, is possible at the ballot box. The state of California, for instance, regularly submits a number of important issues to referenda. Such a process could feasibly be facilitated electronically (Barber [1984: 273ff]).[6] To be sure, this form of decision making removes one of the central elements of Rousseau's model—that decision making be face-to-face. Nevertheless, referenda do provide a viable alternative in a larger society for maintaining the opportunity for participating in decision making. Alternatively, Walzer (1988) has argued that citizens do not need to participate in all democratic decisions. The ideal of participation can be satisfied when citizens participate only in those decisions in which they are keenly interested; not every "public" question is of equal interest to everyone.

There is yet another way to maintain, in the face of the question of its feasibility, the importance of a view of participation as decision making. This involves shifting the locus of those decisions. The challenge to the feasibility or likelihood of participation is often based on the assumption that participation refers to decision making at the national level. Nevertheless, as Mill noted, participation in decision making at the *local level* can foster the sort of expertise that may be necessary for participation at the national level (Mill [1910: 347–48]; Pateman [1970]). That is, democratic decision making does not pertain exclusively to a central government (Mill [1965: 944]; Pateman [1970]). Participation at the local level, therefore, may not be as vulnerable to the charge that participation is neither feasible nor likely.

Democratic participation can also be construed as making a contribution to a *democratic dialogue*. A number of theorists who have focused on civil society and the New Social Movements have enriched our understanding of participation by pointing to this (Barber [1984]; Benhabib [1996]; Cohen and Arato [1992]; Dryzek [1990]; Laclau and Mouffe [1985]; Mouffe [1992]). In this sense, participation means that by words and actions, citizens contribute to the constitution of the political discourse.[7] It is an alternative to viewing participation as *choosing* from a set of options set before them. It means contributing to the constitution of that agenda, in the way that the feminist, environmental, and union movements, for instance, have done. Furthermore, by conceiving of participation in this way, these theorists challenge the "issue orientation" of traditional politics. This theory of participation questions the presuppositions about what properly constitutes the *political arena;* they challenge the boundaries of legitimate concerns for public attention or collective action. "A public sphere is brought into existence whenever two or more individuals . . . assemble to interrogate both their own interactions and the wider relations of social and political power within which they are always and already embedded. Through this . . . association, members of public spheres consider what they are doing, settle how they will live together, and determine . . . how they might collectively act" (Keane [1984: 2–3]).

These analyses also directly challenge New Right arguments about politics pertaining to formal governmental institutions (see also Hardy-Fanta [1993]). They shift the *locus* of participation beyond actions mediated by conventional political institutions. Voluntary associations, for instance, become themselves new arenas within which participation as both contribution to the dialogue as well as decision making takes place. Although the theorists of civil society do not reject the place of conventional political institutions or the importance of finding ways to improve participation in them, these theorists have successfully identified nonstate and nonmarket areas where democratic participation, as both decision making and contributing to the democratic dialogue, takes place.[8] Finally, this alternative conception of the political amounts to more than shifting the locus of the political. These theorists also redefine the political, where politics do not simply pertain to questions of power and the pursuit of interests. Rather, politics is defined "in terms of public debate among deciding how individually and collectively they [will] act and interact" (Dryzek [1990: 153]).

The Benefits of Participation

Having identified a conception of participation as either decision making or as contributing to the constitution of political discourse, generally, I now turn to identifying briefly the primary positive *effects* of participation. It has been argued by a number of theorists that there are three primary functions to a classical theory of participatory democracy.[9] In the first place, participation has an *educative* function. As I noted above, participation provides practical training in the skills necessary for running a democracy. Participation also "educates" one's disposition toward democracy. It fosters psychological development and the feeling of political efficacy. The more that one is able to participate, the more that an individual will feel that her contribution, whether in decision making or in the constitution of a democratic dialogue, is worthwhile. So, participation fosters an attitude of public-spiritedness. Participation enables individuals to recognize and consider other citizens' interests. Additionally, participation allows one to see one's *own interests* more clearly (Bachrach [1967]).

Furthermore, when it is a question of decision making, participation serves the function of *facilitating* the acceptance of these decisions. Individuals affected by public decisions are more likely to accept them when these individuals have contributed in some way to the process. Citizens are likely to accept decisions that are impersonal, decisions not considered to be the expression of any particular individual's or group's will. Such a will would represent an imposition of force on the citizen in question. Closely related to this, participation serves a third, *integrative*, function. Participation increases the feelings of belonging to the community.

Additionally, contemporary theorists of participatory democracy have advanced the models of Rousseau and Mill by articulating the *transformative* function of participation. This transformation concerns the place of interests (Barber [1984]; Dryzek [1990]; Warren [1992]). Typically, liberalism takes individual interests or preferences as given. The important question, from that assumption, is to determine how those preferences can best be protected. Indeed, Rousseau felt that this was a fundamental reason for participation. Even Bachrach's (1967) critique of an elite theory of democracy and his emphasis on participation, namely, that participation enabled one to see one's own interests more clearly, rested on the assumption that one's interests are identifiable and truly one's own. This is also the assumption of pluralists, such as Dahl (1971). Both the pluralists and the classical theorists of participatory democracy agreed that democracy was about the protection of preformed interests. The disagreement was simply over the best means for protecting them.

The contemporary insight of participatory democracy, on the other hand, is the assumption that interests are neither necessarily given nor directly revealed.[10] Participatory democracy expects that new common interests will be forged from the action of political engagement and political debate. New public ends are identified through the processes of public participation. The public choice settled upon may reflect a newly constituted interest. The participatory vision of democracy "emphasizes debate and reasoning about and toward public interests and actions in political communities of citizens who govern themselves, as opposed to liberalism's agglomeration of private individuals governed by their representatives" (Barber [1984: 152]).

Moreover, the *unity* of a self-governing community of citizens does not depend, in contrast to its place in liberal theory, upon a set of homogenous preformed or static interests. Instead individuals become united through a civic education that leads in the direction of constituting political judgment and new interests (Barber [1984: 152]). Political judgment involves the process of willing—to bring about something new. It does not involve simply choosing among existing alternatives.

Furthermore, as politics concerns itself with problems for which there may be no independent ground of judgment, a theory of participatory democracy expects that the terms used in the solution of practical political problems arise from the actions of individuals (Barber [1984: 129f]; Dryzek [1990]). This means that we cannot apply philosophically external norms to the political process, at least not in a mechanical fashion, with the hope of resolving those problems. Their application must be debated and discussed. This is "politics in the participatory mode where conflict is resolved in the absence of an independent ground through a participatory process of ongoing, proximate self-legislation and the creation of a political community capable of transforming dependent, private individuals into free citizens and partial and private interests into public goods" (Barber [1984: 132]). This view, therefore, places transformation at the heart of democracy. A participatory theory of democracy does not aim to eliminate conflict, but to transform it into the constitution of new interests.

The Possibility of Participation

Although the case for participatory democracy has been forcefully made by normative theorists and supported in many places by empirical research, the case is not without its critics. Although the emphasis in this chapter is on identifying a component of participatory democracy rather than on articulating a comprehensive *defense* of participatory democracy, it is useful to address briefly the major critiques of this theory of democracy.

Public opinion research in the 1950s and early 1960s, for instance, tried to show that too many people are too apathetic for participatory democracy to ever function well (Almond and Verba [1963]). Nevertheless, Pateman (1970) has already successfully addressed those conclusions. She has argued and demonstrated, incorporating empirical studies of workplace democracy, that participation begets feelings of efficacy. To be sure, Greenberg (1986) determined in his empirical study of worker participation that participation in the workplace did *not* contribute to feelings of political efficacy. Nevertheless, he also concludes his study generally with the observation that the "bright promise of workplace democracy and self-management can be achieved only if it is part of a larger struggle for popular democracy and equality in the United States" (Greenberg [1986: 171]). This statement effectively questions a broad application of his pessimistic findings on feelings of political efficacy. Greenberg's conclusion recognizes that conditions outside the workplace undermine feelings of political efficacy. So, participation in places other than the workplace must be explored if individuals are going to develop a sense of political efficacy. Indeed, much of the argument for participatory democracy has rested on the empirical research done in the workplace. Since I have already questioned the identification of citizenship with work, it is logical to move beyond the identification of participatory democracy with the workplace.

In addition to making the charge of an apathetic demos, critics have maintained that participatory democracy is unrepresentative, too demanding of time, inefficient, and unnecessary.[11] Sartori (1987), for one, argues that participatory democracy ends up contradicting its own objective of numerical equality. This amounts to the claim that participatory democracy is not possible. He argues that even under such a model, a vocal minority seizes control and may not in fact represent all members. Recounting the familiar story line of Orwell's *Animal Farm*, Sartori argues that a counterelite will simply displace preexisting elites. Similarly, Mansbridge (1980) makes the observation that participatory decision making favors the most savvy and articulate members. Some of these problems with representation have been analyzed by Phillips (1991) in relation to the feminist movement of the 1960s. She notes that the feminist movement typically refused to formalize the structures of decision making. This typically led, in turn, to a refusal to develop procedures for accountability. Although no elites were acknowledged, Sartori's expectation of counterelites, in this example an *unacknowledged* core of elites, did indeed emerge. The refusal to develop procedures for accountability therefore "meant that de facto leaders and elites went unchecked" (Phillips [1991: 127]). Additionally, this absence of formal procedures undermined any claims that the movement might have made to represent women generally. It "could never say for whom or for how many it spoke. It could not then engage with authority in influence outside politics" (Phillips [1991: 127]).

The doubts about the representative limitations of participatory democracy are related to the doubts about the facilitation of interests made possible by such a model. Mansbridge (1980) found that an emphasis on face-to-face deliberation actually submerges conflict. Some participants may not have expressed their interests for fear of disagreeing with other. Alternatively, some feared offending "friends" within the group of participants. Under either scenario, face-to-face meetings ended up preventing some people from expressing their opinions. Consequently, a pressure to conform set in, thereby establishing a false common front. This conclusion challenges the expectation that participation enables a fair airing of interests as well as the opportunity for the transformation of them. Furthermore, on this count, participation may continue to serve the function of integration, but one must begin to question, given Mansbridge's argument, the value of this integration. Is it, in fact, an instance of blind conformism?

Furthermore, the procedures typically associated with participation will not guarantee that all participants feel good about the outcome of a decision. "Permanent" minorities, for instance, might be forever frustrated that their participation has little effect. They therefore may have no reason to feel better about decisions simply because they were made on the basis of a participatory model of democracy. Indeed, many people would like to claim that California's Propositions 187 and 209, having negative implications for particular racial and ethnic groups and for women, represents the will of the people; they were decided by referenda. Nevertheless, the groups opposed to and negatively affected by these propositions may be no less frustrated by this decision, notwithstanding the support for Proposition 209 by some women and minorities.

The concern for the unrepresentative nature of participatory democracy, though not entirely without basis, has been overstated. In the first place, any test of this hypothesis surely cannot focus on specific participatory *events* without considering the longer process within which those events take place. The practice of participatory democracy is an ongoing process, involving the accumulation of knowledge and experience. Given the antiparticipatory habits that individuals may have cultivated for so long, one cannot expect individuals to realize the full potential of participatory democracy with the first attempts. In fact, it may be necessary to wait more than one generation, from the time participatory democracy has been seriously instituted, for its full potential to be realized.

Second, this critique suffers from something of a level of analysis problem. The critique fails to distinguish between the internal dynamics of a group experimenting with participatory democracy and the larger sociopolitical context within which these experiments take place. Even if particular groups, by their internal organization, prove the iron law of oligarchy, and even this cannot be unequivocally established, one must also consider the *effects* that these experiments have on politics generally. It surely cannot be denied that the feminist movement of the 1960s provided access for women to political institutions and to the national political discourse in a way not seen before that time. In other words, social movements must themselves count for the argument for participatory democracy.

Finally, it must be noted that participatory democracy has never been about unanimity. Although such a theory typically expects that identifiable minorities will be included in the process of public deliberation, it does not expect the complete elimination of interests. Whereas some dividing interests may be overcome, others may remain, and new divisive interests may develop. Yet such a prognosis for minority groups does not rebut the argument for participatory democracy, generally.

Critics have also challenged more and new forms of participation because of the demands participation places on people's time. The claim is that participatory democracy is either undesirable or impossible. Walzer (1970) has cautioned that the focus on participation for the purpose of addressing unequal access to decision making inevitably contributes to the exercise of a new form of inequality, namely, an inequality of disposable time; it rewards people with nights to spare. Mansbridge (1980) also links the observation of time constraints with the argument about the *unrepresentative* character of participatory democracy. If a minority of individuals end up constituting a core group of *active* participatory democrats, then the decision this core makes will not necessarily coincide with the range of views and interests held within the group at large. In particular, she suggests that by making *meetings* central to involvement, experiments with participatory democracy end up selecting and limiting their membership. People who do participate are an unrepresentative few. This paradox contradicts the expectation that democratic decision making ought to provide for proportionate outcomes. Moreover, the problem of the time required for participation is especially salient for women. As long as women carry a double burden of unpaid care work and low-paid wage work, a model of participatory democracy will not necessarily incorporate women's interests, nor will it provide an opportunity for women to contribute to the constitution of a democratic dialogue.

In the first place, this critique is not unrelated to assumptions about apathy. There is likely to be a connection between the time that an individual is willing to spend on politics and her feelings of efficacy. In other words, the problem might not always be lack of time, but lack of feelings of personal efficacy. As noted above, the response to this phenomenon is that participation begets feelings of efficacy, which may beget the willingness to devote a night or two to political matters. Additionally, the observation about the excessive burden on women's time is no argument against participatory democracy, but rather an argument distinctly *in favor* of participatory democracy. The goal should not be to unburden women, so that they may focus on "bringing home the bacon, *and* frying it up in a pan." Rather, the goal might be on exploring ways to ease these private burdens, and such a goal could plausibly be effected by improving the prospects for participatory democracy. Finally, the argument for participatory democracy does not stand by the participation of absolutely every individual in society. Participatory democracy, moreover, does not allow that individuals be coerced to participate. The point of participatory democracy is to provide the individual with the *opportunity* to participate—with the opportunity to overcome structures of power. If individuals ultimately choose not to participate, the argument for participatory democracy will still stand.

Participatory democracy is also considered by some theorists to be inefficient and thus, undesirable. Again, Phillips (1991) notes the example in the feminist movement. The movement often tried to expand the principle of equality beyond its strictly political aspects. The movement insisted on an "equalization of involvement and skill " (Phillips [1991: 126]). In this way, the feminist movement undermined the positive benefits of a division of labor; this wasted time and energy. The benefit of a minimalist democracy, on the other hand, is that it demands no more skill than that necessary to cast a periodic vote, and it allows individuals with the most interest and the best skills to participate and "survive" (Sartori [1987]).

Unlike the preceding critiques, this challenge is not internal to the language of participatory democracy. Instead, it imposes an external criterion on the theory of participatory democracy. Yet this theory does not make pretensions to efficiency. In fact, in light of the alternatives, participatory democracy implicitly challenges certain ideas of efficiency. Additionally, the critique suffers from the same limitations I noted in response to the claim that participatory democracy is unrepresentative. Participatory democracy is a learning process that will necessarily involve trade-offs in the short run. Still, taking the long view, participatory democracy may in fact satisfy at least one conception of efficiency. Although the insistence on an equalization of skills may have wasted time and energy in the short run, it may be more efficient in the long run to have a greater number of individuals who have learned these skills.

Finally, participatory democracy has been considered unnecessary under some circumstances, even by people sympathetic to the goals of participation. Assuming that participation is recommended for the reason that it protects interests, Mansbridge (1980) addresses the question about whether interests can best be protected by participation. In this light, Mansbridge articulates a "unitary" model of democracy. She concludes that where there is a *common* interest, the less powerful members of the polity can *trust* that the more powerful members will protect the interests of the less powerful. She does not dismiss participatory democracy altogether, however. Concerning issues that have no common interest, Mansbridge acknowledges the importance of an "adversarial" view of democracy—the pluralist's view of bargaining democracy. In the latter instance, participation, despite some fundamental limitations, will be required for the protection of interests.

Clearly, then, Mansbridge's account of unitary democracy does not undermine the argument for participatory democracy. My response to her, therefore, is not a defense of this theory. Rather, my response is a challenge, in light of a theory of participatory democracy, to her argument for unitary democracy. That is, Mansbridge still assumes that participation is primarily meant for the purpose of protecting or ensuring the expression of one's interests, but this assumption about the merits of participation ignores the transformative function of participatory democracy. Even if one can trust that a representative will protect her interests, in the absence of participation there is no opportunity that new interests could arise by action or discussion. Further, without active participation, one misses the opportunity to correctly articulate one's own interest. Moreover, even if one believes that a representative will protect her interests, in the absence of participation there is no opportunity to develop skills, capacities, a sense of self, and self-respect.

Autonomy and Citizenship

With the meanings and effects of participation set out, I am now in a position to place a conception of autonomy at the center of a participatory theory of democracy. The importance of this step cannot be underestimated. Indeed, much of the theorizing on participatory democracy in the United States in the twentieth century has focused only on that ground that I have just covered, namely, the meanings, benefits, and possibilities (whether persons are interested in or psychologically capable) of participation. Still, less attention has been paid to the social conditions that can either enable or constrain the opportunity for participation in the first place. How does one come to have the capacity to participate? How is it possible, indeed, that men and women come to be in the position in which they can experiment with participatory democracy in a New England town meeting or the women's movement?

I argued above for a view of autonomy as *the status of having been enabled to participate (in some way) in the governing of the state, in an ongoing democratic dialogue, or both.* An individual is free when she has been enabled to participate. So a participatory theory of democracy must include more than simply the meanings and effects of participation, and such a theory must do more than overcome doubts, expressed in the context of psychological assumptions, about its empirical possibilities. A participatory theory of democracy must include the expectation that individuals *will be enabled*—will have the capacity—to participate, in the ways described above. This view of autonomy takes into account social practices and conventions that exclude any individual from political participation. A participatory theory of democracy stands ready to recommend ways to overcome the effects of such practices and conventions.

Who, then, is a citizen within this theory of participatory democracy? And what is the content of citizenship within this theory? I have already claimed that citizens are, by definition, free individuals. Therefore, citizens are individuals who are able to participate in political decision making, and who are able to contribute, by word and deed, to a democratic dialogue. Furthermore, in terms of the treatment of interests by theorists of participatory democracy, citizens are individuals who ought to have the opportunity to participate in the formulation of new interests. Citizenship describes individuals who have received a civic education and who can evaluate goods in public terms (see Barber [1984: 158]). This formulation of interests becomes a public enterprise whose ends are denied by failing to enable individuals to participate, by failing to guarantee that individuals can be citizens. Additionally, a citizen's political experience provides the basis for solving political problems. This allows one to move beyond an appeal to philosophically external norms. Citizenship designates the ability to translate that experience into political solutions. Citizenship is the guarantee of the opportunity to have a voice in solving these problems and to have a voice in the democratic transformation. In short, full democratic citizenship depends on having been enabled to participate in democratic politics.

In contrast to the New Right's exclusive conception of citizenship, the democratic conception of citizenship recognizes when gender roles and employment status undermine the prospects for participation. An argument for participatory democracy must not be articulated strictly in political terms, with no consideration for the social conditions that surround and inform the actual practice of the democratic state. To wit, so-called *natural* social conditions—a phrase whose paradox is overlooked by the New Right—may conflict with or undermine the state of affairs that a democratic state is capable of creating. This argument does more, though, than repeat the important observation that economic and social inequality can undermine political equality and freedom. The limitation of that caveat, as typically offered, is that it remains only contingently related to the logic of participatory democracy. The requirement that one interrogate economic and social conventions must instead be a part of the *internal logic* of participatory democracy and the model of citizenship included therein.

The democratic model of citizenship and its emphasis on participation should also not be confused with the civic republican claim that one is only free when one participates in a democratic polity—that one realizes one's freedom through participation (see Oldfield [1990]; Pocock [1992]; Beiner [1992]). Although, to the extent that participation is a learning process so that by making initial efforts at participation one develops the capacity to participate further and in a more sophisticated manner, autonomy can also be an effect of participation. Still, individuals must maintain the prerogative to remain aloof from political participation, though it is not inconsistent with this theory to maintain that one ought to encourage individuals to recognize the benefits of participation. So an individual does not forfeit the status of full citizenship by refusing to participate in decision making or in the constitution of a democratic dialogue; full citizenship does not depend on participation. Moreover, in contrast to civic republicanism, the democratic conception of citizenship does not insist that citizens express only public interests through political participation. Despite the promise of transformation and for the realization of new interests, it is not inconsistent with democratic citizenship if individuals and groups continue to express personal interests. In the end, an individual is not free, nor can she be considered to have received the status of full citizenship, if she does not have the capacity, by which I also mean the opportunity, to participate.

By making freedom as autonomy central to a model of citizenship, I have eliminated the central place of paid employment. In contrast to the liberal theory of the New Right, this allows citizenship to be a categorical designation. I should note briefly, in light of this, one other way in which the dubious status of women's citizenship, in particular, has been addressed by feminist theorists. A number of feminist theorists have sought to ground citizenship in the distinctive life experiences of women (Hernes [1987]; Jones [1988, 1990]; Piven [1985]; Siim [1988]). If we accept the traditional division between men as paid employees and women as unpaid caregivers, one particular line of feminist theory has laid the groundwork for incorporating the latter within a model of citizenship.[12] The incorporation of women is effected by basing citizenship on *both* paid labor and domestic caregiving. In response, Fraser (1994) has criticized this strategy on the grounds that gender equity cannot be sustained on the distinction between men's and women's work. Indeed, in the spirit of developing a model of citizenship from the contemporary patterns of women's lives, Fraser suggests the need to make citizenship contingent on individuals performing a combination of the two activities. In short, husbands must begin to provide their share of domestic caregiving.

To be sure, Fraser's argument nicely addresses the "motherhood thesis." In general, however, this argument travels a bit off course. I have laid out a model of citizenship that is noncontributory in its design. I have focused on citizenship as being enabled to participate in a range of political activities, and I have focused on citizenship as a categorical designation. Neither by entering the workforce nor by providing domestic care does one, on this account, necessarily satisfy a precondition for citizenship.

Participatory Democracy and the Legitimate State

A democratic polity, therefore, operates on the premise that individuals will be politically autonomous—that individuals will be citizens. Individuals ought to be in a position in which they in fact *can* participate. The model of democratic citizenship then turns to the question of identifying the guarantor of such autonomy. Indeed, to maintain that one ought to have the opportunity to participate suggests that some agent, other than the individual herself, must be charged with ensuring that status. This is precisely what inegalitarian liberalism refuses to do. For it, the status of citizenship depends on the responsibility of the individual. Citizenship depends as much on what one does for oneself as it does on what others forbear from doing. But given the possibilities for social and economic constraints on political participation, the democratic state must *ensure* that individuals who are regularly subject to its laws are autonomous; it must ensure that these individuals have been enabled to participate in democratic politics. In other words, as I am making autonomy central to this model of citizenship, the state must ensure that individuals who are regularly subject to its laws are full citizens.

So the democratic state does not simply guarantee the status of autonomy once it has been established without the aid of the state. If this was true, one would not be far from the inegalitarian liberal claim that the state protects the economic status attained independently of the state. Certainly, many individuals will secure a degree of autonomy without the aid of the state. Many individuals will not in fact be vulnerable to private structures of power that prevent them from participating in democratic politics. Still, the legitimacy of a democratic state will depend on the extent to which it guarantees autonomy for all, even if it actually only delivers the conditions for some.

In contrast to Hayek's theory of minimalist democracy, this participatory theory expects more than periodic, free, and open elections for representatives to formally democratic institutions. Moreover, this participatory theory contrasts with the public/private distinction offered by the New Right, generally, and the legitimate functions of the state that such a distinction defines. The democratic state does not merely respect and ensure the principles of noninterference and noncoercion. Although it still must do so, the democratic state must also ensure that the conditions for participation in that democracy are available to all individuals. In this way, it guarantees a universal application of citizenship. Thus, I am not proposing a universal, abstract conception of autonomy. I have articulated a conception of autonomy as it is related to political participation.

This relationship between autonomy and the legitimate state can also be clarified by examining the relationship between freedom and equality. It has been common in the history of liberal democratic thought to portray freedom and *economic* equality as competing values. Indeed, the problem of poverty highlights nicely this tension within typical liberal democratic discourses; liberty as noncoercion is more important than equality of economic standing.[13] This debate over what value is more fundamental to democracy can be thrown into relief by considering a more fundamental distinction in the status of these two values. Despite what I have said about the substantive conception of liberty among thinkers of the New Right, they still seem to believe that the state of freedom or liberty describes something of a natural state of affairs. In strictly political terms, liberty depends on noninterference by the state. Economic equality, on the other hand, is considered to be a goal to be achieved. Theorists of the New Right think this goal is neither possible nor particularly salutary.[14] In other words, from the latter perspective, economic equality is not a natural state of affairs, and to achieve it, the state would infringe (further) on the naturally occurring state of liberty.

In the first place, economic equality need not be a goal of democracy. New Right liberal theorists are correct to portray this as an elusive goal. I do not, however, make this argument for exactly the same reason that liberal theorists do. Nozick is wrong, for instance, in arguing that taxation is coercive. In fact, if it were indeed possible to realize, and to sustain, there is nothing illegitimate about the state pursuing economic equality. The means to this do not contradict the democratic conception of autonomy. This simply is not something that defines the legitimate state. There is nothing inherently wrong with economic inequality, and neither does the persistence of some degree of economic inequality contradict the goals of a democracy. Indeed, some degree of liberty (as noncoercion) will likely lead to a degree of economic inequality. To the extent that individuals are free to make choices, some will choose the avenues to greater or less personal wealth.[15]

Still, the point about freedom as autonomy in light of the distinction between "naturally occurring" liberty and economic equality as a "goal to be achieved" is that autonomy too must be considered a "goal to be achieved." Autonomy is something that must be achieved; it is not naturally occurring. By this I am not making the claim, as I noted earlier, that freedom is only realized through political participation. Rather, while a democratic state must operate on the premise that its citizens are autonomous, this then requires that the democratic state ensures that the status of autonomy can be attained.

Of course, equality also has a political meaning. In this sense, freedom as autonomy and equality are not in tension. Given this conception of freedom, political equality will mean that autonomy is distributed equally. The opportunity to participate in political institutions and in a democratic dialogue will be available universally. By ensuring that individuals are autonomous, therefore, the state guarantees this equal distribution. This distribution is possible because equality, understood this way, is not a zero sum. Again, this challenges the New Right's claim that the market is the only institution capable of distributing political liberty equally.

Notes

1. By focusing the discussion in this way, I am bracketing questions about who does and does not count as a citizen. I have dealt with this question in a negative manner in the previous chapters: Individuals should not be excluded from a conception of citizenship on grounds that they do not participate in the labor market. Still, I am not contributing to the debate, for instance, whether or not immigrants should be "entitled" to citizenship. I do assume, however, that citizenship is a categorical designation. Everyone subject to the laws made by the demos in which they regularly reside ought to have the prerogative to become citizens of that demos.

2. As we have seen, for example, in Bentham (1843, 3: 433–557) and Hayek (1960: 108). See also Madison, Hamilton and Jay (1987: passim).

3. I do not think that this argument amounts to the claim that the worth of autonomy increases in proportion to the number of options from which to choose. Indeed, an infinite number of options might have the opposite effect: stifling one's ability to make a decision with which she could feel comfortable. But this conception at least maintains that a few choices are better than one.

4. In addition to a definition of autonomy, another important component of an analysis of autonomy is a statement on the reason why we ought to respect autonomy. Indeed, this may not be self-evident. On the liberal conception, Gerald Dworkin (1988) argues that this quality allows us to "recognize" others as persons (31). And Rawls (1971) argues that having a rational life plan, in other words, a plan that one has adopted autonomously, is a necessary condition for "respect" (440).

5. For an alternative equation of autonomy and personal freedom, see Benn (1988).

6. Although, see Pateman (1985) for some doubts about these procedures.

7. This definition should emphasize the point that participatory democracy is not necessarily identified with direct democracy, but neither is participatory democracy identified merely with periodic voting.

8. In addition to constituting political discourse, the forms of association in civil society can be the classrooms for schooling in the skills necessary for decision making in the realm of both local and national politics, that is, an extension of Mill's argument noted above. It should also be noted that this means that a participatory theory of democracy is not incompatible with some actual forms of representative government. The participatory theory of democracy that underlies this argument about the importance of welfare benefits does not hearken to the cantons of eighteenth-century Switzerland.

9. Much of this exposition has been guided by the lucid treatment of participatory democracy by Pateman (1970), especially chapters 2 and 3.

10. For an investigation of the relation between power and the constitution of interests, see Lukes (1974) and Gaventa (1980). They do not, however, connect

their analyses to a mode of redressing those power relationships through a participatory theory of democracy.

11. Phillips (1991: 42–46) provides a clear and concise outline of the major challenges to participatory democracy.

12. Gilligan (1982) has argued for a distinctive feminine psychological profile, and Elshtain (1981) has argued for the merits of motherhood in the contemporary world.

13. The theorists I discussed in Chapters 1 and 2 nicely fit this paradigm, especially Bentham (1973) and Hayek (1960).

14. Of course, given the interference with liberty that the (nonegalitarian) liberal democrats themselves enumerate, liberty would also have to be a *goal*. But removing these constraints seems both possible and desirable to nonegalitarian liberals.

15. Although to suggest that individuals have the option to choose more or less wealth is obviously to describe only a portion of individuals, even in the United States. This option is not available to most of the poor, whether working or not. Moreover, there are limits to the allowance for economic inequality. At some point that inequality has the potential to undermine autonomy.

6

Citizenship and
Welfare Provision

In the preceding chapter I have laid out the principles of democratic citizenship. This model of citizenship is based on a conception of freedom as autonomy, namely, as the capacity to participate in a democratic polity. And this model requires the state to ensure such autonomy. The state must guarantee the conditions of full citizenship. In this chapter I turn to the specific policy that can ensure autonomy, that is, a policy that can guarantee the capacity to participate in democratic politics. The provision of economic resources by a party other than the beneficiary can in fact contribute to one's autonomy. Moreover, to counter the central argument of the New Right's position, this provision by a second party need not be in the form of wages.

Given the focus on the autonomy of the potential welfare recipient, this component of the theory can arguably be made independently of the question concerning the source of that provision, whether that condition can be satisfied by philanthropy (private charity) or state-funded provision. In the end, however, there continues to be an important distinction between public assistance and private charity, and in the interest of full citizenship, the former is superior.

Autonomy and
Welfare Provision

Autonomy depends on access to and control over economic resources, in order that one may satisfy one's human needs for physical survival and psychological health.[1] If these needs are not satisfied, the prospects for participation in the democratic polity are limited. Welfare benefits contribute to one's autonomy because these benefits may enable individuals to participate in political decisions and may enable individuals to contribute to the democratic dialogue. In the absence of benefits, the poor are not as likely to be in a position to participate.

In the first place, poverty may so preoccupy the individual with trying to just stay alive somehow that she has no *time* for participation. This point, it must be emphasized, provides an important counter to the vision of the poor as listless or apathetic. The poor in fact may be forced to be extraordinarily resourceful just to survive. The problem, however, is that all their agency or resourcefulness is directed to this end (see Waldron [1993]). There is little time for engagement in public concerns. Moreover, people who demonstrate agency and resourcefulness in the face of extraordinary odds may recognize that the current state of affairs in this so-called democratic polity is so structured against the interests of the poor that they have determined that there is no outlet for their voice. They may feel a lack of political *efficacy*. Finally, despite the assessment just noted, it cannot be denied that poverty remains, for some, so enervating physically and psychologically that one simply does not have the *energy* to participate.

In sum, poverty presents a barrier to participation because of the constraints poverty imposes on time, efficacy, and energy. Strangely enough, those were the same concerns expressed by critics of participatory democracy, concerns addressed in the preceding chapter. Yet those barriers were not insurmountable. Following the principles of democratic theory, one ought to expect the distribution of welfare benefits to have a number of positive benefits for the nonworking poor.

In the first place, there is good reason to believe that participation will have an educative effect, even for the nonworking poor (Gordon [1990]; Nelson [1984]; Soss [1999, 2000]). The participation enabled by welfare provision ought to provide the poor with practical training in the skills necessary for conducting a democratic government, and this participation ought to educate their disposition toward democracy in the first place. Furthermore, their participation ought to foster psychological development and feelings of political efficacy. The more that one is able to participate, the more that an individual will feel that her contribution, whether as decision making or in the constitution of a democratic dialogue, is worthwhile. In general, the political participation enabled by welfare benefits ought to foster an attitude of public-spiritedness. It ought to enable the poor to recognize and consider others' interests, and it ought to enable the poor to understand their own interests more clearly (see Bachrach [1967]). These are precisely the attitudes, according to neoconservative critics of public assistance, that the nonworking poor lack. Moreover, any reluctance on the part of the nonworking poor to participate at this time might reflect more than a lack of energy or time. Recipients of AFDC may have felt a distinct lack of efficacy, given the institutional design of welfare distribution (see Soss [1999, 2000]). Again, however, one ought to expect their political participation to beget confidence.

Additionally, having been enabled to participate in democratic politics, the poor may develop an interest in public affairs with the added benefit that they will be more likely to accept outcomes of public decisions. The political participation of the poor ought to *facilitate* their acceptance of public decisions, even in the event that such final decisions are contrary to the interests of the poor. Furthermore, as political participation serves the function of *integration,* participation by the poor in particular ought to facilitate their integration in society. Participation by the poor in democratic politics ought to increase feelings of belonging and undermine the social alienation cause by economic inequality. This is especially important for the poor themselves, because the social alienation engendered by poverty is typically less problematic for the nonpoor than it is for the poor.

Finally, the *transformative* function of democracy suggests that new common interests will be forged from the action of political engagement and political debate. New public ends develop through the process of public participation (Barber [1984]; Dryzek [1990]; Warren [1992]). To enable the poor to participate in politics as either decision makers or as contributors to a democratic dialogue is to suggest that the poor themselves will come to see political participation as more than an opportunity to only secure or increase their benefits. On top of this, the poor may come to develop the sorts of skills and attitudes that will enable them to contribute to a wider array of public policy issues.

I should note that poverty only may hinder a participatory sensibility, because there are exceptions. It may be the case, for instance, that poverty is itself the impetus to political action. Or it may be that choosing a life of poverty is an integral part of one's political action, as for the Berrigan brothers or Dorothy Day, for instance. Likewise, one may choose poverty, like Mother Theresa or religious ascetics, at the same time that one chooses to avoid typical forms of political participation. These are truly exceptional individuals, however, and democratic theory must be constructed upon the possibilities for individuals of a more common disposition.

Additionally, poverty presents more than an obstacle to the political participation of the poor themselves. Poverty also undermines the opportunity for the nonpoor to realize the full potential of participatory democracy. So the distribution of welfare benefits, as they enable the political participation of the nonworking poor, will also have positive effects on the nonpoor. The latter, too, are prevented from developing the ability to recognize and consider other citizens' interests, and they, too, suffer from social alienation engendered by poverty. To be sure, the nonpoor lose less from the social alienation of the poor than do the poor themselves. Still, participatory democracy suggests that the nonpoor are missing something as well. By not considering the interests of the poor, the nonpoor also miss the opportunity to inspire the transformative function of participation. The antagonism between the poor and the nonpoor undermines the possibility that new public ends will develop through the processes of the political participation of the poor.

Welfare Benefits and Citizenship

In light of a participatory democratic model of citizenship, public assistance can satisfy the condition of autonomy. Public assistance, when other sources are wanting, can enable participation in democratic decision making and in the constitutions of a democratic dialogue. From these arguments, it is but a short step, and one that should be clear by now, to the kernel of the democratic response to the inegalitarian liberalism of the New Right. Welfare benefits are a central component of citizenship. In contrast to the New Right, the relationship between citizenship and welfare benefits seems similar to the arguments for the right to welfare. Yet aside from the distinction between their emphasis on rights and the democratic emphasis on freedom, there is one other fundamental distinction. For liberals supporting the right to welfare, public assistance is required for the reason that someone already is a citizen. The argument from democratic citizenship, on the other hand, assumes that some individuals, because of their poverty, may not in fact be full citizens at the moment. If their poverty has undermined their opportunity to participate in the democratic polity, they are bereft of an important component of citizenship. Welfare provision is required, therefore, to help constitute the citizenship of the nonworking poor.

As a *justification* for welfare benefits, moreover, the democratic model of citizenship goes beyond the strictly moral or ethical arguments in favor of public assistance. Undeniably, any argument for welfare provision is grounded in some moral assumption about the worth of humankind. Indeed, democratic citizenship assumes that all individuals ought to have the capacity to participate. Still, explicitly moral or ethical arguments that begin and end in appeals to the equal value of all humans typically miss the opportunity to address the political implications of poverty. The problem of poverty is not simply financial destitution. The problem of poverty is one of unfreedom; poverty can be a barrier to political participation. In place of arguments addressed to the "basic material needs" of the poor, welfare benefits can be justified in political terms. Namely, the provision of welfare benefits has positive political consequences. The provision of public welfare can address the unfreedom of the individual, because this assistance can enable her to participate in the democratic polity, thereby contributing to the realization of participatory democracy. Additionally, a justification for democratic citizenship does not rely on a view of poverty as simply a problem of lack of property. To address Reich's argument, property is not central to democratic citizenship, because independence should not be the basis for freedom.

Overall, however, democratic citizenship addresses more than the relationship between welfare benefits and citizenship. I have added that the provision of welfare benefits by the state is a basic aspect of political legitimacy. The state's legitimacy must depend on this provision. In other words, a democratic state's legitimacy depends on the state ensuring the conditions for citizenship. As noted in the previous section, however, if welfare benefits enable citizenship, there seems to be no reason to deny that private charity or philanthropy could satisfy this condition as well. There seems to be no need to focus only on *public* welfare. Indeed, one of the challenges posed by the New Right is to show that one should not be obligated to secure one's economic independence through paid employment in the market. If democratic citizenship does not depend on contributions in general, much less so on working in particular, then in principle there is nothing to deny that philanthropy can satisfy the conditions for democratic citizenship in the same way that public welfare provision can.

The answer to this objection is more prudential than principled. In principle, philanthropy could enable political participation in much the same way that wages, an inheritance, or the support of a spouse may enable an individual to participate in the democratic polity. Nevertheless, the delivery of private charity is simply too contingent to be a basis for citizenship, just as the delivery of a job from the labor market is too contingent to be the basis for citizenship. In the end, state-funded provision is legally enforceable. Among the alternatives, the state is the most certain basis, the Welfare Reform Act of 1996 notwithstanding. Further, the nature of private charity remains, as the name suggests, a private matter. The terms under which it is delivered are off limits to the scrutiny of public discourse (see Young [1990]).

Additionally, the terms philanthropy and private charity are often confused, giving a false impression of the extent of private giving. Although there are indeed a number of private social service organizations directed at the indigent, philanthropy generally, like the welfare state generally, benefits all classes of society. Whereas libraries, museums, and hospital foundations are beneficial to the poor, these forms of philanthropy do not address the autonomy of the poor as directly as does income support. To reiterate, because the democratic state is the best guarantee of this condition for citizenship, the legitimacy of the state will depend on the delivery of this guarantee.

The Terms of Distribution

There is yet another important objection to this model of democratic citizenship that has been offered by critics who are in no way allied with the New Right. Although the provision of welfare benefits can contribute to an individual's autonomy, welfare benefits in and of themselves are not a *sufficient* condition for democratic citizenship. Indeed, the history of the distribution of public welfare benefits to the poor in the United States makes it clear that autonomy depends not only on resources, but also upon the *conditions* under which resources are distributed. A number of theorists have argued that the administration of public welfare has established new structures of power. These structures, then, may undermine the *opportunity* to realize one's citizenship, or these structures may undermine the possibility of even developing the *interest* in expressing one's citizenship in the first place. In general, they may make a mockery of the promise to enable participation through public assistance.

For instance, the distribution of public welfare has '"treated" the poor to more than cash and goods. Some scholars have argued that federal and state welfare programs in the United States and elsewhere have represented an extension of control and surveillance in society.[2] Under the administration of public welfare, individuals have increasingly become the object of state control and are subject to variability and uncertainty (for example, Wolin [1987, 1989]). The poor became "wards" of the state, giving caseworkers the power to be nearly sovereign over the households of the recipients. Caseworkers, for example, had the authority to conduct surprise visits to check for "men in the house." And standards of hygiene were often dictated to recipients. Furthermore, the distribution of public welfare has inculcated dependency by integrating recipients into its massive structure and by imposing a marginalized status on people who refuse to conform to its norms (Foucault [1983]). Additionally, the distribution of public welfare has constituted the category of delinquency or unrespectableness. In other words, the distribution of public welfare has stigmatized the poor. So, although individuals may have received benefits, they did so under conditions that devalued their autonomy and that undermined the possibility that these benefits could enable their political participation. And, to address directly the question of political participation, it has been forcefully argued that the reason for the administration of public welfare in the United States has been to foreclose the opportunities for the poor to mobilize themselves politically (Piven and Cloward [1971]).

Furthermore, feminist critics have identified the patriarchal structure of the welfare state; generally its foundations rest in patriarchal power relations. Accordingly, the welfare state was founded in unfreedom for over half of the population. It was constructed in a sexually divided way, such that women were incorporated on gender-specific grounds—not as the breadwinner, but as the homemaker. Wives did not receive benefits *in their own right* as citizens (Pateman [1989]). And the state has continued to uphold a particular "ethic" of the family unit, namely, one that continues to perpetuate a system of patriarchy (Abramovitz [1988]). Public welfare typically presupposed the wage-labor of the male (Zaretsky [1982]), and was available to women on the condition of their status as mothers and wives. For instance, Aid to Families with Dependent Children (AFDC), the largest antipoverty cash program in the United States, as well as survivors insurance, were established for the purpose of allowing widows to maintain their roles as primary caregivers. To the extent that the role of caregiver has traditionally been relegated to the private sphere and constructed in contrast to male domination and independence, a public policy based on female caregiving devalues the political power of women. Additionally, feminist theorists have noted how the provision of public welfare has stigmatized not only the poor generally, but poor *women* in particular (Fraser and Gordon [1994]).

In addition to "treating" the poor to more than material benefits, the possibility that this might ever be corrected has been questioned. The distribution of public welfare has led to the concentration of state power and an unnecessary centralization of decision making (Foucault [1983]).[3] The welfare state has historically not operated on democratic principles. Its policies have not reflected the will of the community; that is, they have not stood for a popular sovereignty (Walzer [1988]). Basic sustenance may be considered an appropriate object of public action, hence the call for the provision of resources. Still, the administration of those resources has remained private, even when administered by the government (Young [1990]). The bureaucracies of the welfare state have operated without public scrutiny. They have "depoliticize[d] public life by restricting discussion to distributive issues in a context of interest-group pluralism where each group [has] compete[d] for its share of public resources" (Young [1990: 88–89]). It has separated collective action from normative inquiry. Furthermore, the contemporary emphasis on privatization of government-sponsored welfare programs does not, as its proponents would maintain, represent a shift toward the sharing of power (Wolin [1989]). Rather, privatization will continue the control and discipline of the state insofar as it will represent an extension of control over decision making, while marginalizing the welfare recipient. It will represent a collusion between the government and private industry and the exclusion of public accountability. This collusion throws into doubt the relationship claimed by the proponents of privatization, namely, the relationship between the efficiency arguments of privatization and accountability. More important still, this collusion establishes a stronger bulwark in light of which the autonomy and participation of the public welfare recipient may be compromised.

These analyses of the history of the administration and distribution of public welfare demonstrate that resources themselves are not sufficient to guarantee autonomy. I do not, however, take these critiques, as some might be led to do, as a definitive rebuttal to the argument that the state can ensure autonomy through the distribution of public welfare. In the absence of public funds, there is even less possibility that the nonworking poor will be enabled to participate. Indeed, in light of these concerns, one of the objectives of participatory democracy must be to challenge statist or public forms of power. The objective must be to democratize provision—to improve the accountability of bureaucracies.

Additionally, political scientists, historians, and sociologists have demonstrated a promising relationship between the distribution of welfare benefits and democracy. Feminist theorists have also identified the ways in which the administration of public welfare has enhanced the agency of individuals. In the first place, welfare benefits have provided women with the means, albeit meager, to be independent from men. Welfare benefits provide the capacity to form and maintain female-headed households. These households can make decisions, free from the control of the market and husbands. In this sense, welfare benefits represents the decommodification of labor (Orloff [1993]). Although independence should not be the primary objective of public assistance, freedom from structures of power, in this case male domination, is still important. Furthermore, the welfare state has enabled women to develop a political sensibility. Guida West (1981) has argued that participation in the National Welfare Rights Organization (NWRO) of the 1960s and 1970s in the United States politicized women and added women's voices to the debate over welfare reform. "For the first time, thousands of women, previously isolated, stigmatized, and intimidated by the power of the welfare authorities, came together and collectively exerted their influence on public policy to increase income and benefits for their families. For the first time in the history of the federal welfare program, poor women became challengers, rather than passive recipients within the political arena. Thus, the NWRO left indelible marks not only on many of its participants, but also on the federal and state public assistance systems" (West [1981: 6]). Not only has this provided women with new political opportunities, the consequence has been a set of distinctive contributions to the actual policies enacted. In other words, policies have not simply been imposed from above (Jenson [1990]).

Despite the element of social control in the execution of welfare, actual policies have often been the result of contestation. Women have "sometimes been able to use the state in their own interest against more personal oppressions" (Gordon [1990: 5]). Although these arguments focus on the agency of women in relation to the delivery of public welfare benefits, they also suggest the possibility that benefits may enable participation on other political issues. It has been noted that the welfare state has played a part in strengthening the political standing of women generally (Piven [1985, 1990]). The state has created the opportunities to forge a sense of community and to constitute effective social movements among its recipients, whether or not the energy was redirected toward the distribution of public welfare benefits.[4]

Furthermore, the distribution of public welfare has had a positive effect on the conception and organization of the state. Despite Walzer's claim about the undemocratic nature of the welfare state, he contends elsewhere that its consequences for projects other than simply alleviating destitution have made it an important institution (Walzer [1988]). The practice of welfare has gradually and successfully established the principle that the state ought to do something about poverty. Additionally, Walzer argues that by providing welfare benefits, the state has defined its critical function. Namely, the state ought to be defined strictly by its administrative tasks. He adds that the state in particular has an important role to play in dealing with poverty, because only it has the capacity to recognize everyone.

This latter, albeit wide-ranging, set of historical interpretations of the distribution of public welfare benefits, when taken together provide the inspiration for formulating a normative conception of welfare benefits. The distribution of public welfare does not necessarily involve coercion. And public institutions are not necessarily unamenable or resistant to change. Welfare benefits can ensure that individuals have the capacity for autonomy. In particular, welfare benefits can indeed *enable* individuals to participate. So welfare benefits must in fact do more than ensure the physical survival of the poor. Welfare benefits must ensure that one "stay[s] alive in a condition in which one can act freely and purposively" (Plant et al. [1980: 46]).[5] Welfare benefits must ensure that individuals have the opportunity to act *effectively*. They must provide the grounds for human and political agency. Because they can play this role, welfare benefits are an important component of citizenship.

Thus, historical interpretations of the welfare state provided by social control theorists, civic republicans, and feminists should caution one in the execution of specific forms of welfare benefits. In light of these caveats, the aim of participatory democracy must be to criticize measures of public policy that undermine autonomy—measures that undermine citizenship. Through participation, both the formulation and execution of this public policy can cease to be a force of domination, and can become instead a material force for emancipation.

In addition to questions about the form of distribution, one might also ask whether the poor individuals will actually make use of these resources for anything other than their basic needs or personal vices. Indeed, even scholarship meant to support the claim that the poor either are politically apathetic for clearly identifiable reasons, or in fact have been politically active at particular times, for instance through the National Welfare Rights Organization in the late 1960s, suggests that when the nonworking poor do become politically active it is only for the purpose of securing their self-interest as the poor. Under specific circumstances, the nonworking poor mobilize solely for the purpose of wringing economic concessions from the state. Piven and Cloward (1977) argue that it was difficult to sustain the NWRO after the poor secured payments to which they were legally entitled. That does not bode well for the sustained political participation of the poor. The state would seem to be establishing a vicious circle that subsidizes the poor to further loot the national treasury.

There are two distinct responses to this skepticism. In the first place, this reconceptualization of the purpose of welfare benefits does not call for legal enforcement of political participation. Recipients of welfare benefits, like recipients of wages in the market, must make that decision themselves. The point is to make the ability to participate a viable option. Indeed, if government largess, generally, was held to the standard of not subsidizing personal vices, perhaps the U.S. government needs to scrutinize more carefully the numerous and generous tax write-offs it allows. So this theory is not undermined if recipients of public welfare choose to do no more than satisfy their basic needs or personal vices.

On empirical grounds, the nonworking poor are not as politically apathetic or conniving as critics and skeptics would suggest. As I noted earlier, the poor may have simply concluded that it is futile to bring their interests forward, not to mention the structural constraints that inhibit the expression of these interests. Still, the link between feelings of political efficacy and the likelihood that individuals will participate cannot be underestimated (Pateman [1970]), and the political participation of female welfare recipients has already been established (West [1981]). It might be alleged that these women participated solely for the purpose of securing the delivery of a specific good for themselves, but I suspect these New Right critics, if pressed, would likely admit that they expect anyone, rich or poor, to participate in politics solely for the purpose of securing personal interests. Indeed, that is one of the underlying assumptions of the theorists I considered in Chapter 2.

Additionally, Nelson (1984) has concluded that poor single heads of households (all of whom were women) participated in conventional political activities, such as voting, attending political meetings, working for candidates, or giving money, less frequently than all women, and less frequently than men. But, considering the alternative conception of participatory democracy—the contribution to a democratic dialogue—these poor women demonstrated higher rates of participation. These women "reported engaging in political conversations (trying to influence others and being influenced by them) more frequently than all women, and often more frequently than men. From these findings it appears that poor women who head households have a strong interest in politics but may be constrained by resources and responsibilities from participating actively" (Nelson [1984: 217]). In other words, these poor women already are "participating" in one sense of the term, and this observation implies the women's interest in participating, in the other sense, were it not for the hindrances imposed by poverty.

Notes

1. Undoubtedly the capacity to participate depends not only on economic resources but additionally on education, self-confidence, and so on. To stay close to the arguments about public assistance, I want to bracket the policy question about other conditions of autonomy that the state might guarantee.

2. This observation makes the additional point about the relationship between autonomy and privacy. For purposes of my argument, however, I will bracket any analysis of privacy.

3. The similarities with Friedman's (1962) concern for the concentration of power is striking.

4. See also the articles, generally in Gordon (1990). For similar conclusions about the positive consequences for women in the Scandinavian context, see, for example, Hernes (1987) and Siim (1988).

5. Plant et al. (1980) explain the relationship between welfare provision and autonomy through the principle of *need*, to distinguish theirs from an argument about social justice. They argue that the principle of social justice is essentially linked to the principles of merit and desert. These in turn depend on ascertaining one's *contribution* to society. But because of the complex nature of society, individual contributions cannot easily be determined. Therefore, the principle of social justice is not a secure foundation upon which to construct a theory of the provision of welfare benefits. The principle of needs, however, does provide a secure base.

Conclusion

In August 1996, President Clinton "ended welfare as we knew it" when he signed the Personal Responsibility and Work Opportunity Reconciliation Act. Seeming to combine the recommendations of Charles Murray and Lawrence Mead, the block grant mechanism known as Temporary Assistance to Needy Families (TANF) aims in the short term both to remove the incentive for welfare use and to impose work requirements as a condition of assistance. In the long term, TANF will eliminate public assistance for individual recipients altogether by imposing a sixty-month time limit. The new legislation also aims at influencing the incentives of state lawmakers by requiring them to meet work participation rates as a condition of receiving the full level of the federal block grant.[1] In general, the new welfare law seems to reflect the expectation that good citizens will be economically independent of the state—good citizens will typically be workers. And it seems to reflect the belief that good citizens do not expect others to labor for them.

By focusing on personal responsibility and paid employment, the new welfare law also seems to suggest, again following the lead of the New Right, that poverty by itself presents no problem for citizenship. Poverty is only a problem when it is caused by unemployment. The working poor, on the other hand, can be counted as citizens by virtue of their economic independence, however meager and insecure that independence may be. The working poor present no challenge to the liberal virtues of economic independence and responsibility, or to the liberal nexus of rights and obligations. The problem of poverty among people who do work, therefore, is no longer a concern for the New Right or for the supporters of the 1996 welfare reform.

Given that I have developed the argument for democratic citizenship around the question of the nonworking poor, it might be suggested that I share with the New Right this ignorance of working poverty. This is not the case. My concern for the citizenship of the nonworking poor has been inspired by the New Right's commitment to equating citizenship with economic independence and, thus, with paid employment. So this should not be taken as a denial of the political implications of working poverty. The latter is indeed a concern for democratic citizenship, and, although I have argued for welfare provision specifically in relation to the nonworking poor, this argument is not irrelevant for the working poor. In other words, the freedom, or autonomy, of the working poor—their opportunity to participate in democratic politics—may be just as easily undermined by their poverty.

As Chapter 6 demonstrated, poverty may leave little *time* for political participation. This problem may be especially acute for the working poor, who may be forced to divide their time between two or more jobs, or between caregiving and paid employment. Like the nonworking poor, the working poor may also feel a distinct lack of political *efficacy*. The working poor are likely to occupy positions within a workplace hierarchy that do not contribute to self-confidence or general feelings of efficacy. Further, the lessons learned in the workplace are easily transferred to one's appraisal of one's possibilities outside of the workplace, namely, in political affairs. Finally, in connection with conditions that may limit the time available for political participation, working poverty may be physically and psychologically enervating to such an extent that even the working poor may not have the *energy* for participation. In short, democratic citizenship, and its call for public assistance, is equally aware of and responsive to the problem of working poverty.

With a view toward ensuring the opportunity for political participation—that is, toward guaranteeing the full citizenship of all—the New Right and the new welfare law clearly sidestep the real problem. The problem, in light of democratic citizenship, is neither work nor the lack of work. The problems are the obstacles to democratic participation that poverty poses. These obstacles do not discriminate between workers and nonworkers. Thus, given the seriousness of the more general problem of poverty, the emphasis on economic independence from the state and paid employment seems a trifling matter. And if, in contrast to the emphasis just noted, a democratic state ought indeed to guarantee the conditions for citizenship, then a question demanding of more attention in the future—attention that cannot be given within the confines of this book—is which specific policies will guarantee this group's citizenship.

Having argued that work should not occupy any central place in a model of democratic citizenship, I do not mean to suggest that democratic citizens should not include labor conditions as something they might bring to the public table for discussion. Indeed, as I alluded to above, these conditions can undermine citizenship. But the commitment to democratic participation does mean that ideally, the question of constituting full citizenship ought to be separate from the question of labor. Moreover, I do not mean to suggest that work ought to be seen as a derogation of citizenship. Democratic citizenship does not rely, as Aristotle's ideal citizenship does, upon the detachment from the *oikos*. As these alternatives demonstrate, Western political theory has, since Aristotle, divided over whether citizenship involves moving entirely into the public sphere or whether it depends on accomplishments within the private sphere. At the end of the twentieth century, the ideal reflected by the new welfare law is that citizenship is integrally related to the willingness to work (in the private sphere), under any conditions. The problem in all of these cases, then, is a preoccupation with labor. Even Aristotle is preoccupied with it, insofar as citizenship is constructed in sharp contrast to labor, yet at the same time dependent upon the labor of slaves and women. Again, although democratic citizenship is critical of degrading labor conditions and exclusionary labor conventions, this model of citizenship involves neither the embrace nor the explicit rejection of labor. Democratic citizenship depends neither on the freedom from labor nor the freedom to labor.

Aside from the citizenship of the working poor, another issue I have not discussed—but that begs for some consideration—centers on viewing citizenship as the grounds for *unity* among a diverse population. If citizenship ought to be about unity, then how can a policy such as public assistance, which has been subject to so much stigma over the centuries, possibly be the grounds of unity? Indeed, public assistance seems historically to be about separation. The Personal Responsibility and Work Opportunity Reconciliation Act of 1996 may be interpreted in this light as the end of this separation. The injunction to work and the state's commitment to eliminating subsidies for nonwork would seem to enforce the common vision of citizen as worker.

Given what I have already said about the neglect of the problems associated with the working poor, it should be clear that this expectation about unity through work is historically naive. Only within relatively small communities, or within segments of the working class, has work been the basis for unity. But given the nature of market-driven capitalist political economies—given the persistence of class, gender, and racial divisions—work will continue to be a source of division rather than unity. And there is nothing in the 1996 workfare policies to suggest anything new. In this light, democratic citizenship offers a basis for unity that will not be vulnerable to the market.

Other scholars working on the broader question of welfare retrenchment in Western democracies have offered an alternative interpretation of the basis for unity. The refashioning of welfare distribution in Western societies over the past decade or so has been interpreted as the culmination of public outrage at a system that had strayed from its mission of assisting the truly deserving poor. These scholars, many of whom are sympathetic to the nonworking poor, have argued that the problem of means-tested assistance is that it separates the deserving from the undeserving poor, and makes the latter an easy target for stigma (Van Parijs [1991, 1995]; Van Parijs, ed. [1992]; Lawson [1993]). In other words, antipoverty programs undermined their chances for success by targeting the nonworking poor. In conjunction with the claim that the poverty of many people who work is a problem equally deserving of attention from public policy, these scholars have argued that an antipoverty program that does not separate the two classes of the poor would enjoy much broader electoral and legislative support. A Basic Income could be distributed among the working and nonworking poor alike, in a manner that would not offend the basic sense of justice as fairness in a liberal society (Van Parijs [1991, 1995]). A Basic Income would not, therefore, undermine the unity of the particular society.

I have already suggested an answer to the question posed by these scholars (most of whom are British or European). Namely, the *rationale* for a Basic Income—that it elides the distinction between segments of the poor—does not take account of the implications of the 1996 law, both the basic commitment to work and the refusal to consider working poverty to be a problem. If Americans are clearly committed to ignoring poverty among those who work, then the arguments for a Basic Income are unlikely to get any further than the legislation overturned in 1996. Indeed, the most one could say is that TANF is just a form of a *temporary* Basic Income. In short, there is good reason to doubt this proposed solution to the stigma of public assistance in the United States.

To return to the new welfare law, the reforms now seem to enjoy wide support and are indeed having a significant impact on the lives of many people. So it might also be useful to ask what my policy proposals mean in light of the new law. Aside from the question of unity, it might be useful to wonder whether my proposals have any chance of gaining support. I argued in the preceding chapter, for instance, how addressing the poverty of the nonworking poor might serve, at least from their perspective, to facilitate their integration into society by enabling them to participate in democratic politics. But what of the perspective of the nonpoor? In this sense, does the stigma attached to receiving public assistance and the opposition to public assistance from the nonpoor represent an empirical constraint that is as sturdy as the empirical constraint of natural unemployment—a constraint that I used as an argument against equating full citizenship with paid employment?

In conjunction with this, might citizenship in general—not just public assistance—become vulnerable to electoral politics? Once one enters the debate over the empirical conditions for citizenship, one is left open to the empirical possibility that the condition might never be met. I have made democratic citizenship conditional on an alienable plank of public policy. In this view, some people lost the opportunity for full citizenship when AFDC was scrapped in August 1996. I have maintained that an individual is not a full citizen unless she is autonomous, but I have made autonomy conditional upon the actual delivery of welfare benefits for some people. After AFDC, no alternative remains but to hope that the free market will in the end deliver resources to enable the political participation of the poor.

In light of these considerations, one might reasonably ask whether democratic citizenship really marks any advance over the egalitarian liberal models of citizenship I examined in Chapter 4. Indeed, there may be great value in continuing to focus on citizenship as a theory of rights, and that by rights we express something like fundamental equality of all persons. This conception seems to be rock solid. Even if the retrenchment of welfare provision introduced through the Personal Responsibility and Work Opportunity Reconciliation Act of 1996 in the United States amounts to a denial of the benefits of citizenship, that does not threaten the principled conception of citizenship that rights theorists continue to hold. Rights in principle are inalienable. Egalitarian liberal theorists implicitly argue that the condition of citizenship is simply the fact of having been born within a particular jurisdiction; citizenship is a status. One would indeed be on more solid ground here, for the condition for citizenship could be met once and for all at birth or naturalization, and nothing would change it. Mead can make his assertions about the relationship between work and citizenship. Yet in the rights-based view, if an individual was born in the United States, she will be a United States citizen, whether or not she works a day in her life.

Despite these formidable challenges, engaging the New Right on the grounds of citizenship is necessary and not done in vain. As the changes of 1996 ought to demonstrate for egalitarian liberals, having been born in the United States is no guarantee of subsistence, at least not for more than sixty months. People in the United States may all be citizens by virtue of birth or naturalization, but the fundamental equality that such a designation is meant to express can fall just as easily to the free market's ax or hang just as easily by the electorate's noose as can a conception of citizenship as autonomy. To declare that we are all equals by birth will likewise mean little in the face of structural unemployment and low-wage employment. Again, even the democratic model of citizenship depends on a fundamental equality in the worth of human beings, and there is nothing in this model to deny that the language of rights continues to be politically powerful. Still, there is much to gain by incorporating and emphasizing freedom within a conception of citizenship, and citizens have much to gain by designing institutions with a view toward *enabling* human beings to continually challenge social practices that wield considerable control over their lives, and that may be unreflectively accepted as natural.

Citizenship ought to do more than simply provide a catalog of material goods to which one is entitled. A view of citizenship is important for showing and enabling a range of political possibilities when faced with a social structure such as the market, which uses individuals as means to a further end. When one views the grounds of citizenship as autonomy rather than birth or naturalization, it provides a base of expectations against which the social consequences of the free market and the private family can be judged and challenged.

In addition to this empirical question, it might also be supposed that there is no significant conceptual distinction between democratic citizenship and egalitarian liberal citizenship. It may be charged that in fact my arguments for freedom as autonomy are themselves necessarily and directly rooted in a theory of rights and in turn, following Ronald Dworkin's lead, based ultimately in a sense of equality. In other words, in order for the enabling model of citizenship to be taken seriously and to actually ensure that it is enforced, the citizenry must have already convinced itself, and only because it has convinced itself, that individuals have a right to this sort of citizenship.

Some conception of equality is indeed an integral component of democratic citizenship. Yet it is precisely because most parties to the discussion accept this statement that one need not dwell on it. The important political question is about what people think citizenship is likely to engender. Democratic citizenship is a tool of social critique, because in spite of claims to the ontological equality of persons, there are social practices and institutions that contradict such equality. The important question at this point is not to demonstrate that in fact theorists all along have thought that people are equal. Rather, the important point is to draw attention to the fact that social practices give the lie to that assumption. How will people be able to do more than the social and political institutions now allow? How will individuals be able to participate in decision making and in the political dialogue—how will democracy be kept alive and vigorous? For these questions, one needs to focus on the meaning of liberty.

Still, in light of the controversy over the liberty of the property owner or worker and the rights of citizens, freedom must be seen as a democratic value, not as a typical liberal value. The importance of this cannot be overstated. Inegalitarian liberals have claimed that freedom is the check on the egalitarian claims of democracy. This view maintains the public/private distinction that masks all sorts of unequal power relationships in society. In particular, it renders the marketplace immune to critique, because the market is considered the natural arena in which individual wants are negotiated, and to the strongest man the best. In other words, inegalitarian liberalism takes freedom as a standard criterion or critical position, against which the so-called unnatural aims of public discourse in general and democracy in particular must be judged.

Against this, democratic citizenship assumes that the critical position lies with democracy itself. Democracy is a standard against which policies ought to be evaluated, and that involves considering freedom as a value for democracy. So this democratic conception of freedom must not be identified with the goal of independence. In this way, democracy can move beyond the gendered foundations of the independent or dependent dichotomy. This conception of democracy is predicated on interdependent and more solidaristic modes of social interaction. Additionally, to consider freedom qua autonomy as a democratic value widens the field of inquiry and critique. In this light, democracy brings the whole of society within its sights and subjects the marketplace and the family to the sort of critique that is capable of revealing unequal power relationships.

Again, it may be objected that democracy is not really up to the task because too much democracy means individual liberty has been left open to abuses of power by the state or special-interest groups. Such an objection, of course, flows naturally from the inegalitarian liberal position. But the response to such a claim is that a theory of democracy is able to mount a critique against the gamut of social relationships, including those between the state and citizens. There is nothing in a public democratic dialogue that prevents it from acknowledging that the welfare bureaucracy in the United States has gravely threatened the liberty of individual claimants. Inegalitarian liberals maintain that there must a priori be some private sphere that is off limits from the reach of the state. To be sure, even under the democratic model of citizenship one conclusion of public discourse is the definition of private spheres. Moreover, though, there will also be certain things that will be off limits to the interests of (patriarchal) capitalism. What should be off limits is the full expression of citizenship.

But I have strayed from my initial question about garnering public support for public assistance and the contingent nature of democratic citizenship. As I noted in the Introduction to this book, Americans seem keen on guaranteeing liberty. To be sure, that might not be the liberty that lies at the foundation of democratic citizenship—the American public might prize liberty over equality only when that means noninterference over economic equality. Nevertheless, there is reason to hope that a dialogue on freedom and democratic participation may engage the interest of the American public. This book goes a long way toward clarifying exactly what is at stake if the inegalitarian liberal theory of the New Right is fully embraced. It can be hoped that the persistence of poverty and the inability of workfare to address the fundamental problem of poverty will eventually persuade a stubborn public that it is time for new thinking and new policy.

In the end, if citizens are really interested in a democratic state and a democratic society, they must be prepared to ensure that the conditions for that democracy are provided for everyone. This will depend on moving beyond a contributory model of citizenship, retrieving the meaning of liberty from the constraints of liberalism and incorporating it more directly with participatory democratic theory, and acknowledging that poverty undermines the freedom of the poor. At this time, a policy of public assistance is desperately needed to ensure the democratic nature of our state and society.

Notes

1. For descriptions of the 1996 law, see Super et al. (1996) and Albelda and Tilly (1997, chapter 7).

References

Abramovitz, Mimi. 1988. *Regulating the Lives of Women: Social Welfare Policy from Colonial Times to the Present*. Boston: South End Press.

Albelda, Randy, and Chris Tilly. 1997. *Glass Ceilings and Bottomless Pits: Women's Work, Women's Poverty*. Boston: South End Press.

Almond, Gabriel, and Sidney Verba. 1963. *The Civic Culture: Political Attitudes and Democracy in Five Nations*. Princeton: Princeton University Press.

Avineri, Shlomo. 1972. *Hegel's Theory of the Modern State*. Cambridge: Cambridge University Press.

Bachrach, Peter. 1967. *A Theory of Democratic Elitism: A Critique*. Boston: Little Brown.

Bahmueller, Charles F. 1981. *The National Charity Company, Jeremy Bentham's Silent Revolution*. Berkeley: University of California Press.

Ball, Terrence. 1980. "Was Bentham a Feminist?" *Bentham Newsletter,*. vol. 4 (May): 25–32.

Barbalet, J. M. 1988. *Citizenship*. Milton Keynes: Open University Press.

_____. 1993. "Citizenship, Class Inequality, and Resentment." In *Citizenship and Social Theory*, ed. Bryan Turner. London: Sage.

Barber, Benjamin. 1984. *Strong Democracy*. Berkeley and Los Angeles: University of California Press.

Baumgarth, William. 1978. "Hayek and Political Order: The Rule of Law." *Journal of Libertarian Studies* 2, no. 1: 11–28.

Bedau, Hugo. 1968. "The Right to Life." *Monist* 52: 550–72.

Beiner, Ronald. 1992. "Citizenship." In *What's the Matter with Liberalism?* Berkeley and Los Angeles: University of California Press.

Bellamy, Richard. 1994. "Dethroning Politics: Liberalism, Constitutionalism and Democracy in the Thought of F. A. Hayek." *British Journal of Political Science* 24, no. 4 (October): 419–41.

Belsey, Andrew. 1986. "The New Right, Social Order and Civil Liberties." In *The Ideology of the New Right*, ed. Ruth Levitas. Cambridge: Polity Press.

Benhabib, Seyla, ed. 1996. *Democracy and Difference: Contesting the Boundaries of the Political*. Princeton: Princeton University Press.

Benn, S. I. 1976. "Freedom, Autonomy and the Concept of a Person." *Proceedings of the Aristotelian Society* 76, 109–30.

_____. 1988. *A Theory of Freedom*. Cambridge: Cambridge University Press.

Bentham, Jeremy. N.d. *Collected MSS*. London: University College Collection.

_____. 1843. *The Works of Jeremy Bentham, 11 Vols*. Edited by John Bowring. Edinburgh: William Tait.

_____. 1931. *A Theory of Legislation.* Edited by C. K. Ogden. London: Routledge and Keagan Paul.

_____. 1950. *The Theory of Legislation.*Edited by C. K. Ogden and translated by R. Hildreth. London: Routledge and Keagan Paul.

_____. 1968. *The Collected Works of Jeremy Bentham,* Edited by J. H. Burns and J. R. Dinwiddy. London: Athlone Press.

_____. 1973. *Bentham's Political Thought.*Edited by Bhikhu Parekh. New York: Barnes and Noble.

Berlin, Isaiah. 1969. "Two Concepts of Liberty." In *Four Essays on Liberty.* London: Oxford University Press.

Boralevi, Lea Campos. 1980. "Was Bentham a Feminist? A Reply to Ball." *Bentham Newsletter,* vol. 4 (May): 33–48.

_____. 1984. *Bentham and the Oppressed.* Berlin and New York: Walter de Gruyter.

Caird, Edward. 1883. "Preface." In *Essays in Philosophical Criticism*, ed. A. Seth and R. B. Haldane. London: Longmans, Green and Co.

Callahan, D. 1984. "Autonomy: A Moral Good Not a Moral Obsession." *Hastings Center Report* 14: 40–42.

Cohen, Jean, and Andrew Arato. 1992. *Civil Society and Political Theory.* Cambridge: MIT Press.

Cook, Fay Lomax, and Edith J. Barrett. 1992. *Support for the American Welfare State.* New York: Columbia University Press.

Dahl, Robert. 1971. *Polyarchy: Participation and Opposition.* New Haven, Conn.: Yale University Press.

Dean, Mitchell. 1991. *The Constitution of Poverty: Toward a Genealogy of Liberal Governance.* London: Routledge.

Dryzek, John. 1990. *Discursive Democracy: Politics, Policy and Political Science.* Cambridge: Cambridge University Press.

Dworkin, Gerald. 1988. *The Theory and Practice of Autonomy.* New York: Cambridge University Press.

Dworkin, Ronald. 1977. *Taking Rights Seriously.* Cambridge: Harvard University Press.

Dyer, Philip, and R. Harrison Hickman. 1979. "American Conservatism and F. A. Hayek." *Modern Age* 23, no. 4 (Fall): 381–93.

Edgar, David. 1986. "The Free or the Good." In *The Ideology of the New Right*, ed. Ruth Levitas. Cambridge: Polity Press.

Ellwood, David T., and Lawrence H. Summers. 1986 "Poverty in America: Is Welfare the Answer or the Problem?" In *Fighting Poverty*, ed. S. H. Danziger and D. H. Weinberg. Cambridge: Harvard University Press.

Elshtain, Jean Bethke. 1981. *Public Man, Private Woman: Women in Social and Political Thought.* Princeton: Princeton University Press.

Foucault, Michel. 1979. *Discipline and Punish.* New York: Vintage.

_____. 1983. "Social Security," In *Politics, Philosophy, and Culture: Interviews and Other Writings: 1977–1984*, ed. L. Kritzman. New York: Routledge.

Fraser, Nancy. 1994. "After the Family Wage: Gender Equity and the Welfare State." *Political Theory* 22, no. 4 (November): 591–618.

Fraser, Nancy, and Linda Gordon. 1992. "Contract Versus Charity: Why There Is No Social Citizenship in the United States." *Socialist Review* 22, no. 3 (July-September): 45–67.

_____. 1994. "A Genealogy of Dependency: Tracing a Keyword of the U.S. Welfare State." *Signs* 19, no. 2 (Winter): 309–36.

Fried, Charles. 1978. *Right and Wrong*. Cambridge: Harvard University Press.

Friedman, Milton. 1962. *Capitalism and Freedom*. Chicago: University of Chicago Press.

Friedman, Milton, and Rose Friedman. 1980. *Free to Choose: A Personal Statement*. New York: Harcourt, Brace and Jovanovich.

Gamble, Andrew. 1986. "The Political Economy of Freedom." In *The Ideology of the New Right*, ed. Ruth Levitas. Cambridge: Polity Press.

Gaventa, John. 1980. *Power and Powerlessness: Quiescence and Rebellion in an Appalachian Valley*. Oxford: Clarendon Press.

Gilder, George. 1981. *Wealth and Poverty*. New York: Basic Books.

_____. 1987. "The Collapse of the American Family." *The Public Interest* 89: 20–25.

Gilens, Martin. 1995. "Racial Attitudes and Opposition to Welfare." *Journal of Politics* 57, no. 4 (November): 994–1014.

Gilligan, Carol. 1982. *In a Different Voice: Psychological Theory and Women's Development*. Cambridge: Harvard University Press.

Golding, Martin. 1968. "Towards a Theory of Human Rights." *Monist* 52: 521–49.

Goodin, Robert E. 1988. *Reasons for Welfare: The Political Theory of the Welfare State*. Princeton: Princeton University Press.

Gordon, Linda. 1990. "Family Violence, Feminism, and Social Control," In *Women, the State and Welfare*, ed. Linda Gordon. Madison: University of Wisconsin Press.

Gordon, Linda, ed. 1990. *Women, the State and Welfare*. Madison: University of Wisconsin Press.

Gray, John. 1984. *Hayek on Liberty*. Oxford: Basil Blackwell.

_____. 1993. *Beyond the New Right: Markets, Government, and the Common Environment*. London: Routledge.

Green, T. H. 1911. *The Works of Thomas Hill Green, 3 Vols*. Edited by R. L. Nettleship. London: Longmans, Green and Co.

_____. 1911b. "Two Lectures on 'The Elementary School System of England'." In *The Works of Thomas Hill Green, 3 Vols.*, ed. R. L. Nettleship. London: Longmans, Green and Co.

_____. 1950. "On the Different Senses of 'Freedom' as Applied to Will and to the Moral Progress of Man." In *Lectures on the Principles of Political Obligation*. London: Longmans, Green and Co.

_____. 1986a. "Lectures on the Principles of Political Obligation." In *Lectures on the Principles of Political Obligation and Other Writings*, ed. Paul Harris and John Morrow. Cambridge: Cambridge University Press.

_____. 1986b. "Liberal Legislation and the Freedom of Contract." In *Lectures on the Principles of Political Obligation and Other Writings*, eds. Paul Harris and John Morrow. Cambridge: Cambridge University Press.

Greenberg, Edward S. 1986. *Workplace Democracy: The Political Effects of Participation*. Ithaca: Cornell University Press.

Greengarten, Thomas. 1981. *Thomas Hill Green and the Development of Liberal Democratic Thought*. Toronto: University of Toronto Press.

Gutmann, Amy, ed. 1988. *Democracy and the Welfare State*. Princeton: Princeton University Press.

Hamowy, Ronald. 1961. "Hayek's Concept of Freedom: A Critique." *New Individualist Review* 1, no. 1 (April): 28–31.

Hansen, Phillip. 1977. "T. H. Green and the Moralization of the Market." *Canadian Journal of Political and Social Theory* 1: 91–117.

Hardy-Fanta, Carol. 1993. *Latina Politics, Latino Politics: Gender, Culture and Political Participation in Boston*. Philadelphia: Temple University Press.

Harris, Paul, and John Morrow. 1986. "Introduction." In *Lectures on the Principles of Political Obligation and Other Writings*, ed. Paul Harris and John Morrow. Cambridge: Cambridge University Press.

Harrison, Bennett, and Barry Bluestone. 1982. *The De-Industrialization of America: Plant Closings, Community Abandonment and the Dismantling of Basic Industry*. New York: Basic Books.

_____. 1988. *The Great U-turn: Corporate Restructuring and the Polarizing of America*. New York: Basic Books.

Harrison, Ross. 1988. "Introduction." In *A Fragment on Government*. Cambridge: Cambridge University Press.

Hasenfeld, Yeheskel, and Jane A. Rafferty. 1989. "The Determinants of Public Attitudes the Welfare State." *Social Forces* 67: 1027–48.

Hayek, Friedrich A. von. 1944. *The Road to Serfdom*. Chicago: University of Chicago Press.

_____. 1960. *The Constitution of Liberty*. Chicago: University of Chicago Press.

_____. 1978. "Whither Democracy." In *New Studies in Philosophy, Politics, Economics and the History of Ideas*. London: Routledge and Keagan Paul.

_____. 1979. *Law, Legislation, and Liberty, 3 Vols*. London: Routledge and Keagan Paul.

Heater, Derek. 1990. *Citizenship: The Civic Ideal in World History, Politics and Education*. New York: Longman.

Hegel, G. W. F. 1967. *The Philosophy of Right*. Translated by T. M. Knox. London: Oxford University Press.

Held, Virginia. 1984. *Rights and Good: Justifying Social Action*. New York: Free Press.

Hernes, Helga. 1987. *Welfare State and Women's Power: Essays in State Feminism*. Oslo: Norwegian University Press.

Himmelfarb, Gertrude. 1970. "Bentham's Utopia: The National Charity Company." *The Journal of British Studies* 10, no. 1 (November): 80–125.

Hindess, Barry. 1993. "Citizenship in the Modern West." In *Citizenship and Social Theory*, ed. Bryan Turner. London: Sage.

Hohfeld, Wesley. 1919. *Fundamental Legal Conceptions as Applied in Judicial Reasoning*. New Haven, Conn.: Yale University Press.

Hoover, Kenneth R. 1987. "The Rise of Conservative Capitalism: Ideological Tensions Within the Reagan and Thatcher Governments." *Comparative Studies in Society and History* 29, no. 2: 245–68.

Horne, Thomas. 1990. *Property Rights and Poverty: Political Argument in Britain, 1605–1834*. Chapel Hill: University of North Carolina Press.

Jenks, Craig. 1977. "T. H. Green: The Oxford Philosophy of Duty and the English Middle Class." *British Journal of Sociology* 28: 481–97.

Jenson, Jane. 1990. "Representations of Gender: Policies to 'Protect' Women Workers and Infants in France and the United States before 1914." In *Women, the State and Welfare*, ed. Linda Gordon. Madison: University of Wisconsin Press.

Jones, Kathleen. 1988. "Towards a Revision of Politics." In *The Political Interests of Gender: Developing Theory and Research with a Feminist Face*, ed. Kathleen Jones and Anna Jonasdottir. London: Sage.

———. 1990. "Citizenship in a Women-Friendly Polity." *Signs* 15: 781–812.

Jones, Peter. 1994. *Rights*. New York: St. Martin's Press.

Kant, Immanuel. 1964. *Groundwork of the Metaphysic of Morals*. New York: Harper and Row.

Keane, John. 1984. *Public Life and Late Capitalism*. Cambridge: Cambridge University Press.

King, Desmond S. 1987. *The New Right: Politics, Markets and Citizenship*. Basingstoke: Macmillan.

———. 1988. "New Right Ideology, Welfare State Form and Citizenship: A Comment on Conservative Capitalism." *Comparative Studies in Society and History* 30, no. 4 (October): 792–99.

King, Desmond S., and Jeremy Waldron. 1988. "Citizenship, Social Citizenship and the Defence of Welfare Provision." *British Journal of Political Science* 18: 415–43.

Kuflik, Arthur. 1984. "The Inalienability of Autonomy." *Philosophy and Public Affairs* 13, no. 4: 271–98.

Laclau, Ernest, and Chantal Mouffe. 1985. *Hegemony and Socialist Strategy: Towards a Radical Democratic Politics*. London: Verso.

Lake, Marilyn. 1992. "Mission Impossible: How Men Gave Birth to the Australian Nation—Nationalism, Gender and other Seminal Acts." *Gender and History* 4 305–22.

Lawless, Mervyn A. 1978. "T. H. Green and the British Liberal Tradition." *Canadian Journal of Political and Social Theory* 2: 142–55.

Lawson, Roger. 1993. "Social Citizenship, Work and Social Solidarity: Historical Comparisons Between Britain and Sweden." In *Sociology and the Public Agenda*, ed. William Julius Wilson. Newbury Park, Calif.: Sage.

Levitan, Sar A. 1990. *Programs in Aid of the Poor*, 6th ed. Baltimore: Johns Hopkins University Press.

Levitas, Ruth, ed. 1986. *The Ideology of the New Right*. Cambridge: Polity Press.

Lindley, Richard. 1986. *Autonomy*. Basingstoke: Macmillan.

Lloyd, Genevieve. 1986. "Selfhood, War and Masculinity." In *Feminist Challenges: Social and Political Theory*, ed. Carole Pateman and Elizabeth Gross. Boston: Northeastern University Press.

Lukes, Steve. 1974. *Power: A Radical View*. London and New York: Macmillan.

MacCallum, Gerald C. 1967. "Negative and Positive Freedom." *Philosophical Review* 76: 312–34.

MacPherson, C. B. 1973. *Democratic Theory: Essays in Retrieval*. Oxford: Clarendon Press.

Madison, James, Alexander Hamilton, and John Jay. 1987. *The Federalist Papers*. Edited by I. Kramnick. Harmondsworth: Penguin.

Manning, D. J. 1968. *The Mind of Jeremy Bentham*. London: Longmans, Green and Co.

Mansbridge, Jane. 1980. *Beyond Adversary Democracy*. New York: Basic Books.

Marmor, Theodore R., Jerry L. Mashaw, and Philip L. Harvey. 1990. *America's Misunderstood Welfare State*. New York: Basic Books.

Marshall, T. H. 1963a. "Work and Wealth." In *Sociology at the Crossroads and Other Essays*. London: Heinemann.

_____. 1963b. "Social Selection in the Welfare State." In *Sociology at the Crossroads and Other Essays*. London: Heinemann.

_____. 1963c. "Property and Possessiveness." In *Sociology at the Crossroads and Other Essays*. London: Heinemann.

_____. 1963d. "The Welfare State and the Affluent Society." In *Sociology at the Crossroads and Other Essays*. London: Heinemann.

_____. 1963e. "A Note on Status." In *Sociology at the Crossroads and Other Essays*. London: Heinemann.

_____. 1965. "Re-assessment of the Welfare State." In *Social Policy*. London: Hutchinson, chapter 7.

_____. 1981. "The Right to Welfare." In *The Right to Welfare and Other Essays*. New York: Free Press.

_____. 1992 [1950]. "Citizenship and Social Class." In *Citizenship and Social Class*. Concord, Mass.: Pluto Press.

Martin, Rex. 1986. "Green on Natural Rights in Hobbes, Spinoza and Locke." In *The Philosophy of T. H. Green*, ed. Andrew Vincent. Brookfield, Vt.: Gower.

McCloskey, H. J. 1965. "Rights." *Philosophical Quarterly* 15: 115–27.

Mead, Lawrence. 1986. *Beyond Entitlement: The Social Obligations of Citizenship*. New York: Free Press.

_____. 1992. *The New Politics of Poverty: The Nonworking Poor in America*. New York: Basic Books.

Mill, J. S. 1910. *Representative Government*. London: Everyman Edition.

_____. 1965. *Collected Works*. Edited by J. M. Robson. Toronto: University of Toronto Press.

Mises, Ludwig von. 1985 [1927]. *Liberalism in the Classical Tradition*. Irvington-on-Hudson: Foundation for Economic Education.

Moon, J. Donald. 1988. "The Moral Basis of the Democratic Welfare State." In *Democracy and the Welfare State*, ed. Amy Gutmann. Princeton: Princeton University Press.

Morrow, John. 1983. "Property and Personal Development: An Interpretation of T. H. Green's Political Philosophy." *Politics* 18, no. 2: 84–92.

Mouffe, Chantal, ed. 1992. *Dimensions of Radical Democracy: Pluralism, Citizenship and Community*. London: Verso.

Murray, Charles. 1984. *Losing Ground: American Social Policy 1950–1980*. New York: Basic Books.

_____. 1986. "No Welfare Isn't Really the Problem." *Public Interest* 84 (Summer): 3–11.

_____. 1988. "The Coming of Custodial Democracy." *Commentary* 86, no. 3 (September): 19–24.

Nelson, Barbara J. 1984. "Women's Poverty and Women's Citizenship: Some Political Consequences of Economic Marginality." *Signs* 10, no. 2: 209–31.

Nicholson, Peter. 1986. "T. H. Green and State Action: Liquor Legislation." In *The Philosophy of T. H. Green*, ed. Andrew Vincent. Brookfield, Vt.: Gower.

_____. 1990. *The Political Philosophy of the British Idealists*. Cambridge: Cambridge University Press.

Norman, Richard. 1987. *Free and Equal: A Philosophical Examination of Political Values*. Oxford: Oxford University Press.

Novak, Michael. 1987. "Welfare's 'New Consensus': Reply to Gilder." *Public Interest* 89: 26–30.

Novak, Michael, ed. 1979. *The Family, America's Hope*. Rockford, Ill.: Rockford College Institute.

Novak, Michael, and Gordon Green. 1986. "Poverty Down, Inequality Up." *Public Interest* 82: 49–56.

Novak, Michael, et al. 1987. *The New Consensus on Welfare and the Family*. Washington, D.C.: American Enterprise Institute.

Nozick, Robert. 1974. *Anarchy, State and Utopia*. New York: Basic Books.

O'Connor, James. 1971. *The Fiscal Crisis of the State*. New York: St. Martin's.

O'Gorman, Frank. 1989. *Voters, Patrons and Parties*. Oxford: Clarendon Press.

Oldfield, Adrian. 1990. "Citizenship: An Unnatural Practice?" *Political Quarterly* 61, no. 2 (April-June): 177–87.

Orloff, Ann S. 1991. "Gender in Early U.S. Social Policy." *Journal of Policy History* 3: 249–81.

_____. 1993. "Gender and the Social Rights of Citizenship: The Comparative Analysis of Gender Relations and Welfare States." *American Sociological Review* 58 (June): 303–28.

Pateman, Carole. 1970. *Participation and Democratic Theory*. Cambridge: Cambridge University Press.

_____. 1980. "'The Disorder of Women': Women, Love and the Sense of Justice." *Ethics* 91 (October): 20–34.

_____. 1985. *The Problem of Political Obligation*. New York: Wiley.

_____. 1988. *The Sexual Contract*. Stanford, Calif.: Stanford University Press.

_____. 1989. "The Patriarchal Welfare State." In *The Disorder of Women: Democracy, Feminism and Political Theory*. Stanford, Calif.: Stanford University Press.

_____. 1995. "Democracy, Freedom and Special Rights." The John C. Rees Memorial Lecture. Swansea: University of Wales.

Pearce, Diana. 1983. "The Feminization of Ghetto Poverty." *Society* 21 (November/December): 70–74.

_____. 1990. "Welfare Is Not *for* Women: Why the War on Poverty Cannot Conquer the Feminization of Poverty." In *Women, the State, anad Welfare*, ed. Linda Gardon. Madison: University of Wisconsin Press.

Peffer, Rodney. 1978. "A Defense of Rights to Well-Being." *Philosophy and Public Affairs* 8 65–87.

Phillips, Anne. 1991. *Engendering Democracy*. University Park, Penn.: Pennsylvania State University Press.

Piven, Francis Fox. 1985. "Women and the State: Ideology, Power, and the Welfare State." In *Gender and the Life Course*, ed. Alice S. Rossi. New York: Aldine.

_____. 1990. "Ideology and the State: Women, Power, and the Welfare State." In *Women, the State and Welfare*, ed. Linda Gordon. Madison: University of Wisconsin Press.

Piven, Francis Fox, and Richard A. Cloward. 1971. *Regulating the Poor: The Functions of Public Welfare*. New York: Pantheon.

_____. 1977. *Poor People's Movements: Why They Succeed, How They Fail*. New York: Pantheon.

Plant, Raymond, Harry Lesser, and Peter Taylor-Gooby. 1980. *Political Philosophy and Social Welfare: Essays on the Normative Basis of Welfare Provision*. London: Routledge and Keagan Paul.

Pocock, J. G. A. 1992. "The Ideal of Citizenship Since Classical Times." *Queen's Quarterly* 99, no. 1 (spring): 33–55.

Poynter, J. R. 1969. *Society and Pauperism: English Ideas on Poor Relief, 1795–1834*. London: Routledge and Keagan Paul.

Quadagno, Jill. 1990. "Race, Class and Gender in the U.S. Welfare State: Nixon's Failed Family Assistance Plan." *American Sociological Review* 55: 11–28.

Rawls, John. 1971. *A Theory of Justice*. Cambridge: Harvard University Press.

Raz, Joseph. 1989. *The Morality of Freedom*. Oxford: Clarendon Press.

Reich, Charles. 1964. "The New Property." *Yale Law Journal* 73, no. 5 (April): 733–87.

Richter, Melvin. 1964. *The Politics of Conscience: T. H. Green and His Age*. London: Weidenfeld and Nicolson.

Roberts, Dorothy. 1996. "The Value of Black Mothers' Work." In *Radical America: The Politics of Resentment, Part 1: Welfare*. Vol. 26, no. 1: 9–15.

Roberts, Warren. 1979. "Bentham's Poor Law Proposals." *Bentham Newsletter* 3 (December), pp. 28–45.

Roche, Maurice. 1992. *Rethinking Citizenship: Welfare Ideology and Change in Modern Society*. Cambridge: Polity Press.

Rosen, Frederick. 1983. *Jeremy Bentham and Representative Democracy: A Study of the Constitutional Code*. Oxford: Clarendon Press.

Rosenbaum, Alan S. 1986. *Coercion and Autonomy: Philosophical Foundations, Issues, and Practices*. New York: Greenwood Press.

Rosenblum, Nancy. 1978. *Bentham's Theory of the Modern State*. Cambridge: Harvard University Press.

Sartori, Giovanni. 1987. *The Theory of Democracy Revisited: Part One: The Contemporary Debate*. London: Chatham House.

Saunders, Peter. 1993. "Citizenship in a Liberal Society." In *Citizenship and Social Theory*, ed. Bryan Turner. London: Sage.

Schmitt, Richard. 1995. *Beyond Separateness: The Social Nature of Human Beings—Their Autonomy, Knowledge and Power*. Boulder: Westview Press.

Shapiro, Ian. 1986. *The Evolution of Rights in Liberal Theory*. Cambridge: Cambridge University Press.

Shapiro v. Thompson, 394 U.S. 618 (1969).

Sher, George. 1997. *Beyond Neutrality: Perfectionism and Politics*. Cambridge: Cambridge University Press.

Shklar, Judith. 1991. *American Citizenship: The Quest for Inclusion.* Cambridge: Harvard University Press.

Shue, Henry. 1996. *Basic Rights: Subsistence, Affluence, and U.S. Foreign Policy,* 2d ed. Princeton: Princeton University Press.

Siim, Bertie. 1988. "Towards a Feminist Rethinking of the Welfare State." In *The Political Interests of Gender: Developing Theory and Research with a Feminist Face,* ed. Kathleen Jones and Anna Jonasdottir. London: Sage.

Soss, Joe. 1999. "Lessons of Welfare: Policy Design, Political Learning, and Political Action. *American Political Science Review* 93, no. 2 (June): 363–80.

––––––. Forthcoming 2000. *Unwanted Claims: The Politics of Participation in the U.S. Welfare System.* Ann Arbor: University of Michigan Press.

Steintrager, James. 1977. *Bentham.* London: Allen and Unwin.

Super, David, Sharon Parrott, Susan Steinmetz, and Cindy Mann. 1996. *The New Welfare Law.* Washington, D.C.: Center for Budget and Policy Priorities.

Symonds, J. A. 1967. *Letters of John Addington Symonds, 3 Vols.* Edited by H. M. Schuellar and R. L. Peters. Detroit: Wayne State University Press.

Thomas, Geoffrey. 1987. *The Moral Philosophy of T. H. Green.* Oxford: Clarendon Press.

United States v. Guest, 383 U.S. 745 (1966).

Van Parijs, Philippe. 1991. "Why Surfers Should Be Fed: The Liberal Case for an Unconditional Basic Income." *Philosophy and Public Affairs* 20, no. 2 (spring): 101–31.

––––––. 1995. *Real Freedom for All: What If Anything Can Justify Capitalism?* Oxford: Clarendon Press.

Van Parijs, Philippe, ed. 1992. *Arguing for Basic Income.* London: Verso.

Vincent, Andrew. 1986. "T. H. Green and the Religion of Citizenship." In *The Philosophy of T. H. Green,* ed. Andrew Vincent. Brookfield, Vt.: Gower.

Vincent, Andrew, ed. 1986. *The Philosophy of T. H. Green.* Brookfield, Vt.: Gower.

Vincent, Andrew, and Raymond Plant. 1984. *Philosophy, Politics and Citizenship: The Life and Thought of the British Idealists.* Oxford: Basil Blackwell

Waldron, Jeremy. 1993. "Homelessness and the Issue of Freedom." In *Liberal Rights.* Cambridge: Cambridge University Press.

Walzer, Michael. 1970. "A Day in the Life of a Socialist Citizen." In *Obligations: Essays on War, Disobedience, and Citizenship.* Cambridge: Harvard University Press.

––––––. 1988. "Socializing the Welfare State." In *Democracy and the Welfare State,* ed. Amy Gutmann. Princeton: Princeton University Press.

Warren, Mark. 1992. "Democratic Theory and Self-Transformation." *American Political Science Review* 86, no. 1 (March): 8–23.

Weinstein, W. L. 1965. "The Concept of Liberty in Nineteenth Century English Political Thought." *Political Studies* 13: 145–62.

Wellman, Carl. 1982. *Welfare Rights.* Totowa, N.J.: Rowman and Littlefield.

Wempe, B. H. E. 1986. *Beyond Equality: A Study of T. H. Green's Theory of Positive Freedom.* Delft: Eburon.

West, Guida. 1981. *The National Welfare Rights Organization.* New York: Praeger.

White, Lucie. 1996. "On the 'Consensus' to End Welfare: Where Are the Women's Voices." In *Radical America: The Politics of Resentment, Part 1: Welfare.* Vol. 26, no. 1: 17–25.

Wolff, Robert Paul. 1970. *In Defense of Anarchism*. New York: Harper and Row.

Wolin, Sheldon S. 1960. *Politics and Vision: Continuity and Innovation in Western Political Thought*. Boston: Little, Brown.

_____. 1987. "Democracy and the Welfare State: The Political and Theoretical Connections Between Staatsr[aumlaut]son and Wohlfartsstaatsr[aumlaut]son." *Political Theory* 15, no. 4 (November): 467–500.

_____. 1989. "Interview with Bill Moyers." In *The World of Ideas*, vol. 1., ed. Bill Moyers. New York: Doubleday.

Young, Iris Marion. 1990. *Justice and the Politics of Difference*. Princeton: Princeton University Press.

Young, Robert. 1986. *Personal Autonomy: Beyond Negative and Positive Liberty*. New York: St. Martin's Press.

Zagday, M. I. 1948. "Bentham and the Poor Law." In *Jeremy Bentham and the Law*, ed. George W. Keeton and George Scwarzenberger. London: Stevens and Sons Ltd.

Zaretsky, Eli. 1982. "The Place of the Family in the Origins of the Welfare State." In *States and Societies*, ed. David Held. New York: New York University Press.

Suggested Readings

Barry, Norman. 1990. *Welfare*. Minneapolis: University of Minnesota Press.

Benn, S. I., and W. L. Weinstein. 1971. "Being Free to Act and Being a Free Man." *Mind* 80, 194–211.

Bentham, Jeremy. 1988 [1776]. *A Fragment on Government*. Cambridge: Cambridge University Press.

Bremner, Robert. 1956. *From the Depths: The Discovery of Poverty in the United States*. New York: New York University Press.

Briggs, Asa. 1961. "The Welfare State in Historical Perspective." *Archives Européenes de Sociologie* 2: 221–58.

Esping-Andersen, Gøsta. 1985. "Power and Distributional Regimes." *Politics and Society* 14, no. 2: 223–56.

Goodin, Robert E., and Julian LeGrand. 1987. *Not Only for the Poor: The Middle Classes and the Welfare State*. London. Allen and Unwin.

Harris, David. 1987. *Justifying State Welfare: The New Right vs. the Old Left*. Oxford: Basil Blackwell.

Hayek, Friedrich A. von. 1973. *Economic Freedom and Representative Government*. London: Institute for Economic Affairs.

Held, David. 1996. *Models of Democracy*, 2d ed. Stanford, Calif.: Stanford University Press.

Marshall, T. H. 1963a. "Voluntary Action." In *Sociology at the Crossroads and Other Essays*. London: Heinemann.

_____. 1963b. "The Nature of Class Conflict." In *Sociology at the Crossroads and Other Essays*. London: Heinemann.

_____. 1963c. "Changes in Social Stratification in the 20th Century." In *Sociology at the Crossroads and Other Essays*. London: Heinemann.

_____. 1963d. "The Welfare State—A Comparative Study." In *Sociology at the Crossroads and Other Essays*: London: Heinemann.

_____. 1963e. "The Affluent Society in Perspective." In *Sociology at the Crossroads and Other Essays*. London: Heinemann.

_____. 1981a. "Welfare in the Context of Social Development." In *The Right to Welfare and Other Essays*. New York: Free Press.

_____. 1981b. "Welfare in the Context of Social Policy." In *The Right to Welfare and Other Essays*. New York: Free Press.

_____. 1981c. "Changing Ideas About Poverty." In *The Right to Welfare and Other Essays*. New York: Free Press.

Nelson, William. 1974. "Special Rights, General Rights and Social Justice." *Philosophy and Public Affairs* 3, pp. 410–30.

Offe, Claus. 1987. "Democracy Against the Welfare State? Structural Foundations of New-Conservative Political Opportunities." *Political Theory* 15, no. 4 (November): 501–37.

———. 1996. *Modernity and the State: East, West.* Cambridge: Polity Press.

Pateman, Carole. 1985. "Women and Democratic Citizenship." The Jefferson Memorial Lectures. Berkeley: University of California.

———. 1992. "Freeing Citizens: Employment and Democracy." *Wesson Lectures in the Problems of Democracy.* Stanford, Calif.: Stanford University Press.

Skocpol, Theda. 1992. *Protecting Soldiers and Mothers: The Political Origins of Social Policy in the United States.* Cambridge: Harvard University Press.

Trattner, Walter. 1979. *From Poor Law to Welfare State: A History of Social Reform in America.* 2d ed. New York: Free Press.

Ware, Alan, and Robert E. Goodin, eds. 1990. *Needs and Welfare.* London: Sage.

Weale, Albert. 1990. "Equality, Social Solidarity, and the Welfare State." *Ethics* 100, no. 3 (April): 473–88.

Wilensky, Harold. 1975. *The Welfare State and Equality: Structural and Ideological Roots of Public Expenditures.* Berkeley and Los Angeles: University of California Press.

Young, Iris Marion. 1989. "Polity and Group Difference: A Critique of the Ideal of Universal Citizenship." *Ethics* 99 (January): 250–74.

Index

abundance (Bentham)
  equality and, 17
  pauper management and, 17–18
  state role in, 13
aged, government and, 40
Aid to Families with Dependent Children
  (AFDC)
  Gilder's criticism of, 54
  paid employment and, 53
  termination of, 176
  women as caregivers and, 167
anarchy, Friedman on, 44
apathy, democracy and, 149
Aristotle, 173–174
authority. See public authority
autonomy, 139–145
  citizenship and, 154–156
  conceptions of, 139–142
  democratic participation and, 154
  enabling nature of, 144
  freedom and, 142–145
  as goal rather than natural state, 158
  individualistic conception of, 141
  liberal democratic theory and, 140–141
  moral autonomy, 139–140
  personal autonomy, 140–141
  relational nature of, 143
  state as guarantor of, 157
  welfare distribution and, 166
  welfare provision and, 161–164

Basic Income, 175
behavioralists, 60–61
Bentham, Jeremy, 11–26, 43, 82
  on citizenship, 11–12
  Hayek and, 40–41
  liberal democratic theory and, 25–26
  liberty and principle of utility in, 12–15
  on pauper management, 15–21
  on rationality of the indigent, 21–22
  on reasonable expectations, 119
  relationship of indigence and citizenship
    in, 12
  representative democracy and, 91
  security, abundance, subsistence, and
    equality in, 13
  state intervention vs. laissez-faire politics
    in, 11

on suffrage, 22–25, 96
on work, 12
workfare theory of, 98

caregiving
  AFDC and, 167
  women's economic dependency and, 57
  workfare and, 54
Cartesian concepts, 32–33
charity. See philanthropy
citizenship, 88–92. See also citizenship,
  democratic
  Bentham's theories and, 11–12
  criticism of contribution as basis for, 144
  criticism of liberal democratic theories of,
    84–85
  criticism of material basis of, 177
  criticism of New Right conception of, 155
  criticism of work as basis of, 173–174
  exploitation and, 122
  freedom and, 136–139
  limits of, 66–70
  nonworking poor and, 97
  obligations of, 61
  paid employment and, 29, 57–58, 63,
    111–113
  participation and, 144, 156
  political citizenship, 61–62
  poverty as barrier to, 164
  prepolitical conditions for, 55–57
  private sphere and, 128–129
  real freedom and individual self-
    development and, 89
  rights and responsibilities of, 30, 109–115
  rights as basis of, 119
  state promotion of, 92
  unity and, 174
  welfare and, 164–165
  women and, 94–97
  work and, 59, 96
  working poor and, 172–174
citizenship, democratic. See also democracy,
  participatory theory of; participation,
  democratic
  autonomy and, 154–156, 157
  conception of freedom in, 137
  egalitarian liberal citizenship and, 177
  political legitimacy and, 165

unity and, 174
  welfare and, 164
  welfare as insufficient basis of, 166
civic republicanism, 155–156, 169
civil liberties
  denying for the indigent, 12
  property basis of, 107
Cobbett, William, 106
common good
  citizenship and, 89, 90
  real freedom and, 81–82
  state intervention for, 85, 92, 94
community
  citizenship and, 110
  participatory democracy and, 148
  work as basis of membership in, 111, 112
contracts
  for provision of welfare (Dworkin),
    115–118
  for provision of welfare (Held), 119–122
  for provision of welfare (King and
    Waldron), 118–119
cooperation, as primary goal of society, 120
corporate power. *See* power
courts, balancing role of, 126

Dahl, Robert, 148
decision making, 146
democracy
  Hayek on, 36–38
  policies standards and, 178
  representative aspect of, 91
  tension with freedom in liberal theory, 137,
    139
democracy, criticisms of
  apathy as limitation of, 149
  dominance of elites in, 150
  exclusion of minorities in, 151
  inefficiency of, 153
  nonnecessity of, 153
  problems of representation in, 150
  time constraints limit effectiveness of, 152
democracy, participatory theory of, 145–154.
    See also citizenship, democratic;
    participation, democratic
  autonomy and, 143–144
  benefits deriving from participation,
    147–149
  citizenship and, 154–155
  enabling individuals in, 154
  limitations on participation, 149–154
  meaning of participation, 145–147
  noninterference and, 142–143
  state legitimacy and, 156–159
  unanimity not a condition of, 151
democratic dialogue
  participation in, 146–147
  participation of poor women in, 171
  welfare abuses and, 178
  welfare benefits and, 164

democratic model of citizenship. *See*
    citizenship, democratic
dependency
  elimination of, 122–123
  exploitation of, 124
  human nature and, 127
  morality and, 123
  welfare and, 166
disabled, government and, 40
"disappointment-prevention" principle. *See*
    expectations
discretionary benefits, exploitation and, 124
distribution of welfare, 166–171
  abuses of, 170
  benefits of, 168–169, 170–171
  bureaucratic accountability and, 168
  lack of democratic principles in, 167–168
  patriarchal structure of the welfare state
    and, 166–167
  power structures and, 166
  stigmatization of the poor and, 166
duty, 122–128
  as alternative to discretion in welfare
    provision, 125
  contrasted with rights, 122
  dependency and, 122
  moral duties and, 83
Dworkin, Ronald, 115–118
  on autonomy, 140, 142
  on contractual basis of welfare benefits, 118
  on equality, 115–117, 177
  on freedom, 117
  on independence, 142
  on rights as claims, 104
  on social contracts, 116–117

economic equality. *See* equality
economic liberals, 30–42. *See also* Friedman,
    Milton; Hayek, F. A.
  free market policies of, 30
  Hayek and Friedman as spokesmen for,
    30–31
  on liberty, 56
  on private vs. public spheres, 30
education
  democratic method and, 37
  extending opportunities for, 94
  pauper management and, 18
  state provision of, 92, 138
egalitarian liberals. *See also* liberal democratic
    theory
  citizenship and, 177
  right to welfare and, 103
electoral politics, welfare and, 175–176
elites, participatory democracy and, 150
Elizabethan Poor Laws
  Adam Smith's objection to, 106
  "disappointment-prevention" principle
    and, 18
  pauper management and, 16

employment. *See* paid employment
entitlement theory of justice (Nozick), 47–48
equality
  abundance and, 17
  autonomy and, 158
  citizenship and, 136–137
  democratic citizenship and, 177
  economic equality and, 44, 158
  material equality and, 37–38
  maximization of happiness and, 13
  pauper management and, 18
  political equality and, 158
  respect and, 115–118
  state role in, 13
expectations
  "disappointment-prevention" principle
    and, 18
  on not disappointing, 40–41
  welfare benefits and, 119
exploitation
  charity and, 124
  citizenship and, 122
  duty to prevent, 123–124
  family and, 124, 127
  indigence and, 125
  women and, 127–128

family
  effect of welfare on, 50, 54–55
  exploitation patterns in, 124, 127
  moral conservatives and, 30
  patriarchal bias in, 167
  redistributing welfare tasks to, 53–55
  social order and, 53–54
  women as citizens and, 68–69
feminist movement
  interpretation of welfare state by, 169
  participatory democracy and, 151, 153
formal freedom (Green), 80–81
Franklin, Benjamin, 59
freedom. *See also* liberty
  as ability to do things, 137–138
  as absence of coercion, 137
  autonomy and, 142–145
  as basic value of democracy, 178
  Bentham on, 15
  citizenship and, 136–139
  democratic citizenship and, 156
  Dworkin on, 117
  economic and political freedom
    compared, 42–43
  as economic independence, 46
  formal freedom, 80–81
  Friedman on, 42
  Green on, 80–86
  Hayek on, 34–35
  juristic freedom, 81, 90
  as noninterference, 120
  tension with democracy in liberal theory,
    137, 139

welfare policies and, 129
free market. *See* market
Friedman, Milton, 42–46
  criticism of economic equality by, 44
  on economic and political freedom, 42–43
  economic liberalism of, 30–31
  on freedom as economic independence, 46
  on negative income tax, 45–46
  on relationship between freedom and
    power, 42
  on role of public sphere, 44–45
  Rule of Law and, 66
  on value of free market, 43–44

gender biases
  Goodin's failure to address, 127–128
  independence/dependence dichotomy
    and, 109
  labor and, 69
  power and, 70, 168
Gilder, George
  on male/female roles, 57
  on two-parent family, 54–55
Goodin, Robert
  on dependency, 122–123
  on exploitation, 123–124
  failure to address gender-related biases,
    127–128
  failure to address political status of poor,
    127
  on need vs. desire, 122–123
  on non-discretionary approach to welfare,
    124–125
  on relationship of state and market,
    125–126
  on role of duty in welfare distribution, 125
  on state role in enabling market
    participation, 126–127
  on state role in providing welfare benefits,
    123
government
  appropriate role of, 40–42
  proper nature of, 59
Greenberg, Edward S., 149
Green, T.H., 79–98
  on capitalism and laissez-faire liberalism,
    88
  on citizenship, 88–92
  criticism of liberal democratic citizenship
    by, 84–85
  criticism of utilitarianism by, 85–86
  failure to recognize market powers by, 97
  on freedom, 137
  on importance of labor, 87
  on individual self-development, 80–88
  on limits of citizenship, 94–97
  on the nonworking poor, 97
  positive conception of freedom in, 145
  on property, 86–88
  on the role of women, 95–97

on state authority, 86
on state intervention, 92–94
theories as basis of welfare state, 94
tripartite structure of freedom in, 80–86

Hayek, F. A., 30–42, 43, 46
    compared with Bentham, 40–41
    concept of liberty or freedom in, 34–35
    criticism of material equality by, 37–38
    criticism of welfare state by, 39–40
    economic liberalism of, 30–31
    emphasis on free market in, 33–34
    on importance of dispersal of knowledge, 31–32
    on kosmos as spontaneous order, 32–33
    on role of government, 40–42
    on Rule of Law, 35, 66
    on special interest groups, 38–39
    theory of democracy in, 36–38, 157
Hegel, G. W. F., 113
Held, Virginia, 119–122
    on liberty as right to do something, 121
    on provision of welfare benefits, 120–121
    on social cooperation, 120
Hobbes, Thomas, 83
Horne, Thomas, 105–106

income tax, negative, 45–46
independence
    economic independence as basis of citizenship, 58
    economic independence as basis of freedom, 63
    inheritance as basis of, 56
    property as basis of, 105
    relationship to autonomy, 141
    welfare as provider of economic independence, 126
    women as caregivers and, 57
independence/dependence dichotomy. *See also* dependency
    gender biases and, 109
    sense of liberty and, 114–115
indigence. *See also* nonworking poor
    Bentham's definition of, 16–17
    citizenship and, 12
    exploitation and, 125
    government's responsibility for, 40
    Green's theories of, 94
    rationality and, 21–22
    security issues related to, 41–42
individual expectations. *See* expectations
individual rights. *See* rights
inflation, full employment and, 67
inheritance, economic independence and, 56
interest group politics, 38–39

Jones, Peter, 104
juristic freedom, 81, 90

King, Desmond, 118–119
knowledge, dispersal of, 31–32
kosmos (Hayek), 32–33

labor. *See also* work
    citizenship and, 22, 95
    equating with real property, 87–88
    gender inequalities and, 69
    Locke's theory of acquisition by, 48
    market reinforced inequalities and, 67–69
    relationship to poverty, 16
    state intervention and, 92–93
    supply of low-wage labor and, 62
labor unions, 41
laissez-faire liberalism. *See also* liberal democratic theory
    Bentham and, 11
    Green and, 88
legal rights. *See* rights
liberal democratic theory. *See also* New Right
    autonomy in, 140–141, 142
    Bentham's contribution to, 26
    criticism of citizenship in, 156
    Dworkin's challenge to, 117
    freedom, negative conception of, 137
    freedom, positive conception of, 137–138
    good governance and, 11
    Green's contributions to, 79–80
    liberty in, 11, 142
    tension between freedom and democracy in, 139
liberals. *See* economic liberals
libertarians, 46–50. *See also* Nozick, Robert
    compared with economic liberals, 46–47
    on private vs. public spheres, 30
liberty
    control vs. liberty, 14
    Dworkin on, 116
    economic independence and, 42, 63
    economic liberals on, 56
    Hayek on, 34–35
    moral conservatives on, 55
    negative conception of, 138
    noninterference and, 158
    pauper management and, 19–21
    positive conception of, 138, 145
    principle of utility and, 12–15
    property as basis of, 47, 107
    as right to do something, 121
    right to liberty as social contract, 120
    social liberty vs. personal liberty, 20–21
    state role in protection of, 137
    welfare's negative impact on, 49–50
liquor trade, 92–93
literacy, suffrage and, 25
Locke, John
    Green's challenges to, 83–84
    theory of acquisition by labor in, 48

Mansbridge, Jane
  on problems of representation, 150
  on time constraints and democratic
    participation, 152
  unitary model of democracy by, 153
market
  coercive nature of, 67
  controlling power of, 97
  criticism of market as sole means to
    liberty, 159
  equating market participation with
    citizenship, 57–58
  on freedom of, 33–34, 39, 43–44
  labor inequalities and, 67–68
  as mechanisms for public welfare, 125
  principle of noninterference and, 143
  rights and, 128
  right to liberty and, 120
  as source of equal opportunity, 65
  as source of paid employment, 64
  state mediation and intervention in, 67
Marshall, T. H., 109–113
  failure to account for women or
    nonworking poor by, 113
  on historical conceptions of citizenship,
    109–110
  on paid employment as basis of
    citizenship, 111–113
  on social citizenship, 110, 111
material equality. *See* equality
Mead, Lawrence, 59–63
  compared with libertarians, 62
  on obligations and rights, 66
  Personal Responsibility and Work
    Opportunity Reconciliation Act and, 172
  on political citizenship, 61–62
  on relationship between work and
    citizenship, 59, 176
  on role of public authority, 60–62
  on work as exchange, 62–63
membership, citizenship and, 136–137
men
  independence/dependence dichotomy
    and, 109
  male independence contrasted with
    female dependency, 57
  role in two-parent families, 54
Mill, J.S.
  on transformative function of
    participation, 148
  on women's suffrage, 96
minorities, participatory democracy and, 151
Moon, J. Donald
  exclusion of women in theories of, 114
  paid employment as basis of citizenship
    in, 114
  on psychological consequences of welfare,
    113
  on self-respect, 113–114
moral autonomy, 139–140

moral conservatives, 50–55. *See also* Gilder,
    George; Murray, Charles; Novack,
    Michael
  criticism of welfare dependency by, 50–53
  on private vs. public spheres, 30
  on role of family, 53–55
moral duties, 83
Murray, Charles, 50–53
  criticism of welfare dependency by, 51
  on failure to provide incentives for poor,
    51–52
  on individual responsibility, 53
  Personal Responsibility and Work
    Opportunity Reconciliation Act and,
    172
  on racism and condescension in welfare
    policy, 52

National Welfare Rights Organization
    (NWRO), 168, 170
natural rights tradition. *See also* rights
  contrasted with principle of utility, 12–15
  private property in, 19
  real freedom and, 82
needs, desires and, 122–123
negative income tax, 45–46
New Deal, 51
New Right. *See also* liberal democratic theory
  criticism of policies of, 66–70, 157–158,
    159, 173
  democratic participation and, 147
  economic liberals and, 30–42
  egalitarian liberals and, 103
  freedom and, 129
  libertarians and, 46–50
  market participation as basis of
    citizenship in, 57–58
  moral conservatives and, 50–55
  paid employment as basis of citizenship
    in, 29, 63
  property rights and, 105
  public sphere vs. private sphere and, 29
  state intervention and, 29
New Right, theorists of, 31–63
  Charles Murray, 50–53
  F.A. Hayek, 31–42
  George Gilder, 54–55
  Judith Shklar, 58–59
  Lawrence Mead, 59–63
  Milton Friedman, 42–46
  Robert Nozick, 47–50
New Social Movement, 146
noninterference
  applying to market as well as to state, 143
  autonomy and, 142
  liberty and, 158
  participatory democracy and, 142–143
nonworking poor. *See also* indigence; poverty
  autonomy and, 144
  citizenship and, 164

Green on, 97, 138
Marshall on, 113
welfare and, 162, 166
Novack, Michael, 53–54, 57
Nozick, Robert, 47–50
   contrasted with Dworkin, 116, 117
   entitlement theory of justice by, 47–48
   on liberty of welfare recipients, 49–50
   on minimalist state as fundamental to
     individual rights, 47
   political status of poor and, 115
   property and, 47–48
   taxation and, 138, 158
   welfare and, 48–49

O'Conor, James, 67
outdoor relief
   Bentham's objection to, 17
   pauper management and, 16, 18

paid employment
   AFDC and, 53
   citizenship and, 57–58, 63, 128, 156
   conditions of, 64–66
   freedom and, 29
   liberty and, 56
   market factors controlling, 97
   Personal Responsibility and Work
     Opportunity Reconciliation Act and,
     172
   relationship of full employment to
     inflation, 67
Paine, Thomas, 19, 106
parish system relief, 17, 18
participation, democratic. *See also* democracy,
   participatory theory of
   citizenship and, 155
   constraints on, 173
   decision making and, 146
   democratic dialogue and, 146–147
   educative function of, 147, 162
   facilitative and integrative functions of,
     148, 163
   local and nation levels of, 146
   New Right and, 147
   poor women and, 171
   poverty as barrier to, 162
   transformative function of, 148–149, 163
patriarchal biases, 166–167. *See also* gender
   biases
pauper management, 15–21
   abundance and security in, 17–18
   Bentham on, 11
   controversy regarding, 15–16
   distinguishing between the indigent and
     the poor in, 16–17
   Elizabethan Poor Laws and outdoor relief
     and, 16, 17
   equality in, 18
   liberty and, 19–21

rationality and, 21
subsistence in, 18–19
paupers. *See* indigence
personal autonomy, 140–141
   role of choice in, 140
   as self-direction, 141
Personal Responsibility and Work
     Opportunity Reconciliation Act
   citizen as worker in, 174
   as end of welfare, 172
philanthropy
   addressing poverty with, 49
   citizenship and, 165
   distinguishing between rights and charity,
     121
   exploitation and, 124
   utility maximization and, 14
Phillips, Anne, 153
police, 126
political citizenship. *See* citizenship
political equality. *See* equality
political legitimacy, 165
political status
   of individuals, 127
   of welfare recipients, 128
poor, Bentham's definition of, 16–17
poverty
   autonomy and, 162
   citizenship and, 164
   deserving and undeserving poor and,
     51–52
   as economic destitution, 115
   freedom and, 164
   Friedman on, 45
   Goodin on, 123
   labor and, 16
   nonpoor and, 163–164
   political status and, 127
   property and, 165
   working poor and, 172–173
power
   corporate concentrations of, 120
   distribution of welfare and, 166
   economic concentration of, 70
   Friedman on, 42
   gender biases and, 70, 168
   public/private distinction and, 177
   state concentrations of, 167
   state role in balancing disparities of,
     128–129
principle of utility (Bentham), 12–15
private sphere. *See* public sphere vs. private
   sphere
property
   abuses of property by bourgeois class,
     107
   on appropriation of property,
     86–87
   as basis of citizenship, 165
   as basis of civil liberties, 107

challenges to private property rights,
    105–106
equality of respect and, 118
equalization of, 24
equating labor with, 87–88
government as creator of, 106–108
on just and unjust distribution of, 47–48
as qualification for suffrage, 25
state role in protection of, 44, 125
public assistance. *See* welfare
public authority
    Green on, 86
    Mead on, 60–62
    social order and, 59–60
public sphere vs. private sphere. *See also* state
    intervention
    citizenship as challenge to private sphere,
        128–129
    Friedman on, 44–45
    Green on, 95
    Hayek on, 33, 36, 38
    labor and, 95
    New Right and, 29, 30, 157
    role of family and, 53–55
    unequal power relationships and, 177
    welfare and, 55–56

racism, welfare policies and, 52
rationalist constructivists, 32–33
Rawlsian contract theory
    Dworkin derivation from, 115–118
    King and Waldron derivation from,
        118–119
real freedom
    Green's theory of, 81–82
    property as basis of, 87
    state promotion of, 93
Reich, Charles, 106–109
    on abuses of private property, 107
    on civil liberties, 107
    criticism of Reich's property-based
        citizenship, 165
    failure to recognize interdependency of
        relationships in, 109
    on government as creator of property,
        106–107
    on government as grantor of property,
        106–108
    welfare benefits as property, 108
representative government
    Bentham on, 23
    Green on, 89–92
respect, equality of, 115–118
responsibility, welfare and, 53
revolution, security and, 23–24
rights. *See also* natural rights tradition
    Bentham on, 11
    as claims, 104–105
    enabling citizenship with, 89
    as entitlements, 104

equal respect and, 115–118
free market and, 128
legal rights vs. natural rights, 82–84
nature of, 104–105
Nozick on, 47
subsistence and, 118–119
welfare benefits and, 128
Rousseau, Henri
    on democratic participation, 145–146
    Green on, 89
    on transformative function of
        participation, 148
Rule of Law
    coercive nature of, 66
    Hayek on, 35

sanitation, state intervention and, 92
Schmitt, Richard, 143
security
    equality and, 14
    indigence and, 41–42, 49
    liberty and, 19–20
    pauper management and, 17–18
    revolution and, 23–24
    state role in, 13
    suffrage and, 14, 23
self-development, 80–88
self-direction, 141
self-regulation, 139–140
self-respect, 113–114
Shklar, Judith, 58–59
Skidmore, Thomas, 106
Smith, Adam, 106
social conditions, democratic participation
    and, 154
social contracts. *See* contracts
social control theorists, 169
Spence, Thomas, 19, 106
state intervention
    as balance to power disparities,
        128–129
    Bentham on, 11, 13
    cooperating with market as mechanism
        for public welfare, 125
    enabling market participation, 126–127
    enabling political participation, 157
    Green on, 92–94
    as guarantor of autonomy, 157
    as guarantor of common good, 84–85
    as guarantor of human needs, 123
    as guarantor of liberty, 137
    as guarantor of rights, 105
    Hayek on, 33–34
    limiting state power, 51
    market operation and, 67
    New Right and, 29
    noninterference and, 143
    Nozick on, 47
    public education and, 138
    welfare and, 121, 138

subsistence
    consenting to, 118–119
    natural rights tradition and, 19
    pauper management and, 18–19
    post-1996 and, 176
    public assistance and, 17
    right to, 103, 106, 119
    state responsibility for, 13
suffrage
    Bentham on, 22–25
    Green on, 89–92
    security and, 14
    women's suffrage, 94, 95–96

TANF. *See* Temporary Assistance to Needy
    Families (TANF)
taxation
    coercive nature of, 138
    criticism of Nozick's theories of, 158
    negative income tax and, 45–46
Temporary Assistance to Needy Families
    (TANF)
    as a temporary Basic Income, 175
    work requirements in, 172
time constraints, democratic participation
    and
    poverty as cause of, 162
    working poor and, 173

unemployment, 65
unemployment insurance, 65
U.S. Department of Commerce, 67
U.S. Export/Import Bank, 67
utilitarianism, Green on, 85–86
utility, 12–15

wages. *See also* paid employment
Waldron, Jeremy, 118–119
Walzer, Michael
    on limits on democratic participation, 152
    on undemocratic nature of welfare state,
        169
"war on poverty" (1960's), 51
welfare. *See also* distribution of welfare
    abuses of private property and, 107
    autonomy and, 161–164
    citizenship and, 58, 164–165
    contracts for provision of (Dworkin),
        115–118
    contracts for provision of (Held), 119–122
    contracts for provision of (King and
        Waldron), 118–119
    criticism of dependency on, 51
    debate over, 103
    deserving and undeserving poor and,
        175
    Friedman on, 45
    labor and, 95
    New Right and, 29
    nondiscretionary approach to, 124–125
    Nozick on, 48–49
    political status of recipients of, 115, 128
    privatization of, 167
    state provision of, 138
welfare state
    Green on, 94
    Hayek on, 36, 39–40
    historical interpretations of, 169
    lack of democratic principles in, 167, 169
West, Guida, 168
women
    autonomy and, 144
    citizenship and, 114
    dependency of, 57
    exploitation and, 127–128
    Goodin's failure to address inequities
        relative to, 127–128
    Green on, 95–97
    Green's conception of liberty and, 138
    independence/dependence dichotomy
        and, 109
    labor inequalities and, 68
    market roles vs. family roles and, 68–69
    Marshall's theories and, 113
    two-parent families and, 54
    welfare-related stigmatization of, 167
    welfare's role in independence of, 168
    welfare's role in political standing of,
        169
    woman's suffrage, 23, 24, 94
work
    citizenship and, 12, 59, 173–174
    failure to require work in exchange for
        benefits, 62–63
    as paid employment, 61
    provisions for those unable to work,
        48–49
    state requirements for, 61
    value of, 21
work ethic
    elites and slaves and, 59
    welfare policies undermine, 52
workfare
    Green's anticipation of, 98
    Mead recommendations for, 69
    Personal Responsibility and Work
        Opportunity Reconciliation Act and,
        172, 174
    role in undermining women's role as
        caregiver, 54
workhouse
    liberty and, 19–20
    pauper management and, 16
    rationality and, 21
working poor
    democratic citizenship and, 172–174
    Green on, 80
    state intervention on behalf of, 94
    state role in citizenship of, 92
Work Progress Administration, 51

Young, Iris Marion, 141